45 Great Philosophers
and What They Mean *for* Judaism

45 Great Philosophers
and What They Mean *for* Judaism

SHMULY YANKLOWITZ

RESOURCE *Publications* · Eugene, Oregon

45 GREAT PHILOSOPHERS AND WHAT THEY MEAN FOR JUDAISM

Copyright © 2024 Shmuly Yanklowitz. All rights reserved. Except for brief quotations in critical publications or reviews, no part of this book may be reproduced in any manner without prior written permission from the publisher. Write: Permissions, Wipf and Stock Publishers, 199 W. 8th Ave., Suite 3, Eugene, OR 97401.

Resource Publications
An Imprint of Wipf and Stock Publishers
199 W. 8th Ave., Suite 3
Eugene, OR 97401

www.wipfandstock.com

PAPERBACK ISBN: 979-8-3852-0776-3
HARDCOVER ISBN: 979-8-3852-0777-0
EBOOK ISBN: 979-8-3852-0778-7

07/03/25

Contents

Acknowledgments		vii
Introduction		1
1	Confucius (551–479 B.C.E.)	13
2	Buddha (About 480 B.C.E.)	19
3	Socrates (469–399 B.C.E.)	27
4	Plato (427–348 B.C.E.)	35
5	Aristotle (384–322 B.C.E.)	41
6	Avicenna (980–1037 C.E.)	47
7	Averroes (1126–1198)	52
8	Moses Maimonides (ca. 1135–1204)	56
9	Thomas Hobbes (1588–1679)	61
10	René Descartes (1596–1650)	68
11	John Locke (1632–1704)	72
12	Baruch Spinoza (1632–1677)	78
13	Gottfried Wilhelm Leibniz (1646–1716)	82
14	Voltaire (1694–1798)	86
15	David Hume (1711–1776)	91
16	Jean-Jacques Rousseau (1712–1778)	97
17	Immanuel Kant (1724–1804)	102
18	Jeremy Bentham (1748–1832)	107
19	Mary Wollstonecraft (1759–1797)	111
20	Georg Wilhelm Friedrich Hegel (1770–1831)	118

21	John Stuart Mill (1806–1873)	122
22	Søren Kierkegaard (1813–1855)	126
23	Henry David Thoreau (1817–1862)	131
24	Karl Marx (1818–1883)	137
25	William James (1842–1910)	143
26	Friedrich Nietzsche (1844–1900)	148
27	Sigmund Freud (1856–1939)	153
28	Edmund Husserl (1859–1938)	160
29	John Dewey (1859–1952)	165
30	Martin Buber (1878–1965)	171
31	Ludwig Wittgenstein (1889–1951)	176
32	Jean-Paul Sartre (1905–1980)	182
33	Emmanuel Levinas (1906–1995)	187
34	Hannah Arendt (1906–1975)	193
35	Simone de Beauvoir (1908–1986)	198
36	Isaiah Berlin (1909–1997)	203
37	Albert Camus (1913–1960)	208
38	John Rawls (1921–2002)	213
39	Michel Foucault (1926–1984)	218
40	Noam Chomsky (1928–Present)	223
41	Jacques Derrida (1930–2004)	229
42	Daniel Dennett (1942–current)	232
43	Peter Singer (1946–Present)	240
44	Martha Nussbaum (1947–Present)	245
45	Kwame Appiah (1954–Present)	251
Conclusion		256

Bibliography   259

Acknowledgments

JEWISH WISDOM IS NOT always something one can discover or uncover easily. It is a pursuit that takes a lifetime of rigorous study, guidance, perspicacity, and openheartedness. Studying Jewish texts is a journey with infinite steps and no end in sight, a pleasurable pursuit for its own sake.

The opportunity to study and to write about these philosophers has been a delight. In all my years as a Jewish educator, I've never encountered ideas as challenging, eclectic, and rich as these. It was both a rigorous and illuminating experience to approach these ancient ideas and to apply to them to this fraught contemporary moment. It is truly a revelatory encounter with the timeless totality of Jewish wisdom.

The book you hold in your hands was perhaps my most interesting one to write to date. Throughout my life, I have been in and out of texts of secular philosophers. My engagement with their ideas only deepened as my Jewish intellectual engagement grew. Finally, I had the gift, here with this, to wed the two together. It was a dream to bring these two parts of consciousness together.

There were a lot of partners who made this book possible. I would like to start by saying how grateful I am to my publisher, Wipf & Stock Publishers, for allowing me to publish with their team again. I am truly grateful for everything their team has done.

I'm also grateful for the various thought partners I had in this work including Rabbi Zachary Truboff, Rebecca Sacks, Yavni Bar-Yam, Cody Fitzpatrick and No'a bat Miri. Each in their own way added helpful secular and Jewish insights. The assistance from these esteemed colleagues was invaluable as I made my way through my spiritual and intellectual journeys within the philosophers. I'm also grateful to the many students at Valley Beit Midrash who joined me in a class series where I explored earlier versions of these ideas presented here.

Most importantly, this book wouldn't have been possible without the everlasting love of my beautiful and brilliant wife Shoshana, and our wonderful children, Amiella, Lev, Maya, and Shay. Whenever I found myself in need of inspiration, I thought of my family. Thank you for all the joy and light you share with me every day. I love you with all my heart!

Finally, I give my humble thanks to the Creator—the One True God—for giving me life, for giving me hope, for giving me curiosity, for giving me trials and tasks to conquer, and for giving me the ability to pursue a life dedicated to holiness.

Introduction

THERE IS THE SAYING of Socrates, "the unexamined life is not worth living."[1] Having devoted much of my life to secular study in schools and religious study in *yeshivot*, I find this phrase fascinating—it has so much overlap with the Jewish worldview, yet it is so far from entirely encapsulating it.

In my work as an educator of Jewish adults, I'm constantly trying to help people determine what makes up a good life, a meaningful life, and a moral life. While there are all kinds of Jewish paths one can follow in this pursuit—such as studying *musar* for character development, making inward changes via the insights of *Kabbalah* and *Chassidut*, or going out into the world to effect immediate change—I find that people benefit from an eclectic approach that allows them to take something from every perspective they can get their hands on. After all, we learn from *Pirkei Avot*, the Ethics of the Fathers:

> Ben Zoma said: Who is wise? He who learns from every [person], as it is said: "From all who taught me have I gained understanding" (Psalms 119:99).[2]

We find that when we look at our crazy and confusing world from different angles, we can start to make more sense of complex issues, and our understanding of how we should live our lives is enhanced. For thousands of years, though, there's been one particularly controversial way for Jews to gain knowledge outside of the Torah: philosophy.

This word comes from the Greek for "love of wisdom," and it almost begs to be translated into the Hebrew words *ahava* and *chochma*. However, even attempting to make that translation leaves us with the following question: Do the Greek and Jewish understandings of these concepts even mean the same thing? In ancient times, Greek and Jewish civilizations were often

---

1. Plato, *Apology*, 38a.
2. Pirkei Avot 4:1, translated by Dr. Joshua Kulp.

directly at odds, and therefore their understandings of both love and wisdom can hardly be called the same. Additionally, what do we make of the many wisdom traditions that descend from the world's other cultures? Does being a Jew require the Jewish perspective to have a monopoly on the truth over all others?

I think those with an open mind will instantly reject any approach that dismisses all non-Jewish thinking. At the same time, most of us know that we cannot throw away the rich tradition of our Jewish intellectual heritage. There have been times in history when Jewish life was so threatened by the outside world that it made sense for Jews to focus exclusively on the study of Jewish texts and the survival of the Jewish people. Fortunately for us, this is not one of those times.

Today, when there are unprecedented opportunities available to all Jews for Jewish learning and secular study, those bold enough to engage in both can bring these fields into conversation, in the spirit of Talmudic discussion or the Socratic method.

By holding up Jewish values side-by-side with the wisdom of the philosophical world, we can work to bring the intellectual rigor and moral clarity of philosophy to our Judaism and all of our thinking. Foreign ideas need not be seen as a threat to Judaism nor as a replacement for it, but as a tool enabling us to be the best Jews we can be.

When we study philosophy, we're not trying to, God forbid, assimilate into a secular and academic orientation, automatically embracing whatever the leading academic thought of the day is as the highest truth. Nor do we romanticize philosophers as bringing down direct prophecy from Heaven. Instead, the gift and the challenge of being a Jew in modernity is the task of engaging with the thinkers who have shaped our world and understanding the implications this may have for Judaism.

The old debates of whether we should accept or reject foreign thinking has become anachronistic. Today, we have the task and the opportunity to do something much greater: to bring the best of the outside world into dialogue with the Jewish tradition, which for far too much of history has been forced to keep its ideas to itself. We should want to fearlessly open our minds to other ways of thinking even while we bring Jewish wisdom to a world that doesn't fully understand what we have to offer.

On a personal level, we can see that the wider philosophical world can enhance our own lives. I know it has with mine. At times when we're grappling with questions of despair and the ultimate purpose of life, existentialism can provide us a powerful lens with which to look at our lives. When we're struggling with difficult political problems around contemporary issues, we can access a worldwide and time-tested conversation about human ethics. By accessing different thinkers from throughout history and seeing how they grapple with dilemmas similar to our own, we can find new ways to access our source of resilience in an ever-changing world.

And so, over the course of a year, my community of learners and I have tried to look at some of the greatest philosophers—past and present, Jewish and gentile, famous and underappreciated—and see what we might gain from them from a Jewish perspective. We weren't trying to dive deeply into everything these people wrote and thought, we were seeking to explore different ideas relevant to Jewish practice and ethical living. Our goal was not to be sophisticated scholars of philosophy, but to understand what we could and use it to make progress in our personal meaning-making and deploy its wisdom for the benefit of ourselves and the rest of the world.

One could analyze these thinkers and their ideas within their respective historical times, exploring what influenced each one toward their philosophical orientation. But that's not what we're doing here. Here, we're dealing with their ideas and honoring the insights of thinkers beyond their context and circumstances, asking specifically what we, as a Jewish community, can learn from them. In a sense, we approach them as Jews would the Torah. Rather than assuming their writings have an esoteric truth preserved only for a select few, we assume that they are relevant to all who would turn to them.

In our time, we can see value in different ideas without taking them as dogma. Rather than rejecting a flawed idea, we can redeem its good points, its *nekudot tovot*, to give the world just a little more momentum in its journey toward justice.

For example, much of philosophy's history sees freedom as the goal of human life. The Jewish tradition, however, really isn't concerned with freedom in the same way, but with justice. For sure, we value freedom, and we explicitly celebrate it every Passover. But by bringing Judaism into the conversation about freedom, we recognize that freedom is a way of actualizing justice. For many philosophers, freedom is seen as an end unto itself even if it does not lead to justice, and we need not reject their thinking. But as Jews, we understand that we have a higher purpose than just freedom for its own sake.

Toward the end of the Torah, God exhorts us:

> I have put before you life and death, blessing and curse. Choose life—if you and your offspring would live—by loving the Lord your God, heeding [God's] commands, and holding fast to [God].[3]

---

3. Deuteronomy 30:19–20, translated by JPS.

We see that we're given freedom, but what is its purpose? We're given the freedom to embrace life and its blessings, something that is only truly possible through a commitment to morality, sanctification, and ethics, which allows us to actualize the greatness of our human potential, not necessarily by making ourselves bigger but by making ourselves smaller. What's important to God is not just that we have the freedom to choose, but that this freedom provides a path toward embracing morality and affirming life.

And so, we chose to deepen our sense of morality and our commitment to life by exploring 45 different philosophers and what they mean for Judaism. Of course, narrowing the world of philosophy to 45 individuals is by necessity going to leave many out. We chose philosophers who didn't *necessarily* represent the best of human thought, but those who represented distinct approaches and offered unique ideas that have influenced human history.

That said, this list is still limited. Until modernity, all the philosophers we look at here are men. They are predominantly white, and they are predominantly Christian. (A good handful are Jews living largely assimilated lives in Christian cultures.) Almost invariably, these thinkers enjoyed elevated social status in their respective societies, and therefore rarely understood the perspective of the marginalized and oppressed. It is only when we get to modernity and post-modernity that we find voices that have only recently been brought into the conversation of philosophy.

The selected philosophers are presented in this book by the order of their birth, and they are also ones that have been a part of my own intellectual journey over the last 25 years. After hearing Martha Nussbaum speak when I was in graduate school, I was immediately inspired to go vegetarian. Reading the work of Peter Singer, I felt his ideas resonated so much with the Jewish ethical tradition that they helped inspire my decision to donate a kidney to a stranger. Though only the former appears in this book, both Kwame Anthony Appiah and Alasdair Macintyre have been deeply influential on my understanding of virtue ethics and human rights, which has amplified my study of *musar*.

Part of why I have long found this compelling, is that it's not obvious that philosophy, mostly taught by non-Jews, and the Torah should come into contact with each other. We might hold that the Torah is incomparable and that any attempt to bring it into dialogue with outside thought can only tarnish it. Or we might dismiss a Jewish perspective as insular and unfounded and instead try only to live with the wisdom of philosophy. For me, the tension between them is what makes learning them together so beneficial.

We care what non-Jewish philosophers have to say, and that's because Judaism lives not in a vacuum, but in dialogue with the world, for as Maimonides wrote, "One must accept truth from whomever says it." It's not that Judaism encounters the world as an outsider, but rather that we're immersed within it at all times. Whether we like it or not, Judaism is molded by the places and times in which Jews live. Developments such as globalism, democracy, socialism, and feminism affect everyone, whether we are aware of it or not. Part of the journey of this book is about understanding the history of that influence and deciding which developments we want to discard, adopt, or modify. We will gain a far greater grasp of Judaism when we understand how different transformational ideas throughout history have contributed to Judaism's unfolding.

Judaism ought never to seek out isolation. Torah is about life, and we must learn from all aspects of life, just as we learn from Ben Zoma in *Pirkei* Avot. We can appreciate the great contributions that emerge from science, anthropology, psychology, sociology, and yes, philosophy—even though philosophy's claim that it answers life's big questions can make it religion's biggest competitor. A young, contemporary rabbi and philosopher has observed:

> Jesus never laughs and Socrates never cries. Why?
> Perhaps because religion lacks a sense of humor, but not a sense of suffering, while philosophy lacks a sense of tragedy, but not a sense of irony.
> If we accept this crude dichotomy, then many things which pass as philosophy should really be considered religion, and vice versa.[4]

In our study of Judaism and philosophy, we will find profound philosophy in our Judaism, and we will find religious values in the work of philosophers. We will also see that neither field makes a perfect substitute for the other and therefore neither can ever fully subsume the other.

It shouldn't be our view that philosophy is the sole contributor of what academic thought can contribute toward religion. Yet, at the heart of Torah is imitating the Divine, and that is a moral project. In studying Judaism and moral philosophy together, what we really seek is to explore and learn how to refine our moral instincts, how to explain our moral reasoning and our passion for empathy and human dignity. Studying philosophy in a Jewish context is about trying to become more Godly. We're here to honor progress and the new forms of thinking that enhance Torah.

While we're committed to honoring different eras, we're not moral relativists. It's not true that, say, anything goes given a certain historical context. We're in search of an ultimate sense of morality, and I know no

---

4. Zohar Atkins, *Are You Religious or Philosophical?*

better system for finding that than the way it is continually revealed through Judaism. But Judaism, we must know by now, cannot be separated from the world we live in.

Diving into these ideas has been a thrilling personal journey of discovery, and I've grown immensely working through them. I hope you will too.

In this book, I will set out to put the broad world of philosophy into contact with Jewish thought through a series on 45 philosophers. Each has been chosen with care. And yet, there are so many more I wish there was time to include. Truly there should be 200 chapters instead of 45! But then again if we had 200, we would still need 200 more. The world of ideas is rich and vast.

On that note, here we will now acknowledge a range of thinkers beyond what we will cover in this book, but that nonetheless deserves our attention.

This series opens with Confucius and Buddha. Confucianism and Buddhism constitute two of the three main schools of Chinese thought. The third school, unaddressed in our series but important to know about, is Daoism (or Taoism), which traces its origins to the 6th-century BCE Chinese thinker Laozi and was further shaped by late-4th-century philosopher Zhuangzi.[5] Daoism calls for a life lived in harmony with Tao, which itself is not a concrete concept but can be loosely translated as "path," although we might also understand it as continued transformation.[6]

We did not touch upon Japanese philosophy in this course, but if we did, we would have studied Dōgen Zenji, the 13th-century Buddhist priest and philosopher, who was an important figure in Japanese Zen. Much of what we know about him comes to us from the scholarship of 20th-century Japanese philosopher Watsuji Tetsurō, whose writing put Western ethics into contact with Eastern philosophy.[7] A course on Japanese philosophy would also highlight the contributions of Hajime Tanabe, who in the first half of the 20th-century brought together Eastern and Western thought from Buddhism to Christianity to Marx.

For many people, philosophy begins with the great Greek thinkers, Socrates, Plato, and Aristotle, which we do cover, but these men are not the only Greek philosophers who shaped human thought. There are, for example, a long list of pre-Socratic philosophers to consider: Thales, Anaximander, and Anaximenes, all of Miletus; Xenophanes, Heraclitus, Parmenides, Protagoras, Democritus, and Pythagoras. Later, we have Epicurus

---

5. Hansen, *Daoism*.
6. Hansen, *Daoism*.
7. Carter and McCarthy, *Watsuji Tetsurō*.

founder of Epicureanism, who notably allowed women and enslaved people to join his school; Zeno of Citium, founder of Stoicism and his predecessor, Diogenes of Sinope, founder of Cynicism; and Pyrrho, the first skeptic philosopher.

From there, the course jumps ahead in time to the Islamic Golden Age, which lasted from the 7th to the 13th centuries CE. In addition to the thinkers we do cover, other giants from the era include the first true scientist, Alhazen; the father of Algebra, al-Khwarizmi; and the great mystic Jalāl al-Dīn Mu☒ammad Rūmī, often called simply Rumi. Rumi's writing in particular has had a lasting influence, especially the way he exalts love as an experience of the divine.[8]

What's more, in the years we jump over there are exciting developments in thought during the shift from Late Antiquity into the Medieval period, such as Boethius and Abelard. And we can't forget Saint Augustine of Hippo—not only a brilliant theologian (although deeply problematic on the topic of Jews) but author of the intimate autobiography *Confessions*. Other notable Christian thinkers of the Medieval period include Saint Anselm of Canterbury, famous for his ontological argument for the existence of God; Boethius, who translated the Greek classics into the more accessible Latin; Saint Jerome, biblical translator; and Thomas Aquinas, who synthesized Christian theology with the rationalism of the Greeks philosophers. Aquinas's influence in particular cannot be emphasized enough. A foundational figure of Western philosophy, his writings launched centuries of philosophical thought on God, free will, perception, matter, and ethics.[9]

Covering the 15th and 16th centuries, the Renaissance period is a rich place for human development. We could easily have a whole supplementary course on Renaissance thinkers: the Dutch humanist Erasmus, Polish astronomer Copernicus, English social philosopher Thomas More, German theologian and reformer Martin Luther, French philosopher Michel de Montaigne (famous for popularizing the form of the literary essay), English natural philosopher Francis Bacon, and of course, the father of modern political science—the Italian statesman Niccolò Machiavelli, who deserves just a bit of extra attention. Born at the tail end of the 15th-century, Machiavelli would go on to write *The Prince*, perhaps the most famous book on politics ever written on how one gains and maintains power.[10] The book was influential on Enlightenment thinkers.

---

8. Chittick, *RUMI, JALĀL-AL-DIN vii. Philosophy*.
9. Pasnau, *Thomas Aquinas*.
10. Mansfield, *Niccolò Machiavelli*.

In the eras before specialization, philosophy and the sciences were far more intertwined than now. Nobody illustrates this better than 17th-century mathematician, philosopher, and scientist Rene Descartes, who is covered in this course. But many other philosophers made significant contributions to our understanding of the natural world and mathematics. Additional names to know include Blaise Pascal, Galileo Galilei, and George Berkeley, whose 18th-century writings on physics are considered a precursor to Einstein.[11] Blaise Pascal is especially interesting. A contemporary of Descartes, his work in mathematics and physics shaped both modern economics and social science; his engagement with Catholicism gave us the much-cited Pascal's Wager, which takes a probability-based approach to belief.[12]

This course covers several thinkers from the Age of Enlightenment, occurring in 17th- and 18th-century Europe, but to those we could add Cesare Beccaria, Denis Diderot, Montesquieu, and Hugo Grotius. Of this period, the Scottish philosopher Adam Smith might deserve particular attention, as he is often seen as the father of modern capitalism with his masterwork *The Wealth of Nations*. Other notable theorists of a similar type might have included the 18th-century statesman Edmund Burke and—jumping ahead—the present-day philosopher Amartya Sen, who writes on the economics of social justice.

Our coverage of German idealism, which emerged in the late 18th and early 19th centuries, does include Immanuel Kant and G.W.F Hegel, might have also included Friedrich Schlegel[13], Johann Gottlieb Fichte, and F.W.J. Schelling, as well as the later thinker Ludwig Feuerbach[14] whose thought was deeply informed by Hegel and greatly influenced Karl Marx. Lamentably, we did not get to discuss the Frankfurt School at length. Emerging between the World Wars during the Weimar Republic, this institute of social research led to a wealth of cultural and political thinkers: Walter Benjamin, Herbert Marcuse, Max Horkheimer, Theodor Adorno, Jurgen Habermas, Erich Fromm, among others. As much of the world polarized into political extremes in the 20th-century, there were some voices of social liberalism that bear mentioning: Miguel de Unamuno and Jose Ortega Y Gasset, both of Spain.

Following Freud, whom we do cover, there has also been a robust movement of psychanalysis entering the field of philosophy and helping us

---

11. Duignan, *George Berkeley*.
12. Clarke, *Blaise Pascal*.
13. Although, Schlegel may have been more of a romantic than German Idealist.
14. Feuerbach was a response to German Idealism (Hegel primarily) but he was not really a German Idealist himself.

consider how meaning is made. By far the psychoanalyst who has had the most influence on philosophy since Freud is Jacques Lacan, a 20th-century thinker who as well as making contributions to psychoanalysis (most notably, perhaps, the notion of the 'mirror' phase'), is also known for applying Freudian concepts of the unconscious to a wide range of other disciplines. His impact can be felt strongly in the realms of cultural theory, especially disciplines that challenge power structures such as post-structuralism, feminist theory, and even in disciplines that emerged after his passing in 1981, such as queer theory.[15] I'll address queer theory shortly.

One of the primary inquiries of modern philosophy is the relationship between language, logic, and meaning. In the first half of the twentieth century, philosophers began to think deeply about linguistics and its relation to meaning-making. This led to the emergence of semiotics, the study of signs, spearheaded by notable thinkers including Ferdinand de Saussure. The great Ludwig Wittgenstein, who is covered in this course, is often considered the greatest philosopher of the twentieth century and offered a deeply influential philosophy of language. Wittgenstein was a student of the philosophical giant Bertrand Russell, who together with his former teacher Alfred North Whitehead wrote seminally on classical logic.[16] For much of the twentieth century, many philosophers wrestled with the relationships between language, logic, and truth. These include Rudolf Carnap, AJ Ayer, Karl Popper, and Willard Van Orman Quine, as well as influential pragmatists George Santayana.

Not all thinkers were completely convinced by logic. French philosopher Henri Bergson emphasized the importance of intuition; he can be considered a forerunner of phenomenology, the study of the relationship between objective reality and lived experience.[17] Along with Edmund Husserl and Martin Heidegger, covered in this course, there is Maurice Merleau-Ponty, Max Scheler, Hans-Georg Gadamer, Michel Henry, Alva Noë, J. L. Austin. Though not a phenomenologist, Richard Wollheim wrote notably on the mind and emotions.

In the later twentieth century, popular culture itself became the subject of philosophical inquiry in the form of Cultural Studies, which considers culture in relation to power. Some major early figures of this movement hailed from the University of Birmingham: Richard Hoggart, Stuart Hall, and Raymond Williams.

---

15. Johnston, *Jacques Lacan*.
16. Monk, *Bertrand Russell*.
17. Lawlor and Moulard-Leonard, *Henri Bergson*.

One of the most significant philosophical movements of the last decades of the twentieth century is postmodernism, which famously rejects objectivity and stable identity. Though not every thinker associated with the term would identify with that label, we explore two prominent figures, Michel Foucault and Jacques Derrida, in this course. Also notable are Jean Baudrillard, Roland Barthes, Gilles Deleuze, Pierre Bourdieu, Jean-Francois Lyotard, Anthony Giddens[18], Julia Kristeva, Helene Cixous, and Luce Irigaray. Even pragmatism—which first emerged in the 19th century under Williams James and John Dewey (both covered in this course) and Charles Sanders Peirce—was given a postmodern iteration in the form of the neopragmatism developed by Richard Rorty.

This is a good time to acknowledge that the history of recorded philosophy is dominated by men until we get to the more modern period, at which point women thinkers begin claiming space in the institutions of thought. We cover Simone de Beauvoir and Mary Wollstonecraft, but I wish we had time to do more: Iris Murdoch, Simone Weil, and Helene Cixous (whom I mentioned above). Not to mention the Black feminists who awoke us to the urgency of intersectional feminism, for example, Sojourner Truth, Audre Lorde, bell hooks, and of course Kimberlé Crenshaw who herself coined the phrases "intersectional feminism"[19] and the ever current, "critical race theory." From the world of Jewish feminism, I'd be remiss not to highlight Professor Judith Plaskow, perhaps the best-known feminist Jewish theologian whose work explores the tensions between patriarchal Judaism and feminist thought;[20] and Professor Tamar Ross, an Orthodox Jewish Israeli and a feminist who resists the notion that these two identities are at odds.

Another important avenue of modern thought, and one we will not get to in this course, is Queer Theory, which formally emerged in the early 1990s and was deeply influenced by Michel Foucault (whom we do cover in this course). While many people may misunderstand queerness as purely an issue of sexuality, queer theory is in fact the robust examination of how gender and sexual identities are in many ways social constructs and not just to be viewed as biologically determined. Primary thinkers of Queer Theory include Gloria Anzaldúa, David Halperin, Judith Butler, and Adrienne Rich. A newer avenue of queer theory is the advent of trans philosophers such as Talia Mae Bettcher, Robin Dembroff, Sophie Grace Chappell, Susan Stryker, and C. Riley Snorton. Without a doubt, our understanding of the world and

---

18. Some would argue that Giddens was very much a modernist.

19. Steinmetz, *She Coined the Term 'Intersectionality' Over 30 Years Ago. Here's What It Means to Her Today.*

20. Adler, *Judith Plaskow.*

ourselves is richer when our philosophers are not coming exclusively from the points of view of white, straight cis-men.

On that note, I must emphasize the importance of the work of liberation being done by Black thinkers who have made white supremacy more visible to all of us. We can trace Black existentialism, also called African critical theory, back to Frederick Douglass and Anna Julia Cooper in the 19th century, on to W. E. B. Du Bois in the first half of the 20th century. Du Bois is most known for his writing on the "double consciousness" faced by those who must live both as American and Black.[21] His legacy continues today in the work of Lewis Ricardo Gordon.

Critical thought about race shares a significant overlap with Postcolonialism, which emerged as thinkers began to wrestle with the painful, complex legacies of colonialism and imperialism. To learn more about this important field, you might check out Henry Odera Oruka and his concept of "sage philosophy," Edward Said on Orientalism, Aimé Césaire on Black consciousness, Franz Fanon on subjugation, Gayatri Spivak on the subaltern, Achille Mbembe on necropolitics, and Ngũgĩ wa Thiong'o on decolonializing the mind.

As we continue to think about global warming, environmental philosophers, naturalists, and philosophers of science will continue to be relevant. Foundational thinkers of this ilk include John Muir and Henry David Thoreau (the latter whom we do cover), with more recent examples including Arne Naess, Margy Midgley, Paul Feyerabend, and Bill McKibben.

Even as new fields of philosophy flourish—from the queer to the postcolonial—there are still ongoing debates about virtue and logic that can be traced back to Aristotle. Questions of virtue continue to be explored by Alasdair Macintyre, Martha Nussbaum, and William Macaskill. Macaskill is especially relevant at this moment. He's only 36, but already has profoundly shaped the way that we talk about altruism, the nature of philanthropy, and the relationship between wealth and charity; that said, it remains to be seen how his legacy will be affected by his associations with now-disgraced crypto CEO Sam Bankman-Fried.[22]

One of the more visible contemporary philosophers is one not covered in this course: Slavoj Žižek, a deeply provocative and sometimes funny philosopher who has been called "the Elvis of cultural theory."[23] His willingness to comment on current affairs—for example in newspaper op-eds—have

21. Vereen, Wines, et al., *Black Existentialism: Extending the Discourse on Meaning and Existence.*

22. Alter, *Exclusive: Effective Altruist Leaders Were Repeatedly Warned About Sam Bankman-Fried Years Before FTX Collapsed.*

23. Shannon, *The Elvis of Cultural Theory.*

brought Hegelian dialectics, Lacanian psychoanalytic theory, and Freudo-Marxism into popular culture.[24] One of his major contributions to political theory is bringing the psychoanalytic concept of the unconscious into an understanding of how ideology is formed.[25]

As a final note before we jump in, I should add that this work is primarily concerned with putting non-Jewish philosophy into contact with Jewish ideas. For the most part, the thinkers covered in this course are not engaging with Judaism, with some notable exceptions including Maimonides, Martin Buber, Emmanuel Levinas, and Hannah Arendt. On your own, you might look into Herman Cohen, specifically his writing on Judaism as fundamentally ethical in belief and practice;[26] Hermann Cohen, whose work on synthesizing philosophy and theology are nearly as fascinating as his complex personal biography. What makes Cohen and the Jewish philosophers mentioned above unique is the impact they had not just on Jewish thought but on the history of philosophy as a whole.

As I said at the beginning of this introduction, the world of ideas is rich and vast. If you take away only one lesson from this course, let it be that our Jewish engagement should include exploring broadly in the world of ideas. We should not be afraid of encountering thinkers across the spectrum.

---

24. Parker, *Slavoj Žižek*.
25. Parker, *Slavoj Žižek*.
26. Edgar, *Hermann Cohen*.

1

Confucius (551–479 B.C.E.)

WHAT MAKES SOMEONE A *mensch*, or a good and honorable person? Why must children honor their parents? What is the point of carrying on old traditions? What is the most important rule of all for everyone to follow?

These are all questions that we can find ample answers to within the texts of the Jewish canon. But I believe Jews are called to learn from the knowledge of the world, just as the world can learn from us. And Confucius provides us with some deep and ancient food for thought.

One of the most influential thinkers of all time, and arguably the most influential thinker in the history of East Asia, Confucius lived in Lu, China, at about 500 B.C.E. His surname was *Kong* and *Fuzi* meant "master." While there aren't clear historical records, it is said that he was an official in the upper echelons of government until, dissatisfied by the duke's lack of morality and character, he abandoned his post for a totally different life.[1]

As a philosopher, Confucius championed tradition and character development, placing special emphasis on hierarchies. He stressed the importance of parents and government, but he also believed that this natural order was not enough. One must also cultivate a life of virtue, he taught, in order to become a *junzi*, or a gentleman.[2]

In this system, one becomes righteous, a *mensch*, we might say by practicing a series of core behaviors: benevolence, righteousness, ritual propriety, wisdom, and trustworthiness.[3] These are all ideas that, no matter what tradition we were raised with, we should find familiar.

---

1. See YouTube: The School of Life, *Eastern Philosophy – Confucius*.
2. Csikszentmihalyi, *Confucius*.
3. Csikszentmihalyi, *Confucius*.

One of the disruptions that Confucius made was that, in the world he was born into, Chinese society was built around strict social hierarchies. Confucius, though he valued those established positions of status, was much more interested in a person's merit than their *yichus*, the prestige of the family members that preceded them. More important to him was virtue, which was not exclusive to the ruling class, nor issued by the heavens, but something sought and cultivated by the masses.

Additionally, he saw value in the traditional religion and practices, but not for theological reasons. He stayed silent about the traditional gods and mythologies[4], instead emphasizing the human-constructed moral order, while defending religious practice as instrumental in maintaining that order.

In these ways, Confucius could be described as conservative[5], traditional, and past-looking. He had great respect for ritual (believing that ritual and music can transform one's character) and for past ancestors, much like we do in Judaism. We too are ritual-oriented, carrying on the traditions of our ancestors, and we are conservative in the sense that we want to preserve the truths and values we've inherited rather than create entirely new principles. Confucius' thought should not feel all too foreign to us.

Meanwhile, four-and-a half thousand miles away, the Jewish world had been facing major upheaval in Confucius' time. The First Temple had recently been destroyed, and the 10 lost tribes had been carried off to Babylon, with only Judah, Benjamin, and part of Levi remaining. This is famously memorialized in Psalm 137, which says:

> By the rivers of Babylon,
> there we sat,
> sat and wept,
> as we thought of Zion ...
>
> If I forget you, O Jerusalem,
> let my right-hand wither;
>
> let my tongue stick to my palate
> if I cease to think of you,
> if I do not keep Jerusalem in memory
> even at my happiest hour.[6]

---

4. Although he was engaged with the sacrificial offering system.

5. We will see a similar type of conservativeness in the Greek philosophers around the same time in history.

6. Psalms 137:1, 5–6.

However, Confucius' lifetime would turn into a time of resiliency for the Jewish people. Many Israelites were able to come back from exile, Zechariah served as a prophet, and the building of the Second Temple began. It's also possible that the story of Esther and Purim takes place during this time. It was after the return to Zion and during the period of the Second Temple that what we know today as the rabbinic tradition would begin to develop. Many of the ideas developed by the rabbis find a distinct resonance in the thought of Confucius.

For example, Confucius is considered one of the first progenitors of the "Golden Rule." It is recorded in the *Analects*, a book containing his traditional sayings[7]:

> Zi Gong [Confucius' student] asked ... "Is there one word which may serve as a rule of practice for all one's life?" The Master said, "Is not RECIPROCITY such a word? What you do not want done to yourself, do not do to others."[8]

Students of the Talmud will see a direct parallel between this and Hillel the Elder's summary of Judaism to a prospective convert. (Hillel lived about 400 years after Confucius.) The stranger comes to Hillel saying, "Convert me on condition that you teach me the entire Torah while I am standing on one foot." That is to say: Teach me the entire Torah quickly. And Hillel replies to him, "That which is hateful to you do not do to another; that is the entire Torah, and the rest is its interpretation. Go study."[9]

This idea, of treating others the way you want to be treated being the foundation of a just society and a good life, of course shows up across many world philosophies and religions. That being said, it should be noted that Judaism does not limit itself only to a negative formulation of the Golden Rule, but also advocates a proactive positive formulation as well: "You shall love the neighbor as yourself."[10]

Another parallel is the value of honoring one's parents. In the *Book of Filial Piety*, written after Confucius' death but based on his teachings, Confucius is said to have taught:

> The child derives their life from their parents, and no greater gift could possibly be transmitted; his ruler and parent ... Hence, he

---

7. Scholars of Confucius largely believe that Confucius wrote, or at least edited, many of the classical Chinese texts including "The Five Classics" but the Analects were compiled many years after his death.

8. Chinese Text Project: *The Analects*: Wei Ling Gong, 24.

9. Babylonian Talmud, Shabbat 31a. A similar statement can also be found in the Second Temple literature. See Book of Tobit 4:15, "That which you hate, do to no man."

10. Leviticus 19:18.

who does not love his parents, but loves other men, is called a rebel against virtue; and he who does not revere his parents, but reveres other men, is called a rebel against propriety.[11]

One writer[12] saw a direct parallel between that passage and the medieval Jewish text *Sefer ha-Chinuch*, the *Book of Education*, which says:

> [A person] should take to heart that the father and the mother are the cause of his being in the world; and hence it is truly fitting to honor them in every way and give every benefit he can to them, because they brought him to the world, and worked hard for him when he was little. And once he fixes this idea in his soul, he will move up from it to recognize the good of God ... And he should think at length about how very fitting it is to be careful in his worship of God.[13]

Hakimi pointed out that "Judaism views filial piety as a model for the ultimate service of God, while Confucianism sees it as a model for the service of the state."[14] While Judaism, by contrast, does not reject government in favor of anarchy, the tradition is certainly to be deeply skeptical of government officials. While there may be a mitzvah to honor one's parents, there is no mitzvah to honor the king or the head of state. In fact, it is written in *Pirkei Avot*, the *Ethics of the Fathers*:

> Be careful [in your dealings] with the ruling authorities for they do not befriend a person except for their own needs; they seem like friends when it is to their own interest, but they do not stand by a person in the hour of their distress.[15]

Yes, Judaism makes important space for special roles: parent, kohen, Levite, rabbi, prophet, king, judge, and even the secular state. But more important are the values each person is commanded to live by. Confucius, too, while not rejecting the social hierarchies, believed that the social order is insufficient to make someone virtuous, hence his values of benevolence, righteousness, ritual propriety, wisdom, and trustworthiness. Confucius's emphasis on meritocracy, that people should be awarded status not on the basis of their birth but by the knowledge and virtue they had achieved, also finds similarities in rabbinic thought.

---

11. Sacred Books of the East, Volume 3, Chapter 9, Trans. James Legge.
12. Isaac Hakimi.
13. Sefer HaChinukh 33:2.
14. Isaac Hakimi: "Of all Man's acts, none is greater than Filial Piety."
15. Pirkei Avot 2:3.

> Rabbi Shimon says: There are three crowns: the crown of Torah, the crown of priesthood and the crown of monarchy - but the crown of a good name outweighs them all.[16]

Priesthood and kingship are inherited but the Torah is available to everyone who is willing to put in the time and energy to learn. The Mishnah also makes clear that yichus or Torah knowledge must be complemented with virtue. As great as the kind or Torah scholar may be, without ethics (a good name), their achievements are worth little.

One of these traits that Jews in particular might have a particular kinship with is "ritual propriety." In a world that wants us to do away with seemingly archaic traditions, both Confucianism and Judaism uphold the importance of ritual continuity. The idea of *mesorah* (tradition) is central to Judaism and essential to its survival throughout the centuries. As the Passover Haggadah makes clear, the wicked son is not one who rejects God. Rather his challenging question, "What does this ritual mean to you?" is understood as a rejection of the Jewish past.

Perhaps the best reflection in the Jewish tradition of Confucius' concept of *menschlichkeit* is in the Musar movement, the 19th-century Jewish ethical renewal movement that emphasized the development of a person's *middot* or character traits. Some examples of *middot* include loving-kindness, honesty, slowness to anger, and commitment. These are all also characteristics of God in the Bible, whose model we are called to imitate.

After Confucius' life, his ideas became profoundly influential in Chinese culture.[17] Confucianism became one of the "Three Pillars of Chinese Culture," alongside Buddhism and Daoism. Despite attempts by the communists to stamp out the cultural influences of Confucianism,[18] it remains, alongside the other two pillars, a key component of the religious and philosophical lives of many people in China, as well as elsewhere in Asia.

Similar to our concern today with Jewish assimilation, Confucius wanted to revive traditional values that he saw being abandoned. For example, he wanted to strengthen the family unit and felt that was good for the

---

16. Pirkei Avot 4:13.

17. His ideas also influenced the west. Jesuit missionaries were more receptive to neo-Confucian ideas identifying them as less problematic than what they deemed as idolatrous approaches found in Daoism and Buddhism. A 17th century philosopher Gottfried Wilhelm Leibniz similarly celebrated Confucius for his early developments on embracing universal natural laws independent of the dogma of religious authorities. At a time in early enlightenment when thinkers were trying to keep ethics intact while breaking from the church, Confucius set a model for them.

18. The Communists found the Confucian approach of maintaining traditional hierarchies to be a threat to their new approaches that sought to eradicate certain inequalities built into those hierarchies.

collective society. As Jews we can appreciate the commitment to conserving the past and the rituals we've inherited while also looking to the present within our character development. In seeing Confucius with a similar trajectory and teaching some similar values, we can appreciate how humanity 2,500 years ago was thinking similarly even while not in touch at all. And yet, while Judaism, in its evolutions, is constantly layering new ideas on top of old ones, we can appreciate the conservative approach, also found in Judaism, that some values are not to be abandoned easily. Today, we often get the sense that family, character, and tradition are less important than progress. Confucius can help to remind us that those are actually anchors in our lives and in society at large.

2

Buddha (About 480 B.C.E.)

How should we address the problem of human suffering? Does it demand action in the world, or first an adjustment of the mind? Can a person be Jewish and a Buddhist at the same time? What is the role that earthly pleasures, such as wine, sex, and food, should play in our lives? These are all discussions that come up when we examine the common ground and the differences between traditional Judaism and the philosophy of the Buddha.

We should perhaps begin by saying that "Buddha" is not a name, but a title, meaning "awakened;"[1] one who attains "bodhi" has reached enlightenment. It's believed that many people have been Buddhas, such as the Dalai Lama today. "The Buddha," however, refers to Siddhārtha Gautama, who lived as an ascetic religious teacher in India[2] approximately 2,500 years ago, only to be called "the Buddha" centuries after his death.

Tradition says that the Buddha was born into royalty in Nepal, where he lived an extremely privileged life, not leaving his palace. When he was 29, it is said, he wandered out of the palace and was stunned to find out about the existence of violence, illness, and death. Choosing to embark on an intellectual life to find out what to make of these challenges, he meditated on how, when a lawn is mown, insects living in it are certainly killed. He'd built on this sense of compassion for the world he'd discovered until he reached an enlightened state.[3] A Buddha is someone who can now see the true reality of the world and is completely removed from destructive internal forces like ignorance, hate, and even desire itself.

---

1. Siderits, *Buddha*.
2. He was born in Nepal.
3. See YouTube: The School of Life, *Eastern Philosophy - The Buddha*.

This enlightenment, or Nirvana, led him to teach the "Four Noble Truths," all of which center around the theme of suffering. In the words of the Stanford Encyclopedia of Philosophy, these truths are:

1. There is suffering.
2. There is the origination of suffering.
3. There is the cessation of suffering.
4. There is a path to the cessation of suffering.[4]

These four truths are predicated on the idea that we perpetually find ourselves attached to and desiring things that are fundamentally impermanent. Until we recognize that neither ourselves nor the world truly exists in the way that our egos perceive them, we are trapped to pursue that which is illusory. Buddhism offers a host of practices and ways of thinking that are intended to liberate us from attachments in order to see reality as it truly is.

This path, whose end goal is the cessation of suffering, is called the Noble Eightfold Path, which entails:

1. Correct View
2. Correct Intention
3. Correct Speech
4. Correct Action
5. Correct Livelihood
6. Correct Effort
7. Correct Mindfulness
8. Correct Concentration[5]

The Buddha struggled with whether or not to teach the Dharma to others. He believed most are too far removed some such noble truths for these spiritual practices to have any real value. One can't live half with anger, jealousy, and greed and then partially with spiritual bliss. It's all or nothing. But ultimately the Buddha embraced many monks and then sent them out to teach and ordain many more monks so they could grow and transform the world.

Jews have long been attracted to Buddhism, and there are many reasons for this. For American Jews who saw Jewish life as limited to stale synagogue rituals, Buddhism provided a series of practices that could make

4. Siderits, *Buddha*.
5. Lopez, *Eightfold Path*.

spirituality more real and accessible to the individual while leaving some cultural and communal baggage behind. Buddhism's truths can also be seen as orienting one towards a universalist orientation, something that was important for American Jews, who found Judaism to be too parochial. That being said, it's easy to see how Buddhism's values can find similar expression in Judaism, albeit with the Buddha's philosophy paying particular attention to the discipline of the mind. It makes sense, then, that those disillusioned by mainstream Judaism often dabble in Buddhism to find heft in areas they see Judaism as lacking. From this, we have the caricature of the JewBu, the Jewish Buddhist.

Although there is great diversity of beliefs within Buddhism, the Buddha is generally not seen as a god or prophet[6]. He's a person of reason rather than revelation. In that respect, one might argue that Buddhism is more of a philosophy or way of life than a religion—a concept largely understood through the dominant lens of Christianity and Islam. Many eastern traditions, such as Daoism, Buddhism, and Confucianism, don't fit well either inside or outside the purview of what we might call "religion."

I think that, if we pay close attention to the Buddha's ideas, we'll see that many aspects of Buddhism are compatible with Judaism provided that a Jew has an understanding of who they are and the Jewish community they are an indispensable part of.

First of all, similar to the Jewish sages, the Buddha was concerned with living the right life and the cultivation of virtue that living a good life requires. He was deeply troubled by suffering, much like Judaism is. Like those in Judaism, he knew that sensual pleasure is not the purpose of existence. He rejected both asceticism and gluttony in favor of a "middle way." His goal was then to use this middle way as a pathway toward people's enlightenment. Furthermore, the Buddha wanted people to reduce their suffering, which in his philosophy comes from "attachments."

One can see both of these ideas clearly expressed by Maimonides, whose emphasis on the golden mean eschews embracing extremes for a proper balance in one's life. This applies both to character attributes and how one lives one's life. In the Guide for the Perplexed, like the Buddha, he specifically highlights the danger of material attachments and the suffering that it can bring about.

> The soul becomes familiarized with, and accustomed to, unnecessary things and consequently acquires the habit of desiring things that are unnecessary . . . and this desire is something

---

6. Scholars suggest that the earliest Buddhist texts do not suggest that the Buddha was omniscient; however, some later texts do.

> infinite... If for instance, your desire is directed to having silver plate, it would be better if it were of gold... In most cases such a man exposes himself to great dangers, such as arise in sea voyages and the service of kings; his aim therein being to obtain these unnecessary luxuries."[7]

Because our desire for material objects knows no bounds, it never quite feels we have enough. For Maimonides, it is the risks we take to pursue our desires that so often serve as the source of our pain. Like Buddha, Maimonides felt we must do our best to release ourselves from attachments, so that we can reduce our suffering. The Buddha, however, took it a step further and emphasized that we cannot only reduce our suffering but eliminate it entirely. We must learn to let go of our selfishness and our very sense of self, the ego that is the cause of it.

The Buddha's "middle way," however, is less materialistic than the Jewish one. In Judaism, things like sex, food, and money are generally viewed as good—we just must learn to take breaks from them, knowing that they're not everything and need to be channeled towards holy purposes. In Judaism, the pleasures of the world and attachments within this world are real and mostly good, while for the Buddha they are necessary only to keep suffering to a minimum.

Whereas Buddhism tends to see desire as the root of suffering, Judaism tries to find some place for it. It is taught in Tractate Yoma of the Talmud that, in the time of the prophet Zechariah, the evil inclination for idol worship emerged from the Holy of Holies in the Temple, symbolized by "a fiery lion cub." The people then captured it and put it in a lead container, freeing themselves from the inclination toward idolatry. Then, they captured the inclination toward sexual activity, but Zechariah, the Talmud says, said to them: "See and understand that if you kill this inclination the world will be destroyed because as a result there will also no longer be any desire to procreate."[8]

The legend continues:

> They followed his warning, and instead of killing the evil inclination [for sexual sins] they imprisoned it for three days. At that time, people searched for a fresh egg throughout all of Eretz Yisrael and could not find one. Since the inclination to reproduce was quashed, the chickens stopped laying eggs. They said: What should we do? If we kill it, the world will be destroyed. If we pray for half, i.e., that only half its power be annulled, nothing

---

7. Maimonides, *Guide for the Perplexed*, 3:12, Pines translation, 445-446.
8. Babylonian Talmud, Yoma 69b.

will be achieved because Heaven does not grant half gifts, only whole gifts. What did they do? They gouged out its eyes, effectively limiting its power, and set it free.[9]

This story teaches that we can't kill the sex drive, or there will be no procreation. You cannot kill the desire for personal profit or there would cease to be businesses and products that consumers need. For the rabbis, the *yetzer hara*, the self-interested inclination, is necessary for the world to function. Judaism wants to elevate attachments: such as relationships and the desire for food and drink, rather than break them. We can even use these pleasures as ways of connecting to God. However, much like in Buddhism, the last thing we want to do is mistake these things for the purpose of life.

Another similarity between Judaism and Buddhism is that both want a perfected world without hardships. The Buddha's model, however, is Nirvana, the cessation of the inner struggle. In Judaism, the desire for redemption is not just directed inwardly but outwardly as well. Some of the most inspiring words of the prophets are their vision of world peace, as described in Isaiah chapter 11, where it says, "The wolf shall dwell with the lamb" and "A babe shall play over a viper's hole,"[10] and Isaiah chapter 2:

> God will judge among the nations
> And arbitrate for the many peoples,
> And they shall beat their swords into plowshares
> And their spears into pruning hooks:
> Nation shall not take up
> Sword against nation;
> They shall never again know war.[11]

In this approach, it appears that not only has there been an inner transformation of human beings, but it has resulted in a dramatic improvement of the broader, physical world. The personal transformation alone is not sufficient in the Jewish perspective. It must become global. Both Judaism and Buddhism care about reducing suffering and both have a vision of what that will look. For Judaism it's the messianic era and for Buddhism it is Nirvana. However, the pathways of each aren't the same.

For Judaism, ending suffering requires us to go out into the world and dedicate our efforts towards healing the sick and helping the poor. It tends to be focused on external action rather than a change in mindset—though

---

9. Babylonian Talmud, Yoma 69b.
10. Isaiah 11:6, 8.
11. Isaiah 2:4.

there's a place for that too. We don't deny the objective reality, and we don't claim that the ego or the self is merely illusory.

Yes, the Hasidic tradition teaches *bitul hayesh*, abandonment or negation of the self, but it is not meant to be a permanent state of being, rather it lives in tension with the overarching Jewish tradition of self-preservation. The simultaneous holding of both of these values is reflected back in one of the most famous quotes of Hillel the Elder:

> If I am not for me, who will be for me? And when I am for myself, what am I? And if not now, when?[12]

The goals of life on earth in both traditions are about ending suffering. But for the Buddha, it's about the personal path toward abandoning the ego, while Judaism aspires to a global reformation on a societal level, and even on a religious level it's more communal.

But yes, I think it's true that the Buddha's teachings *can* enrich a Jew's life, particularly by building their inner strength and character that we can translate Jewishly into how we show compassion in our actions toward others. In an interview for Valley Beit Midrash, the Modern Orthodox rabbi David Almog, who's studied Buddhism intensively, told me:

> I don't believe I understood *tefilah*, prayer, until I had a meditation practice where I regularly invoked very definitive forms of *kavanah* [intention] ... But also, specific *mitzvot*, specific commandments, specific deeds, like how to do *tzedakah* ... how to give ... to somebody in need while recognizing that their needs and your needs, that there's no difference in dignity. Their needs are as important to me as my needs are to me, and that their person is equal to my own. There were very specific practices in Buddhism that informed that ... having an ability to perform them [*mitzvot*] with *kavanah* that I didn't learn when I was in a Jewish setting ... I may have been taught it, but I wasn't ready to hear it.

I also asked Rabbi Almog for one teaching of Buddhism that can be of the most help to Jews. He said it was a mental-training practice called *lojong*. By reflecting closely on our actions, Rabbi Almog explained, we can learn to develop empathy for all people, including our enemies.

There is a Torah commandment:

---

12. Pirkei Avot 1:14.

When you see the donkey of your enemy lying under its burden and would refrain from raising it, you must nevertheless help raise it.[13]

Almog explained that *lojong* trains a person to, when disgruntled by an enemy, ask themself questions such as:

- "What do I gain from my experiences with this person?"
- "How is this person teaching me to be more patient?"
- "How is this person teaching me to confront my hatred?"
- "How is this person making me realize that I'm selfish?"
- "How am I going to act justly even if the person really is doing something that is unjust or is provoking anger?"

"Those steps," Rabbi Almog said, "help me keep the mitzvah of helping my enemy's beast of burden better."

More general is the question of whether the Buddha's primary purpose, to end suffering, is compatible with Judaism. A contemporary Renewal-affiliated rabbi, David Ingber, would say it absolutely is. In a dialogue with Buddhist monks and the professor Lobsang Tenzin Negi, of the Center for Contemplative Science and Compassion-Based Ethics, Ingber said:

> I like to say had it not been for the Buddha, I wouldn't be Jewish. Had it not been for the Buddha, I would not have known that Judaism could have been not just an identity, not just a culture, and not just something that you did a couple of times a year, but it could be a full practice. That Judaism offered a way into what the Buddha called Nirvana, or the cessation, the extinguishing of the crazy mind, the fire mind, the mind that is always on fire.[14]

To summarize, in Buddhism the mind is central but in Judaism, action (the mitzvot) is central. Buddhism is atheistic and accepting of emptiness whereas Judaism is theistic and embracing of the fullness. Buddhism is stoic and encouraging us to detach from our emotions whereas Judaism is passion-driven and emotional. Buddhism largely rejects the reality as we perceive it whereas Judaism sees a deeper reality but affirms the surface reality as not merely an illusion (there are multiple layers of truth). Both promote the middot (focus on our character development) but they will often promote different character traits. Both can suggest a middle path is healthy and generative.

13. Exodus 23:5.
14. See YouTube: SpiritPeaceLove, *Buddhist Jewish Dialogue*.

So, can a JewBu be a good Jew? I would say so. And I would say, for all of us, we should not be afraid of the Buddha. He's not a god, he's not a threat, and his aims are noble. We can all be inspired by him, even those of us who don't dive into the deep waters of Buddhism.

3

Socrates (469–399 B.C.E.)

WHAT DOES IT MEAN to live a good life? Is it more important to say what is true than what is diplomatic? Can we actually know anything at all? These are questions posed by the thought of Socrates, the first of the philosophers to be unignorable by Jewish thought, and by the rest of the world.

Before we jump into Socrates, we should zoom out and think about the relationship with the Jews and Greeks. The Jews generally weren't super impressed with their surrounding cultures but they certainly were with the Greeks. Here we see engagement with rational thought, the birth of western philosophy, and attempts to synthesize tradition with philosophical thinking. The Jews are also ambivalent about the Greek emphasis on aesthetics and the obsession with beauty and hedonism. Famously Rabban Gamliel, one of the greatest sages, was in the bathhouse where there was a statue of Aphrodite[1]. Yavan is considered to represent Greece and he is considered to be a descendent of Yefet (a son of Noah). The Torah was translated into Greek (the Septuagint) and the Jews had an ambivalent relationship to this[2]. The Jews were accessing Greek thought through Roman society, which has a new flavor, since Rome was obsessed with imperialism and with power in general. But Roman culture is still an extension of Greek thought. This is why we often refer to Greco-Roman influence (like some today talk about Judeo-Christian influence on the western world). The Jews were deeply

---

1. Babylonian Talmud, Avodah Zara 3:4.
2. "On the 8th of Tevet, the Torah was rendered into Greek during the days of King Ptolemy, and darkness descended upon the world for three days." Megilat Ta'anit, Last Ma'amar. On the other hand, we learn: "Our Rabbi, Shimon ben Gamliel, says the only language [other than Hebrew] the books of the Bible can be written in is Greek." Babylonian Talmud Megillah 9b.

influenced by this society much as we are today by American society. Josephus Flavius wrote:

> [They were] desirous to leave the laws of their country, and the Jewish way of living according to them, to follow the king's laws, and the Grecian way of living. Therefore, they desired to build a gymnasium in Jerusalem. And when they had been given permission, they also attended to the circumcision of their genitals, that even when they were naked, they might appear to be Greeks. Accordingly, they left off all the customs that belonged to their own country, and imitated the practices of the other nations.[3]

Was Jewish assimilation into Greek culture all bad? Some didn't think so.

> A frank appraisal of the periods in which Judaism flourished will indicate that not only has a certain amount of assimilation and acculturation not impeded Jewish continuity and creativity, but that in a profound sense, this assimilation and acculturation was a stimulus to original thinking and expression, a source of renewed vitality. To a considerable degree, the Jews survived as a vital group and as a pulsating culture because they changed their names, their language, and their patterns of thought and expression.[4]

The rabbis also teach, or imagine, that some Greeks had some level of respect for the Jews. One Talmudic passage records:

> As soon as Alexander the Great met Shimon HaTzaddik face to face, he descended from his chariot and bowed down to him. The servants protested, "Such a great king as yourself bows to that Jew?" Alexander replied, "This face," explained Alexander, "appeared to me before every battle which I won..."[5]

Some will respect the Jews when we talk, dress, and act like them but not if we are distinct and different. Napoleon Bonaparte famously said: "To the Jews as French – everything. To the Jews as Jews – nothing." That is a popular attitude toward to Jews in America today too. If they Jews are mostly assimilated and you can't tell any difference between them and us, but those orthodox Jews who look, talk, and eat differently, we're not so interested.

3. Flavius, *Antiquities of the Jews*, book 12, Chapter 5:1.
4. Prof. Gerson Cohen, "The Blessing of Assimilation" (JTS commencement address, 1966).
5. Babylonian Talmud, Yoma 69a.

Unfortunately, it's not only gentiles but also Jews who are embarrassed of Jews who look and act different than the norms in Christian society.

With Socrates, we see the beginning of Greek philosophy and western philosophy as we know them. But, despite his influence, we cannot know for sure what he actually said, as, like many impactful figures in Jewish thought, he didn't leave any of his own writings. Instead, we know only what's written about him, in the works of his student Plato.

Among the most famous of his sayings written down by Plato is "The unexamined life is not worth living," or perhaps more accurately: "The unexamined life is not worthy of a human being."[6]

For me, this is a feeling those in the Jewish community should find relatable. Many of Judaism's most common rituals cause us to reflect on our lives and ask questions. If we are to pray, we must first ask ourselves what is it that we are in need of to pray for. When the High Holidays come, we must engage in teshuvah, a process that forces us to ask ourselves about where we have gone wrong in our lives. Shabbat, whether we're conscious of it or not, causes us every week to reflect on our lives. So too, contemplative prayer or meditation can bring us to this kind of much-needed inner work. The role of knowledge is seminal among the Jewish virtues.

More broadly, Socrates pushes us from being mindlessly obedient to being questioners. He's considered the founder of western philosophy precisely because he doesn't take anything for granted. The Socratic method, which is inherently dialectical, is an attempt to create a dialogue between opposing ideas. One can find a similarity to this in the Jewish tradition. When learning Jewish texts, the goal is not to take the text at face value, but to ask questions that emerge from a close reading of it. These questions focus on what about the text doesn't make sense or how the text might be contradictory with other Jewish texts. Through the process of asking and answering these questions, the meaning of the text is discerned. According to the rabbis, this a process that never ends, for there are "seventy faces of Torah."[7]

Socrates was additionally a courageous figure; however, his pursuit of philosophy caused him to be accused of corrupting the youth with his unique thinking and having "irreverence toward the gods."[8] He was eventually convicted of his crimes by Athens, but rather than fleeing as many expected, he bravely stayed and voluntarily accepted his punishment.

---

6. Plato, *Apology*, 38a.
7. Bamidbar Rabbah 13:16.
8. Nails, *Socrates*.

Abraham, the founder of Judaism, is understood as having followed a similar path. According to the midrash, Abraham destroys the idols in his father's shop, and as a result is brought before the king for blasphemy. When the king urges him to worship idols on penalty of death, Abraham refuses. However, unlike Socrates, who died by drinking hemlock, Abraham was thrown into a fiery furnace and saved by God.[9]

Socrates was the original "gadfly," someone unafraid to say controversial things about the ruling political powers in order to provoke change. According to Plato's *Apology*, Socrates says in his trial:

> If you put me to death, you will not easily find another, who, to use a rather absurd figure, attaches himself to the city as a gadfly to a horse, which, though large and well bred, is sluggish on account of his size and needs to be aroused by stinging.[10]

His form of philosophy cannot be separated from the political realm, which means that his work is inherently engaged with questions of justice.

Socrates' courage was additionally reflected in how Socrates didn't philosophize for the purpose of defending political positions, winning arguments, or making money—but simply to move toward a more just society with more thoughtful citizens.

The controversies Socrates provoked through his constant questioning of established norms, can best be understood in light of Pirkei Avot, the Ethics of the Fathers, where it differentiates between controversy that is constructive and controversy that is destructive:

> Which is the controversy that is for the sake of Heaven? Such was the controversy of Hillel and Shammai [a good-faith debate for the purpose of finding truth]. And which is the controversy that is not for the sake of Heaven? Such was the controversy of Korah and all his congregation [a rebellion for the purpose of acquiring power[11]].[12]

We would recognize Socrates' constant questioning as an attempt to offer controversy for the sake of heaven. It was his belief that this would lead to a greater understanding of the truth.

While it makes sense why Socrates would annoy so many of those who encountered him, his approach was not to directly preach truth, but to expose, through a dialectical method, others' contradictions and lack of

---

9. Genesis Rabbah 38.
10. Plato, *Apology*, 20e.
11. Sacks, *Arguments for the Sake of Heaven*.
12. Pirkei Avot 5:17.

knowledge. Socrates is commonly credited with the phrase, "All I know is that I know nothing." However, this is a simplification. The fuller quote according to Plato is:

> I am wiser than this man; for neither of us really knows anything fine and good, but this man thinks he knows something when he does not, whereas I, as I do not know anything, do not think I do either. I seem, then, in just this little thing to be wiser than this man at any rate, that what I do not know I do not think I know either.[13]

In a way that is similar to Socrates, there are a lot of Jewish texts that emphasize how important it is for us to know the limits of our knowledge. We often think we know more than we actually know, and if we are to learn, we must recognize there is much that we do not. This is a major theme in Maimonides' Guide for the Perplexed, where he argues that too often people try to understand complicated philosophical questions without the proper preparation. As a result, they are drawn to answers that are incorrect and perhaps even antithetical to the Torah. Socrates' statement also finds similar expression in the mystical teachings of Rabbi Nachman of Breslov would frequently say, "the culmination of all knowledge is when one realizes that one knows nothing."[14] That being said, even though the Jewish tradition values a degree of humility, it still believes that knowledge is possible. In Pirkei Avot[15], it is recorded:

> Ben Zoma said: Who is wise? One who learns from every person, as it is said: "From all who taught me have I gained understanding."[16]

From this, it is clear that we must be humble about what we know, because no matter how learned we may be, there is always something to be learned from others, even those we think to be beneath us.

Socrates wanted each person to fulfill the good life, but he asks, "What is good?" "What is right and just?"

He believed that virtues, *aretê*, are absolute, for all human beings, and not relative. That makes him profoundly ancient and very pre-modern. This appears to differ slightly from an approach taken by Judaism's Maimonides, who was influenced by Aristotle and taught the golden mean. He wrote:

---

13. Plato, *Apology*, 21d.
14. *Likutei Moharan, Tinyana* 7:6.
15. Pirkei Avot 4:1.
16. Psalms 119:99.

> If a person finds that their nature tends or is disposed to one of these extremes ... they should turn back and improve, so as to walk in the way of good people, which is the right way. The right way is the mean in each group of dispositions common to humanity; namely, that disposition which is equally distant from the two extremes in its class, not being nearer to the one than to the other."[17]

However, Plato's point is an epistemological one (concerned with truth) and Aristotle's point is one of behavior (how we should live). Nonetheless, we might wonder how absolute truths might translate into practice in extreme or moderate ways. To be sure, Socrates emphasized philosophy as a process of discerning virtue even if it wasn't always clear exactly what that means. Plato and Aristotle each take the idea and interpret it in their own ways.

It is crucial to note here that Socrates, on the other hand, believed that people fall into vice due to a lack knowledge. People do wrong because they don't know right, but if they know what is right, they will do what is right. That is why knowledge is the primary pursuit of life: other virtues will flow from it. In this way, he differs somewhat from the Jewish tradition. For the rabbis, making moral mistakes is not the result of a lack of knowledge but caused by the desires we have, what is often referred to as the yetzer hara, the "evil will." While knowledge is seen as essential for improving oneself, knowledge alone is never enough. One must also directly grapple with one's desires, take responsibility for them, and learn how they can be channeled appropriately.

It does appear that Socrates, when his father died, inherited a significant amount of money, so he didn't need to earn a living. It also appears that when he was sentenced to death, Socrates was given the choice of exile, but instead he accepted a guilty verdict and the death penalty.

In the time of the massively impactful Greek philosophers, Jewish thought was entering the era when it was to be forever influenced by these thinkers. Greek philosophers are not, for example, quoted in the Talmud, and the rabbis go so far as to say that it is forbidden for one to teach their son "Greek Wisdom."[18] However, the Greek ways of thinking, such as inductive reasoning, begin to influence other cultures. With Socrates, at the classics at large, we see the beginning of the process of Greek philosophy coming to define what it means to be intellectual.

---

17. Maimonides, *Mishneh Torah*, Human Dispositions 1:3.
18. Babylonian Talmud, Sotah 49b.

While Judaism learns from philosophy, it does not define itself by it. "The Greeks worshipped human reason, the Jews, divine revelation," Rabbi Jonathan Sacks wrote in his book *The Great Partnership*. "The Greeks gave the West its philosophy and science. The Jews, obliquely, gave it its prophets and religious faith."[19] This distinction is of great importance. Reason alone cannot serve as a source of transcendent meaning in our lives. While it can help us navigate the world more effectively and efficiently, it cannot easily explain those things that are most important to us. The ones we love and the values we see as worthy of dedication and sacrifice are rarely if ever fully explicable by reason. Rather, they are best understood through the religious idea of holiness. As Rabbi Sacks summarized it: "Judaism is about relationships. The Greeks asked, 'What exists?' Jews asked, 'What is the relationship between the things that exist?'"[20] It is through revelation that we learn what it means to be in relation with God, and it is through our relationship with God we learn how our lives should be directed towards holiness.

Rabbi Sacks expounded on this by saying[21]:

> The Greeks, and many in the Western World who inherited their tradition, believed in the holiness of beauty ... Jews believed in the opposite: *hadrat kodesh*, the beauty of holiness: "Give to the Lord the glory due to His name; worship the Lord in the beauty of holiness."[22]

A couple hundred years after Socrates, the Hebrew Bible would be translated into Greek, which Jews would consider both miraculous and a watering down of Jewish knowledge. Relatedly, it would lay the groundwork for Christianity to spread by way of gentiles familiar with the stories of the Hebrew Bible from visiting Greek-speaking diaspora synagogues.

Infamously, Greek culture and even religion would come to take over the wider Jewish culture and even the Jerusalem Temple, culminating in the Maccabean revolt, and the story of Hanukkah, which literally means "Dedication," a reestablishing of what we see as the proper Judaism.

However, purity from Greek influence is not something that is actually possible, nor is it something we should strive for. In fact, the Pesach Seder, one of the most popular and beloved Jewish rituals, is based on the Greek symposium, a night of question-asking and critical inquiry. Afikomen, the ritual in which we hide matzah at the Seder, comes from the Greek word

---

19. Sacks, *The Great Partnership*, 46.
20. Sacks, *Future Tense*, 182.
21. Sacks, *Ceremony & Celebration*, 86.
22. Psalms 29:2.

epikomon, or dessert[23]. Like the symposium, the seder includes leaning, dipping, drinking, and discussion. The design of the Pesach experience, by the rabbis, in a sense, we owe to Socrates.

The ancient Greek philosopher Athenaeus explained:

> The leader of the symposium "took pride in gathering about him many persons of culture and entertaining them with conversation . . . now proposing topics worthy of enquiry, now disclosing solutions of his own; for he never put his questions without previous study or in a haphazard way, but with the utmost critical, even Socratic acumen, so that all admired the keen observation showed by his question.[24]

But, in other ways, the rabbis distanced the seder from the approaches of the Hellenistic world. To start, the symposium was mostly about philosophical discussion about food, drink, love, and beauty whereas the seder was about God's miracles. Further, the symposium was reserved for the elite whereas the seder was designed to be for all ("let all who are hungry come and eat") and is more specifically geared toward the questions of children. Additionally, after the symposium would often continue with drinking after-parties whereas the Jewish approach didn't permit this.

> To be clear, the rabbis differentiated the Passover meal from some of the more frivolous and indulgent aspects of the symposium by forbidding after-dinner drunken revelry at neighbors' homes—this is the original meaning[25] of the prohibition against having afikomen (dessert/after-party) after the Passover sacrifice.[26]

Whether we admit it or not, our lives and thinking and even ritual as Jews has been changed by the life of Socrates. The task throughout history—as well as now—has been to filter and discern for what outside methods bring us closer to the truth.

---

23. Zion, *How Passover Customs Have Changed and Developed Over Time*.

24. Athenaeus, *Deipnosophists*, 2nd, c. Greece.

25. "This point was made by, among others, Saul Lieberman, Ha-Yerushalmi kifshuto (Jerusalem: Hotsa'at Darom, 1934), 521; and Chanoch Albeck in his classic commentary on the Mishnah (m. Pesaḥim 1:8)."

26. Hidary, *How is the Passover Seder Different from all Other Symposia?*

4

Plato (427–348 B.C.E.)

How do we know what is truly real? Does a perfect world exist? If not, can we create one? What is the nature of the human soul? Are all people equally valuable?

Alfred North Whitehead once said that "All of Western philosophy is but a footnote to Plato," whose metaphysical thought covered everything from religion to human nature to science to love and sexuality.

While the Jewish tradition doesn't generally adopt the same positions on these topics as Plato, Plato was the one to lay the groundwork for philosophical debates that have gone on throughout the world over thousands of years. And Judaism, intentionally or not, has been in dialogue with him. Neoplatonism was most deeply influenced by Christian and Islamic influences.

Plato's view of philosophy bears a likeness to what we might think of today as mysticism. It assumes that there are higher, hidden truths one must discern that can shed light on the way the world is to ideally function. Though Plato doesn't speak of God in the way that Jews do, he does believe that the highest of philosophical truths is "the good" which shed lights on all other ideas.

We tend to think of Plato as just a student of Socrates in Athens from around 2,400 years ago, but he was also influenced by the pre-Socratic thinkers, such as Pythagoras, Heraclitus, and Parmenides. For almost all these people, what we know of them we know from the writings of Plato. And, unlike with Socrates, whose teachings we don't have directly, we believe we have the totality of Plato's work. It is worth noting that Plato is just his pen name given by his wrestling coach due to his physical size but his actual name was Aristocles, son of Ariston.

But, when we talk about Platonism, what we're primarily referring to is Plato's theory of forms. In the theory of forms, there are two worlds: our material reality and the unseen world of forms, or ideals. While the very first verse of the Torah already distinguishes between heaven and earth, it may not be until Plato that we understand the binary in such a new light. We might understand Plato's world of forms to consist of the abstract blueprints for how things would ideally be.

The classic example used to explain this is a table. Yes, you have a table in your house, but it is not the "ideal" table, which exists only in the heavenly image of "table-ness." A real table is known through your senses, but the ideal table, the form of a table, you can conceive of only through pure reason.

For Plato, there is the messy world we live in and the ideal, perfect world of forms. In a way, this is similar to Jewish mysticism which also conceives of an ideal heavenly realm that runs parallel to our own world. However, one of the unique innovations of Jewish mysticism is that we see it as our goal not only to gain knowledge of this heavenly realm but also to perform actions in this world which can positively impact the one above. Hassidut places a great emphasis on this idea as can be seen in the writings of the Maggid of Mezeritch, the successor of the Baal of Shem Tov, who taught it this way:

> This is the meaning of [the title] "The Song of Songs" —
> One who sings a song below
> Can arouse many songs on high![1]

For Plato, the world here is trying to copy the perfect world above, in Judaism we are repairing both the world here and the world above. Judaism's picture of heaven, then, is not a blueprint, but a mosaic shaped by the repairs we've made.

Plato's best-known teaching might be his Allegory of the Cave, which teaches about the ascent of the soul to achieve enlightenment. According to Plato, to better understand the way we experience the world, we must imagine it as if we are chained to the wall of a cave. A fire sits behind us and men carry objects in front of the fire which then cast shadows on the wall of the cave upon which we look. We look at them thinking they are real but can't recognize they are illusions. However, if one was able, they could free themselves from their chains, find their way out of the darkness cave, and behold the world as it is illuminated by the sun. For Plato, the philosopher

---

1. Green and Holtz, *Your Word Is Fire: The Hasidic Masters on Contemplative* Prayer, 21.

is able to achieve this when they use reason to recognize that the world of appearance is an illusion. Rather, they discover that true world is that of the ideal forms.

However, in believing human beings could free themselves from the cave, Plato was for better or for worse an elitist. Democracy is developed by the Greeks yet they had an elitist approach to who should govern: the educated[2]. He did not believe that most had the capacity to philosophize. Those few who were capable of it were unique and should be appointed as political leaders, empowered to make decisions for the collective. Listening to anyone else would mean putting in charge those who only know the shadows of things rather than how they truly appear. The theory of forms, reflected in Plato's parable of the cave, is about the relationship between human perceptions and truth. Most people are fools because they are led primarily by their senses, which can deceive them, rather than by reason. They fall into the trap of empiricism, that perception is reality and that our senses alone can provide us with something objective.

Plato's Allegory of the Cave is also similar to a legendary story in the Talmud, in which, Rabbi Shimon bar Yochai, is sentenced to death for criticizing the Roman government and goes into hiding in a cave, along with his son, Rabbi Elazar. There, they are miraculously given a carob tree and a spring of water, and for 12 years they stay in the cave praying and studying Torah. (Tradition holds that during this time Shimon bar Yochai received the mysteries of the Zohar, the foundational text of Jewish mysticism.) Then Elijah the Prophet comes and tells Shimon bar Yochai that the emperor has died and he's no longer in danger. So Rashbi and his son leave the cave, where they see workers plowing and sowing.

"These people abandon eternal life of Torah study and engage in temporal life for their own sustenance," Shimon bar Yochai says, and he and his son shoot fireballs from their eyes at the common people.

A voice from heaven then says to them, "Did you emerge from the cave in order to destroy My world? Return to your cave."

A year later, they emerge from the cave, and see an elderly man preparing for Shabbat. "See how beloved the *mitzvot* are to Israel," Shimon bar Yochai says to his son. "Their minds were put at ease," the Talmud teaches, "and they were no longer as upset that people were not engaged in Torah study."[3]

---

2. This raises fascinating questions today around the duties of citizenship and the responsibilities involved with being a voter to understand the issues one is voting on.

3. Babylonian Talmud, Shabbat 33b.

While both stories involve individuals being forced to live in a cave rather than the real world, the story of Rabbi Shimon bar Yochai makes clear that there are times when the enlightened may be condemned to dwell there. Rather than glorify those with knowledge of the supernal realms, the Talmud is wary that such knowledge may cause individuals to show disdain for the world as it is because it pales in comparison to the ideal world. For Plato, the goal of the philosopher is to bring enlightenment to all people, whereas in the Talmud, it is enough for the scholars and "regular" people to each find fulfillment in their own way.

It is not coincidental that, just as Plato is the founder of the field of the philosophy of mysticism, Rashbi is by tradition a key figure of Jewish mysticism. They're both people thought to possess a special kind of knowledge, Plato's knowledge through reason and Rabbi Shimon's knowledge through study and revelation.

Plato's ideas also overlapped with Jewish thought regarding the nature of the soul. It makes sense that, for Plato, we're obviously not merely bodies, but souls. He primarily associates it with the mind and intellect as what governs the body, even as it remains separate from it. The soul, unlike the body, is the essence of who we are. Plato believed in the immortality of the soul, and engaged in several long dialogues about the afterlife and reincarnation.

This is not too far from Jewish conceptions of the soul, however, in Jewish thought, the soul is identified not only with the intellect but is said to consist of multiple parts: the *nefesh*, the breath of life; the *ruach*, the spirit; the *neshama*, the part that connects us to God; and the *chaya* and *yechida*, two higher levels that transcend this world. So too, in traditional Judaism the soul might be thought to reincarnate (according to some) or be immortal (according to all).

There are also commonalities between Plato's views on gender and those of the Jewish tradition. In the Book of Genesis, it says:

> And God created humankind in the Divine image,
> creating it in the image of God—
> male and female God created them.[4]

Rashi notes that, according to the midrash, this means that the first person contained both genders, only to be divided later.[5] So too, for Plato, the fullest form of a person is not a man or a woman, but both.

> In the first place, there were three kinds of human beings, not merely the two sexes, male and female, as at present: there was a

---

4. Genesis 1:27.
5. Rashi on Genesis 1:27:3.

third kind as well, which had equal shares of the other two, ... For 'man-woman' was then a unity in form no less than name, composed of both sexes and sharing equally in male and female ... There was one head to the two faces, which looked opposite ways; there were four ears, two privy members, and all the other parts, as may be imagined, in proportion.[6]

The rabbis may very well have been influenced by the Greeks for they directly cite the Greek word "androgyne" to describe the first human beings, who were a combination of both male and female. It says in the Midrash:

> Said R. Yirmiyah ben Elazar: In the hour when the Holy One created the first human, God created them [as] an androgyne [a Greek word], as it is said, "male and female God created them." Said Rabbi Shmuel bar Nachman: In the hour when the Holy One created the first human, God created them double-faced, and sawed them and made them backs.[7]

Unlike Judaism, Plato believed that human beings could be broken down as having one of three kinds of souls, which aligned with a rigid class system: a soul of the appetite, for the working class; a spiritual soul, for the warrior class; and a soul of reason, for what he called the philosopher-king, the kind of person he envisioned as a ruler. While Judaism doesn't generally divide people strictly into hierarchies, it does have a lot to say about how to run a just society. And so, Maimonides, who learned deeply from the works of Plato's student Aristotle, by way of the works of Islamic philosophers, had his own conception of a philosopher-king. He wrote in his *Guide for the Perplexed* about how a leader must learn from the attributes of God. He derives this from when Moses asks to see God's face, and God responds that this is impossible. Even so, God is willing to pass before Moses, thus revealing what has become known as the thirteen attributes of mercy: " a God compassionate and gracious, slow to anger, abounding in kindness and faithfulness, extending kindness to the thousandth generation, forgiving iniquity, transgression, and sin."[8] In his great philosophical work, the Guide for the Perplexed, Maimonides writes:

> It behooves the governor of a city, if he is a prophet, to acquire similarity to these attributes, so that these actions may proceed from him according to a determined measure and according

---

6. Plato, *The Symposium*, 189d–190b.
7. Genesis Rabbah 8.
8. Exodus 34:6-7.

to the deserts of the people who are affected by them and not merely because of his following a passion.⁹

According to Maimonides, God's attributes are not to be discerned by contemplating some hidden divine realm but can be found when one pays close attention to the natural world and the way that it functions.

> For instance, one apprehends the kindness of God's governance in the production of the embryos of living beings, the bringing of various faculties to existence in them and in those who rear them after birth - faculties that preserve them from destruction and annihilation and protect them against harm and are useful to them in all the doings that are necessary to them.¹⁰

The way Plato would articulate it, the basis of being moral and constructing a just society is one where people have acquired the wisdom to understand the form of the good. Only the knowledgeable, Plato and Rambam would agree, are fit to rule. One might say that Plato came to deify logic and we might question if reason should be so primary when there are so many other human faculties as well.

Before concluding, it is worth noting the most commonly referenced popular culture idea emerging from Plato: the idea of platonic love. Although never called that by Plato himself, he did suggest that there is a type of love that is non-romantic and non-sexual. This is a type of friendship where one transcends attraction toward another's body to a higher level of attraction to one's soul. Interesting enough, in the Symposium, Plato addresses this through the lens of pregnancy. One can have a sexual encounter that produces a pregnancy of the body but one can also have a platonic love encounter that produces a pregnancy of virtue. There is a ladder of love where one can ascend to higher forms of love for self, other, and the Divine.

So, does Judaism either approve or disapprove of Plato? His thought was so wide-ranging that one can't really arrive at a binary conclusion. The questions posed by Plato's work, however, are ones that Judaism has had, and will continue to have, the challenge of wrestling with. It is exciting that the Greek philosophers, who had financial means, transcended cultural norms to be obsessed with riches, food, and pleasure and to move to the realm of ideas. In our day as well, we have a Jewish community that can be infatuated with power and wealth, like all other communities in this age of materialism, and we can work toward a Jewish renaissance that is once again fascinated by the power of ideas and ideals.

---

9. Maimonides, *Guide for the Perplexed*, 1:54.
10. Maimonides, *Guide for the Perplexed*, 1:54.

5

Aristotle (384–322 B.C.E.)

How do we know an idea is true? Is the observable more important than the speculative? Does everything have a purpose?

Aristotle is the Greek philosopher to have maybe the greatest direct impact on the path Jewish thought will later take in the Middle Ages, and the ideas he raises are ones that, unlike with other thinkers, we have used extensively as points and counterpoints in many of our essential books throughout Jewish history.

Aristotle was the third and final of the classic sequence of the chain of essential Greek philosophers: Socrates, Plato, and Aristotle. Just as Plato was a student of Socrates, Aristotle was a student of Plato. These appear to have been his main influences since his parents died when he was around 13 years old and he was raised by a guardian (Proxenus of Atarneus) who later married Aristotle's sister. Aristotle's father, Nicomachus, who was the personal physician to King Amyntas of Macedon and it seems he had an early influence on him by teaching him science.

Aristotle began learning with Plato later in Plato's life, when he was around 60, and studied with him until Plato's death around the age of 82. However, Aristotle's philosophy dramatically diverged from Plato's path. He seems to have been shocked not to be chosen as Plato's successor[1], so he left Athens for Ionia. Aristotle tutored Alexander the Great starting in 343 BCE. He also taught other future kings: Ptolemy and Cassander.[2]

Aristotle founded the Peripatetic school which was a philosophical academy in Athens whose members conducted philosophical and scientific

---

1. Instead, Plato's nephew, Speusippus, was chosen to lead.
2. Green, *Alexander of Macedon*, 58-59.

inquiries. The school declined after the middle of the 3rd century BCE, but it was revived later in the Roman era. Only about one-third of Aristotle's writings have survived and it's not clear that what remained was ever intended to be published at all. These writings include the first formal studies of logic. He had a huge influence on medieval Muslim thinkers where some referred to him as "The First Teacher." He also had a large influence on medieval Christian scholars where Thomas Aquinas would refer to him as "The Philosopher" and Dante would refer to him as "the master of those who know." As we shall explore, Maimonides was blown away by Aristotle as well referring to him as the "chief of the philosophers."[3] In a letter to Shmuel Ibn Tibbon, Maimonides writes that there is no need to study any philosophy that precedes Aristotle.[4]

In substance, Aristotle's philosophy was more methodical and dependent on observation of the world and how it functioned as opposed to Plato's emphasis on intuition. Because of this, Aristotle ultimately rejected Plato's theory of forms. He could not accept them because they could not be proven by Aristotle's scholarly scrutiny. While Plato was occupied with ideals, Aristotle was interested in studying things as they were observable. Why do we need to be distracted, Aristotle thought, by the unprovable and hypothetical?

Aristotle was instead a pioneer in the field of logic, believing in the power of reason. He developed the principles of syllogism and deductive reasoning. That is to say, one can create an "argument whose *structure* guarantees its validity."[5] The most commonly taught example of this is: "All men are mortal. Socrates is a man. Therefore, Socrates is mortal."

Aristotle applied his methods to his study of the natural world, taking an interest in animals and the earth. While Plato's background was in the more abstract field of math, Aristotle's father was a physician, rooted in science and the practical.

In the Jewish realm, Aristotle's thought heavily influenced the thought of Maimonides, who lived in the 12th century C.E., and, as a renowned physician was one of the most impactful Jewish philosophers and Torah scholars of all time. He picked up Aristotle's philosophy from his Muslim neighbors and modified it for a Jewish worldview.

Beyond the significant number of times Rambam references Aristotle in his own works, we can see Aristotle's footprint in how Maimonides also

---

3. Davidson, *Moses Maimonides: The Man and His Works*, 98.
4. Kellner, *Maimonides on Judaism and the Jewish People*, 77.
5. Shields, *Aristotle*.

placed such a strong emphasis on this-worldly matters, focusing on how halacha, Jewish law, was central to Jewish life.

While it's tempting for anyone to think excessively about what will happen after this life and after this world, Rambam believed we can't know too much about what is coming, so we should focus on this life.

> All these and similar matters cannot be definitely known by people until they occur for these matters are undefined in the prophets' words and even the wise people have no established tradition regarding these matters except their own interpretation of the verses. Therefore, there is a controversy among them regarding these matters.[6]

In that respect, we can say Aristotle's worldview feels somewhat Jewish; yes, Judaism has deep thought on mysticism and eschatology, but it is primarily a lived practice is about sanctifying this life and this known reality.

Perhaps living in the world of physicians rooted both Aristotle and Maimonides in the tangible, in the here and now. While a Jewish mystic might feel a connection to Plato, with his belief that "forms" or "ideals" can be recognized innately, a Jewish rationalist can easily feel represented in part by Aristotle, who was a proponent of study.

Now, to be sure, both Aristotle and Rambam placed a great emphasis on philosophizing as a form of metaphysical contemplation. The worldly matters are necessary but ultimately just a distraction from where we should ideally direct our energies. This is why Rambam writes in the Mishneh Torah that the messianic age is about having the free time to contemplate God. So they are both focused on the virtues (and laws) we should live by daily in this world but the ideal, for Maimonides, is indeed to escape this world toward a deeper contemplative life. As usual, Maimonides is full of contradictions. Is life about this world or beyond this world? Yes, and yes!

For Maimonides, the Torah and philosophy convey similar truths, and therefore one cannot contradict the other. Because of this, he read the Torah non-literally in such a way that allowed him to show how it conveyed philosophical truths such as God's incorporeality and God's oneness. Additionally, he viewed it as essential that the mitzvot be understood as neither arbitrary nor containing mystical secrets but rather reflecting a rational purpose. To determine this purpose, he took a teleological approach drawn from Aristotle, who taught that there are four causes for why things come to be:

1. The material cause, which is what something is made of.

---

6. Maimonides, *Mishneh Torah*, Kings and Wars 12:2.

2. The formal cause, the shape, the stuff it's made up of.
3. The efficient cause, how it is brought into being.
4. The final cause, which means the purpose of a thing.

So too regarding the mitzvot, Maimonides argued how they were to bring about certain goals of philosophical and ethical importance. For example, practices such as eating meat and milk together were understood as being connected to idol worship, and therefore the Torah forbid them so as to ensure Jews would stay as far away from idolatry as possible.

Here there is an overlap between Aristotle and the Jewish mystics, who believe that everything in creation is encoded with a Divine purpose. It is written in the Tanya, a foundational text of Chabad Hasidism:

> This ... thought was expressed by the Ari [Isaac Luria, the originator of Lurianic Kabbalah], of blessed memory, when he said that even in completely inanimate matter, such as stones or earth or water, there is a soul and spiritual life-force— that is, the enclothing of the "Letters of speech" of the Ten Utterances [of creation] which give life and existence to inanimate matter that it might arise out of the naught and nothingness which preceded the Six Days of Creation.[7]

The ultimate purpose of creation, then, is for human beings to elevate the spiritual life-force in all things to bring us to a better world.

However, *all* traditional Jewish philosophers would disagree with Aristotle's belief that the world was not created at all—that it simply always existed. Maimonides writes in his *Guide for the Perplexed*:

> If we were to accept the Eternity of the Universe as taught by Aristotle, that everything in the Universe is the result of fixed laws, that Nature does not change, and that there is nothing supernatural, we should necessarily be in opposition to the foundation of our religion, we should disbelieve all miracles and signs, and certainly reject all hopes and fears derived from Scripture.[8]

Rambam adds later on that, if the universal is eternal, there is no way for humanity to meaningfully improve it, and therefore there is no greater purpose for the human being. He writes:

> Aristotle, who assumes the Eternity of the Universe ... needs not ask to what purpose does man exist, for the immediate

---

7. Shneur Zalman of Liadi: *Tanya*, Shaar Hayichud Vehaemunah.
8. Maimonides, *Guide for the Perplexed*, 2:25.

purpose of each individual being is, according to his opinion, the perfection of its specific form. Every individual thing arrives at its perfection fully and completely when the actions that produce its form are complete. The ultimate purpose of the species is the perpetuation of this form by the repeated succession of genesis and destruction, so that there might always be a being capable of the greatest possible perfection. It seems therefore clear that, according to Aristotle, who assumes the Eternity of the Universe, there is no occasion for the question what is the object of the existence of the Universe.[9]

If the universe is static, as Aristotle says it is, Maimonides argues: Then what is the purpose of our lives except to live, procreate, and die? Surely, if everything has a purpose, the purpose of the human being goes beyond that sad cycle, because the universe itself must have a purpose too.

So, what do we make of Aristotle 2,300 years later? Obviously, even with his brilliance, Aristotle's understanding of areas such as geography and astronomy were proven flawed by human advancement. His scientific advancements were replaced later in the Enlightenment. So too, his ethics proved to be badly mistaken, as he supported slavery and deemed women to be inferior human beings. Further, he appears to have been rather ethnocentric advising Alexander the Great to be "a leader to the Greeks and a despot to the barbarians, to look after the former as after friends and relatives, and to deal with the latter as with beasts or plants."[10] But every thinker has their errors and their own historical and moral context that they're immersed in, so we cannot blame Aristotle simply for being ancient.

More applicable for us today are the things he got right, which were truly revolutionary for the advancement of human knowledge. His method of proving arguments with science and logic were so convincing that Maimonides believed, when scientific evidence is indisputable, the Torah must be reinterpreted to find a new meaning. This remains an important principle of Jewish religion; it is not the Torah *against* science, but the Torah *with* science as complementary realms of knowledge and wisdom.

So too, Aristotle was very serious about ethics and virtues, and Rambam adopted his idea of the "golden mean," that a virtue lies between two vices. In the *Guide for the Perplexed* he applies this to sex and the commandment to "be fruitful and multiply," saying:

> We must keep in everything the golden mean; we must not be excessive in love, but must not suppress it entirely; for the Law

9. Maimonides, *Guide for the Perplexed*, 3:13.
10. Green, *Alexander of Macedon*, 58-59.

commands, "Be fruitful, and multiply."[11] The organ is weakened by circumcision, but not destroyed by the operation. The natural faculty is left in full force, but is guarded against excess.

While the science of this might be dubious, we can still learn from the idea Aristotle and Maimonides were teaching: virtue is found not in the extremes—to use Rambam's example, either having sex constantly or avoiding it altogether—but in tempering desires to live a guided and optimal life. The fact that Maimonides thinks the goal of circumcision is limiting sexual pleasure is perhaps yet another great influence that Aristotle had on him as Aristotle believed physical sensations were a very lower access point to truth and did not think highly of sexual matters.

For both Aristotle and Maimonides, we are led not by ideals but by behaviors, what Aristotle thought of as habit, and what we might call *halacha*. According to Maimonides, it is better, for example, to give just a little bit of *tzedakah* every day than to give a large sum of money all at once. Why? Because by giving each day, you are training yourself to be in the habit of pursuing justice, rather than exhausting your funds in one day and not doing this justice work for the rest of the year. In the virtue ethics of Aristotle and Maimonides, the primary goal of ethical behavior is character development.

As modern Jews, there is much of the philosophy of Aristotle that we can appreciate. Whether one is a mystic or a rationalist, we tend to believe it is best to invest our moral and spiritual energy in what we can logically show to be worthwhile pursuits. Further, by believing in the purpose of all things, we can gain the consciousness necessary to fulfill the purposes of our own lives.

---

11. Genesis 1:22.

6

Avicenna (980–1037 C.E.)

WHO ARE WE? WHAT are we? Are we our bodies? Or are we something greater? Today we skip about 1350 years to the philosophy of the Islamic thinker Avicenna, who brought the work of Aristotle into the realm of soul.

Just about the entire development of rabbinic Judaism as we know it occurred during this gap of time since Aristotle, from the lives of Hillel the Elder and Rabbi Akiva, to the codification of the Mishnah, to the redaction of the Talmud, to the prevalence of early medieval rabbis such as Saadia Gaon.

But Jewish "philosophy," meaning systematized thought about knowledge itself, doesn't really emerge until the medieval period. Of course, much went on in history both inside and outside of the Jewish world, including the destruction of the Jerusalem temple, but in the realm of philosophy, the time between the ancients and medievals is considered something of a footnote.

One reason for this gap in our timeline is that, during the intellectual prominence of the Muslim world during the Islamic Golden Age, Aristotle's works weren't translated into Arabic until around 800–950 C.E. Avicenna is a Latin name and his Arabic name was Ibn Sina (son of Sina) which was what he would have been referred to in the region of Persia where he lived (today known as Iran and Iraq).

Avicenna, then, became the primary Muslim philosopher to engage with the thought of Aristotle, joining the conversation we left off with over 1,300 years prior. Before Maimonides became the key Aristotle-influenced philosopher of the Jewish tradition, and before Thomas Aquinas did the same with Catholicism, Avicenna, or, as he was called in Persia, Ibn Sina, was among the great philosophers of Islam.

Unlike Rambam and Aquinas, though, Avicenna was not primarily a theologian, and he did not adhere rigidly to the doctrines of Islam. Although he did feel that he could radically challenge Aristotle at times, Avicenna affirmed the Aristotelian view that the world is eternal, not created, even though that clashed with Islamic theology.

He differed with Aristotle, though, in that, for Aristotle, the soul is associated with the intellect. It can in a sense exist beyond one's death but only as a manifestation of the rational knowledge that one acquired in life. To Avicenna, the mind is fundamentally distinct from the body, and it includes not only the knowledge we might ascertain but also our experiences and our very sense of self. Because it is immaterial, the soul is immortal and able to endure after our physical bodies have perished.

Traditional Jewish thought both agrees and disagrees with Avicenna. Yes, the soul exists after death and can go to be with God. However, there is also the doctrine of the resurrection of the dead, that these souls will be put back in our resurrected bodies, at least for an earthly messianic period.

Avicenna arrived at his view that our selfhood persists after our death through a thought experiment he called the "floating man," a kind of precursor to the thought of René Descartes. The "floating man" is recorded in his treaty "On the Soul" in his *Book of Healing*.

Avicenna proposes that we imagine the following:

> One of us must suppose that he was just created at a stroke, fully developed and perfectly formed but with his vision shrouded from perceiving all external objects – created floating in the air or in the space, not buffeted by any perceptible current of the air that supports him, his limbs separated and kept out of contact with one another, so that they do not feel each other. Then let the subject consider whether he would affirm the existence of his self. There is no doubt that he would affirm his own existence, although not affirming the reality of any of his limbs or inner organs, his bowels, or heart or brain or any external thing. Indeed, he would affirm the existence of this self of his while not affirming that it had any length, breadth or depth. And if it were possible for him in such a state to imagine a hand or any other organ, he would not imagine it to be a part of himself or a condition of his existence.[1]

According to this model, if we had just come into existence, but we didn't have any senses—we were, for example, blindfolded and floating in

---

1. Avicenna's De Anima, *Being the Psychological Part of Kitab Al-Shifa*. Edited by F. Rahman. That work is quoting this one: Goodman, L. E. (2013). *Avicenna: Arabic Thought and Culture*.

the air—we would still know of our own existence, even without any senses. So, what makes me, me? It can't be my body, Avicenna argues, because I can know that I exist without it.

Similarly, Descartes later imagined a demon trying to tell us we don't know anything. But the one thing we can know, Descartes says, is our own existence—because one can know that they're the one having thoughts. Hence his famous phrase, "I think. Therefore, I am."

Both Avicenna and Descartes, in their thought experiments, seek to demonstrate that the mind or self is the primary thing that we know exists, even more than we know our bodies exist. Even without, or ignoring, our bodies and senses, Avicenna argues, we can know the self exists. Therefore, we can know the self exists independently of the body. And, if the soul doesn't live and die with the body, the soul must be immortal.

Now, this was somewhat problematic in Muslim theology, because, in Islam, the soul lies dormant with the body until the whole person, body and consciousness, is resurrected in the afterlife. And so, Avicenna was attacked as a heretic for this view that the soul lives forever outside of the body.

Techiyat HaMetim, the physical resurrection of the dead, is also one of Maimonides' 13 principles of the Jewish faith. (The soul in Jewish thought preexists the body, lives in the body, goes to be with God after the body's death, is put back in the resurrected body in the messianic period, and ultimately back to the world of souls.) Nonetheless, Avicenna's dualism became popular among Christian theologians, who liked how he made Aristotle's ideas translatable to a worldview with an immortal soul.

By the 13th century, though, the Christian thinker Thomas Aquinas argued that Avicenna was wrong—that a more accurate interpretation of Aristotle intertwines the mind and body more. Aquinas believed the mind to be the same self as the body. For example, you feel a pain in your leg differently than you notice a hole in the wall. That must be because the pain is affecting *you* and the hole in the wall isn't; your body and self must be truly linked.

But Descartes, in the 17th century, returned the dominant mode of thought to a dualism, a conception that is metaphysical like Plato's, not materialist like Aristotle's.

Today, most philosophers reject mind-body dualism because of neuroscience developments. Avicenna was very interested in physiology in his time, but he didn't have access to the scientific tools that move most thinkers closer to Aquinas' view, that the mind and body are connected; we can explain how different parts of the brain—in the physical body—are in control of different parts of what we are thinking.

Gilbert Ryle critiqued dualism as arguing for a "ghost in a machine." We can explain how the machine works, he thought, without suggesting there's a ghost in there. Even though current philosophers reject Avicenna's dualism, they do agree that there is a self with a first-person view, like an eye, which is not something that can be totally explained by scientific theories.

What should Jews think of all this? Judaism does not have much of a dilemma with mind-body separation. Judaism is less concerned with the exact location of consciousness and more concerned with the soul, how that consciousness connects and relates to God. We don't have a problem with the (not fully proven) idea that the mind is located within the brain. But the fact that that aspect of human consciousness cannot be definitively located in the brain does indicate the potential for the immateriality of the soul.

Whatever the case, we imagine the soul as the connecting point between the material and spiritual world. And, in this life, it is stuck with our body.

Avicenna forces us to deal with the question of what it means to have the gift of consciousness and what it means to have a body that does not seem to be fully unified. These questions, about what it means to be alive, resonate for those of us spiritually engaged.

Rabbi Ahron Soloveichik wrote that after experiencing a stroke and suffering from partial paralysis on his left side, he felt that, "It is as if I have become completely detached from my left leg and my left arm."[2] With this realization, he argues that he gained a new awareness of the way in which the body and soul are not one and the same:

> The fact that I am now constantly under the impact of a biological sensation of carrying a foreign, detached object consisting of the left side of my body corroborates the proposition that the human soul is a separate entity having an identity of its own and extraneous to the body ... in a normal person, the body and soul are synthesized and integrated in such a beautiful and well-integrated pattern that for all practical purposes the soul appears to be immanent in the body.[3]

However, other thinkers, such as Martin Buber, tend to emphasize the fundamental unity of body and soul. Even if the soul ultimately remains separate from the body, we should strive for a harmonization of the two as

---

2. Soloveichik, *A Glimpse at Eternity from a Hospital Dungeon*; Soloveichik, *Logic of the Heart, Logic of the Mind*, 31.

3. Soloveichik, *A Glimpse at Eternity from a Hospital Dungeon*; Soloveichik, *Logic of the Heart, Logic of the Mind*, 31.

much as possible. He wrote in The Way of Man: According to the Teachings of Hasidism:

> What is meant by unification of the soul would be thoroughly misunderstood if "soul" were taken to mean anything but: the whole man, body and spirit together. The soul is not really united, unless all bodily energies, all the limbs of the body, are united. The Baal-Shem interpreted the biblical passage: "Whatsoever thy hand finds to do, do it with thy might[4]" to the effect that the deeds one does should be done with every limb, i.e., even the whole of man's physical being should participate in it, no part of him should remain outside. A man who thus becomes a unit of body and spirit — he is the man whose work is all of a piece.[5]

There are the *taryag mitzvot* (613 Biblical *mitzvot*) and one returns until all of them have been properly fulfilled.

Different from Avicenna's view that our bodies and souls are fundamentally distinct, in Judaism, in Buber's articulation, we find that the body and soul, while not necessarily the same, are both essential and are deeply connected to one another.

---

4. Ecclesiastes 9:10.
5. Buber, *The Way of Man: According to the Teachings of Hasidism*.

7

Averroes (1126–1198)

DO REASON AND RELIGION contradict? If so, what are we supposed to do? These questions are far older than we might imagine, as we learn from studying the work of Averroes. By examining how this debate played out almost 900 years ago, perhaps we can gain a better understanding of how we should address these topics today.

Averroes, known in Arabic as Ibn Rushd, was a scholar of both philosophy and religion, the first of our philosophers to be deeply entrenched in religious life. Born in Córdoba,[1] he was a *qadi*, or an Islamic judge; he decided matters of Islamic law by issuing fatwas,[2] the direct equivalent of rabbinic responsa. In effect, he was in Islam what Judaism would call a rabbi.

He worked under a very strict regime, but still found time for his philosophical efforts and spent his nights writing commentaries on Aristotle. Inspired by Aristotle, Averroes believed only the social elite were really capable of complex, higher-order thought, and that most Muslims should accept the Quran literally, at face value. However, this approach wasn't unusual for his era. In the Jewish tradition, Maimonides felt similarly and made clear that he only wrote his *Guide for the Perplexed* for those educated sufficiently in the ways of philosophy.

What *is* exceptional is that Averroes embraced the philosophy of Aristotle and rejected religious fundamentalism. He believed the Quran didn't accurately portray the universe in a literal sense and that philosophy was needed to better understand religious truths. Rather, the Quran was better

---

1. Present-day Spain
2. Dutton, *The Introduction to Ibn Rushd's "Bidāyat al-Mujtahid,"* 188–205.:10.2307/3399333. JSTOR 3399333.

understood as a poetic expression of religious truth conveyed allegorically to make the truth accessible to the masses.

A similar view was held by another religious thinker from Córdoba, about four centuries later, the 16th century Kabbalist Rabbi Moshe Cordovero (the Remak). He too criticized the simplistic notions of God held by the masses and argued that through learning, they could achieve a more sophisticated understanding. He wrote:

> An impoverished person thinks that God is an old man with white hair, sitting on a wonderous throne of fire that glitters with countless sparks, as the Bible states[3] ... Imagining this and similar fantasies, the fool corporealizes God. He falls into one of the traps that destroy faith. His awe of God is limited by his imagination.
>
> But if you are enlightened, you know God's oneness; you know that the divine is devoid of bodily categories—these can never be applied to God. Then you wonder, astonished: Who am I? I am a mustard seed in the middle of sphere of the moon, which itself is a mustard seed within the next sphere. So it is with that sphere and all it contains in relation to the next sphere. So it is with all the spheres—inside the other—and all of them are a mustard seed within the further expanses. And all of these are a mustard seed within further expanses.
>
> [As you learn to understand God as truly infinite,] your awe is invigorated, the love in your soul expands.[4]

The major difference between the Remak and Averroes is that Averroes was less bothered that the unlearned masses would maintain a simple theology while only the educated would strive for a more scientific and philosophical worldview. The Remak, however, seemed to want all Jews to move beyond a literal meaning of religious language and replace it with a more sophisticated system of mystical symbolism.

Averroes believed those with access to education had a religious obligation to engage in theology with a philosophical lens, however this only applied to the elite and not the masses. Within this way of thinking, Averroes held that any time Aristotelian thought contradicts the Quran, Muslims must reinterpret the Quran in order to reconcile it with the truths of philosophy. This is a crucial intellectual move for people committed to traditional religion, to be able to say, "I am committed to the truth of my

---

3. In the Book of Daniel.

4. Moses Cordovero, *Or Ne'erav*, 2:2 (18b–19a), translated by Daniel C. Matt in *The Essential Kabbalah: The Heart of Jewish Mysticism*, 22.

sacred text, *and* I am committed to what we understand about reason, and therefore the sacred text must be reinterpreted so philosophy and religion are compatible."

Rav Saadia Gaon taught[5] that when reason and revelation contradict, one must go back and reexamine both. If there seems to be a clash, it must be the case that there is just a misunderstanding. Either our reason is flawed or the revealed text has a different meaning than we originally thought. Either way, we must be willing to engage in serious intellectual work to ensure the two become aligned.

For Averroes, his study of Aristotle ultimately caused him, to give up the traditional Islamic notion that the world was created by God. Instead, he affirmed the Aristotelean view that the world did not have a beginning but was instead eternal. It has always existed and will remain to do so.

On the other hand, Averroes also reinterpreted Aristotle. For instance, he maintained the fundamental Islamic belief in the resurrection of the dead, and felt that rejecting the immortality of the soul was heresy. Where many traditional Islamic theologians criticized philosophers for not believing in bodily resurrection, Averroes sought to defend the belief and understand it in a more nuanced way. He argued that one is reborn in the world beyond after they die, but their body will not be the same as it was in this world. Rather, it will take on elevated attributes necessary for a higher spiritual existence that we cannot yet fully grasp.

The afterlife, in this way of thinking, is highly intellectualized. Averroes is saying, if one grasps eternal truths, they live forever through those truths. But, if one doesn't grasp them, they die with their body by not attaining what is eternal. This is radically different from a typical fundamentalist reading of religious texts, or the Hollywood image of heaven that consists of people holding hands with their loved ones and dancing through the clouds.

Due to his willingness to reinterpret religion in light of philosophy, Averroes, at times, received strong opposition from his fellow Muslims. They banned his books, and, in 1195, he was personally exiled. Though the ban was subsequently canceled two years later, and he returned to Cordova, he died the next year.

In the 13th and 14th centuries, his works were translated into Latin and Hebrew, which enabled him to have an enormous influence on Christian and Jewish thinkers, particularly those who had an interest in Aristotelian philosophy

What should the thought of Averroes mean for Jews in our time?

---

5. I learned this teaching from Rabbi Saul Berman when I was in rabbinical school.

While we're not beholden to Aristotelian philosophy today, there remains a need to reconcile theology with reason. Because reason is God-given, holy, and true, it must be granted as much weight if not more than the literal readings of religious texts. Without reason, religion easily falls into fundamentalism, and therefore it is crucial that one maintain a commitment to both the integrity of religious texts and the need to frequently reinterpret them. This ensures that religion's timeless values survive while religious texts can still remain open to new layers of meaning that reason can help us unlock.

Part of the way Judaism manages this tension is through the idea of the Oral Torah, which serves to expand upon the Written Torah. The ongoing process of Midrashic interpretation of the Written Torah compels us to constantly engage the text in new ways and develop new understandings and applications for it.

In religious life today, there is a tendency to eschew tradition in favor of progress or rigidly cling to simple understandings of the past at the expense of letting religion breathe and grow in the present. Averroes can serve as an example for how to pass on eternal truths while maintaining our intellectual integrity.

"Judaism is layered," Rabbi Arthur Green teaches. "The rules of the game were: You never deny the truth of the prior layers. You just reinterpret them." Such a statement feels almost directly in conversation with Averroes, who thought, when his religion didn't make sense, he needed not to throw away his religion, but to add to it.

Confronting the problems and contradictions of religious thought in a direct manner is sometimes scary. It often requires great courage to challenge religious dogmas that no longer make sense in order to make way for the more sophisticated truths that faith can enable. Averroes, we see, paid a price for doing this.

Today, we may not think of academic life as overly brave. For the most part, scholars are not courageous truthtellers who go against the prevailing currents or cultural critics charged with taking on the religious or political establishment. But many philosophers of the past, like Averroes, and even some in the present, continually challenge religion to live up to its claim of holding the highest form of truth.

Perhaps we should allow these philosophers to inspire courage in us to re-evaluate some of the mainstream ways of thinking as well. In the end, we may not need to choose religion or reason, but rather sometimes live with paradox and the mystery of multiple truths.

8

Moses Maimonides (ca. 1135–1204)

WHAT IS GOD LIKE? Can we even really know? Is the debate over the meaning of the written Torah only about how it is to be applied in our world, or does it point us to deeper, philosophical truths? Is it our responsibility to just accept the Torah as it is or does it reflect specific values?

In some ways, we can't discuss Judaism after the 12th century at all without at least implicitly talking about Rambam (an abbreviation for Rabbi Moshe[1] ben Maimon, or, in Latin, Maimonides). His application of philosophical principles to Jewish thought and practice forever changed what it meant to be Jewish.

Maimonides composed three major works including a commentary on the entire Mishnah, the first comprehensive and influential code of Jewish law known as *Mishneh Torah*, and *The Guide for the Perplexed*, which attempted to bridge between the truths of philosophy and Judaism.

In effect, the *Mishneh Torah*, quite controversially, simplified the Talmud for the masses. Instead of needing to ask a rabbi how the more-than 2,700 winding pages of the Talmud translate into Jewish practice, someone could simply refer to the *Mishneh Torah*, which would tell them what they needed to do. To get the fullness of the Jewish tradition, though, with all the debates and stories, one received no help from Maimonides, and still needed to go to the Talmud itself.

A Spanish-born immigrant to Egypt, Rambam, in addition to being a *halakhist*, was an all-around intellectual, renowned as a physician[2] and sci-

---

1. He knew he was great, as he truly was. He thought there had never been another Moshe since the original Moses. He felt his role for Jewish thought was monumental perhaps almost akin to the original Moses.

2. He even served as a physician to the sultan Saladin.

entist. His most indelible mark on the world, Jewish and otherwise, though, was as a philosopher, his principal work being *The Guide for the Perplexed*.

Like the Islamic philosophers of his era, Maimonides was heavily influenced by Aristotelianism. He accessed Greek thought through the Islamic philosophers like Al-Farabi, Ibn Sina (Avicenna), and Ibn Rushd (Averroes). For example, he subscribed to Aristotle's idea of the Golden Mean, which we've discussed in relation to Socrates and Aristotle. He also embraced the Greek idea of the perfection of the intellect and believed one achieves eternal life by attaching themself to perfect truth. Unlike other rabbis who desired for Jews to embrace a culture of learning and debate, Rambam wanted Jews to adopt the correct practices and beliefs (such as with his innovation of articulating 13 attributes of faith) that would enable them to cling to the eternal divine truth. The effect of this was that as a legalist, he made Judaism simpler than it typically is understood to be, and as a philosopher, he made Judaism more complicated than it had been.

Rambam summarized the correct beliefs a Jew must know and affirm in his 13 Principles of faith, which begin with:

1. God exists; God is perfect in every way, eternal, and the cause of all that exists. All other beings depend upon God for their existence.
2. God has absolute and unparalleled unity.
3. God is incorporeal–without a body.[3]

Further, Rambam believed that virtues are cultivated through practice and habituation, and therefore he simplified the Jewish faith into 13 principles and Jewish law into a code. Without a clear path to follow, Rambam was concerned that Jews would find themselves going astray.

While one might think that the marginalization of questions and debate along with the formalization of dogma doesn't sound very 'Jewish,' his ideas have largely been accepted. But even so, they were not without controversy during and after his own life. This was largely due to Rambam's reliance on Aristotelean philosophy, which had previously been considered outside of Judaism. Professor of Jewish Philosophy Dr. Alan Mittleman explains it in the following manner:

> Part of the controversy is ... about the limits of intellectual openness, but also the nature of intellectual integrity. Is it possible to have full intellectual integrity, full mature stature as a human being, just within the ... four cubits of the Torah, or do you need to go outside the special learning and tradition of the

---

3. Septimus, *The Thirteen Principles of Faith*.

Jews? Maimonides welcomes the outside because he believes it's the duty of the Torah to welcome truth wherever it comes.[4]

To reconcile the Torah with philosophy, Rambam argued that the Torah cannot be understood literally. An overly simple reading of the Torah, for example, might lead someone to believe that God physically walks in the Garden of Eden, or brings the Israelites out of bondage in Egypt with a literal outstretched arm, or sits as a white-haired man on a throne. Maimonides was adamant that God does not have a physical body, and that anyone who disagrees with this was to be considered outside the fold of Jewish belief.

Instead, Biblical verses must be understood allegorically, a point Rambam makes clear in the introduction to *The Guide for the Perplexed*. Only then can it be seen how they point to deeper philosophical truths:

> Taken literally, such expressions contain wisdom useful for many purposes, among others, for the improvement of the condition of society ... Their hidden meaning, however, is profound wisdom, conducive to the recognition of real truth.[5]

Instead of accepting the Bible's descriptions of God at face value, he developed his negative theology—which is to say, we can't know what God is; we can only identify what God is not. God has no definable "essential attributes", because God exists beyond language. Whatever labels we attempt to apply to God, they can only define God in a limited and therefore incorrect fashion. Further, we cannot talk about God's "accidental attributes," traits that define how God is all-powerful or all-good, since they require evolution and adaptation and God is unchanging.

Even if we can say little about what God is, Rambam makes clear we can know God's actions and seek to imitate God. For instance, God took us out of slavery in Egypt, and so too to be like God, we should be liberators of others.

Even though Rambam was Jewish—and was the most influential Jewish thinker of the past 1,000 years— we can still question whether we, as contemporary Jews, wish to be Maimonidean?

I believe some of his ideas can be powerful while others might require modification. First of all, we *can't* separate Rambam from the Judaism we've inherited. His impact is too great. In many ways, we are all Maimonidean in that we *don't* believe God has a human form and sits on a physical throne up

---

4. See YouTube: The Jewish Theological Seminary, *Persecuting Ideas: The Case of Maimonides*.

5. Maimonides, *Guide for the Perplexed*, #21.

in the heavens. We can, in part, thank Rambam for making this understanding the standard Jewish belief.

Still, if we hold too rigidly to Rambam's ideas, we will conceive of God as distant and unable to understand our spiritual needs. Many times, we want to engage with a personal God of emotion, whom we'd call our Father and our King, or our source of Motherly knowledge (*binah*) or the Divine feminine presence (*Shechinah*). Even though we don't believe these to be literal descriptions of God, they capture the different ways we relate to God. By not only focusing only what God isn't, we can paint a far richer and more accurate picture of our relationship to God. As a Maimonidean, it is hard, if not impossible, to meaningfully pray to God as God is described in the traditional Jewish prayer book.

And, while Rambam shies away from bogging his readers down with Talmudic debates, he does want us to understand the reasons for Jewish practice. In his *Sefer HaMitzvot* and in The Guide for the Perplexed, he lays out the reasons for the commandments. Rambam knew that we are rational, meaning-making beings, and that we will always seek to understand the religious rituals and practices we engage in. Rambam provides reasons for the commandments, thereby showing how they point to higher philosophical truths and ethical maxims. Rambam left us his famous eight levels of tzedakah challenging us to give more anonymously and sustainably. Where he might have lacked a desire to satisfy that need of ours, though, was in how he refused to make meaning of God's Being. We want to know who and what God is but Maimonides pushes us away from this.

In deciding how we understand the Jewish tradition, we might ask ourselves: Is an emphasis on negative theology too restrictive? Though we don't necessarily understand the Bible literally, that doesn't mean we must only understand it philosophically as well. For example, why not take a more mystical path of understanding Torah as done by Ramban, a younger contemporary of Rambam? Further, there are benefits to Jewish law being codified made simple in a way that makes it accessible to the masses. However, there is also a cost. The true beauty and power of Jewish law can often only be grasped when seeing its complexity and diversity.

Maimonides is the most important Jewish philosopher of all time, but its critical to keep in mind he's not at all the only thinker in the Jewish tradition. Whatever we decide to make of him, his ideas should be put in conversation with other, competing and complementary, views. While Rambam was the one to in large part make the Jewish tradition what it is today, Judaism's understanding of God is not defined by him alone.

In addition to influencing the world at large and Judaism at large, he had a unique contribution to Sefardic heritage given that's the world he emerged from and was speaking to (working in Spain, Morocco, and Egypt). He's buried in Tiberias today if those visiting Israel want to pay their respects.

9

Thomas Hobbes (1588–1679)

How do we prevent our neighbors from doing bad things? Left to our own devices, will human beings primarily do evil? How do we keep our worst impulses in check? What powers must be given to the government?

Although his work was all-compassing, and he was a noted scholar of humanities and classics, Thomas Hobbes is known first and foremost as a political philosopher and as one on the most important thinkers at the cusp of pre-democratic modernity.

Hobbes was deeply influenced by the advent of modern science; he met the impactful astronomer Galileo Galilei and was engaged with the philosopher-politician Francis Bacon. Embracing the newly established reliance on science, Hobbes believed science could answer virtually all of our questions.

In this worldview, humans, like all animals, were thought to be totally knowable, and best understood almost like machines that could be taken apart and reverse-engineered. He was critical of Descartes' view of duality, that mind and body can be distinguished. In Hobbes' view, our knowledge is derived from our sense experience, which the imagination then constructs into ideas. Because Hobbes viewed the human being as solely a biological entity, he did not seem to account for consciousness, because, for him, everything is entirely physical, including our human experience.

And, just as a human being is akin to a machine, there was no reality beyond that of our senses. All things to Hobbes were material, made of physical matter. Hobbes' emphasis on empiricism has led many scholars to suspect he was an atheist. However, he also repeatedly emphasized like Maimonides that the human mind cannot grasp something like God—God is the only thing we can't know.

Hobbes applied his thinking to the realm of politics in his main work, *Leviathan*[1], which actually takes its name from the sea monster in the Hebrew Bible. The Leviathan in Tanakh is seen as perhaps God's mightiest creation. In the Book of Isaiah, God is described as destroying the Leviathan when the world is brought to a state of justice:

> In that day the Lord will punish,
> With God's great, cruel, mighty sword
> Leviathan the Elusive Serpent—
> Leviathan the Twisting Serpent;
> God will slay the Dragon of the sea.[2]

In the Psalms, the Leviathan is also described as the only animal powerful enough physically to play with God. It says in Psalm 104:

> There is the sea, vast and wide,
> with its creatures beyond number,
> living things, small and great.
>
> There go the ships,
> and Leviathan that You formed to sport with.[3]

And, in the most poetic section of the Book of Job, God explains God's own greatness to Job by saying that only God can defeat the Leviathan. God asks Job rhetorically:

> Can you draw out Leviathan by a fishhook?
> Can you press down his tongue by a rope?
>
> Can you put a ring through his nose,
> Or pierce his jaw with a barb? . . .
>
> Can you fill his skin with darts
> Or his head with fish-spears?
>
> Lay a hand on him,
> And you will never think of battle again.[4]

---

1. This work is a great example of how much Hobbes cares about religion. Some have wrongly suggested that because Hobbes wants to bring religious affairs under the control of the political sovereign that he is anti-religion. But that move for him is about preserving political and social stability until times are unsettled.

2. Isaiah 27:1.

3. Psalm 104:25–26.

4. Job 40:25–26, 31–32.

In Hobbes' book *Leviathan*, the title illustration contains a Latin rendering of Job 41:25, in which God says of the sea monster:

> There is no one on land who can dominate him,
> Made as he is without fear.

For Hobbes, the Leviathan is not a monster that wreaks havoc on humanity, but a source of power symbolizing the sovereign authority of the state. Yes, there may be a king or queen, but only because a head is necessary to ensure the preservation and stability of the body. Hobbes' *Leviathan* embraces social contract theory as the foundation of the state. In this theory, a social contract is "an actual or hypothetical compact . . . between the ruled or between the ruled and their rulers, defining the rights and duties of each."[5] However, Hobbes' social-contract theory is a bit different from what we might be familiar with regarding modern democracies.

For America, the Declaration of Independence is an actual moment in history where people came together to form a new republic. It makes clear that the government gets its powers "from the consent of the governed." Hobbes' social-contract theory, however, is more of a myth. For Hobbes we must make the assumption that:

> In primeval times . . . individuals were born into an anarchic state of nature . . . They then, by exercising natural reason, formed a society (and a government) by means of a social contract.[6]

The reason we must assume such a thing even if it cannot be factually proven is because it is essential that the people see the sovereign as legitimate. Any undermining of the sovereign's authority can lead to its removal and a descent into chaos.

Hobbes' theory of government is not inherently monarchist, but it was shaped by the English Civil War, which took place in his lifetime. When the people rose up against the monarchy, Hobbes sided with the king. He supported having a strong government, because he felt that without a sovereign, humans were condemned to a brutal state of nature, what he calls a "war of all against all." It is not so much that Hobbes thought human beings are particularly violent, but that without any law or authority to mediate between people, individuals would have no choice but to violently pursue their self-interest in order to protect themselves against others. In the state of nature, human life is in Hobbes' memorable words, "solitary, poor, nasty,

---

5. Encyclopedia Britannica, *Social Contract*.
6. Encyclopedia Britannica, *Social Contract*.

brutish, and short."⁷ The only way to ensure that people can live together peacefully is if there is a sovereign who can make the law and enforce it by force if necessary.

In the Jewish tradition, Hobbes' sentiment about the dangers of collective life without sovereign authority is shared in *Pirkei Avot*, the Ethics of the Fathers, compiled over a thousand years earlier. There, it is recorded:

> Rabbi Hanina, the vice-high priest said: pray for the welfare of the government, for were it not for the fear it inspires, every man would swallow his neighbor alive.⁸

Furthermore, it is a repeating refrain throughout the book of Judges, a time when the Jewish people were without a king, that: "In those days there was no king in Israel; every person did as they pleased."⁹

Though Hobbes derives his model of political sovereignty from the biblical example of God's sovereignty, a closer look reveals the ways in which his political thinking differs dramatically from that of the Torah. For Hobbes, it was essential not only that there be a sovereign who is granted authority over the state but that the sovereign's power must be absolute. Unlike modern democracies which depend on a separation of powers and checks and balances, Hobbes argued against these things out of fear that they could undermine the sovereign's authority and usher in chaos. Hobbes shows a remarkable lack of concern for the potential abuses of power that the sovereign may inflict upon his or her subjects, which stands in marked contrast to the Torah's approach to sovereignty. When the Jewish people approach the prophet Samuel to appoint a king for them, he makes clear that giving one person so much power will inevitably lead to its abuse.

> "This will be the practice of the king who will rule over you:
> He will take your sons and appoint them as his charioteers and horsemen, and they will serve as outrunners for his chariots . . .
>
> He will take your daughters as perfumers, cooks, and bakers.
>
> He will seize your choice fields, vineyards, and olive groves, and give them to his courtiers.
>
> He will take a tenth part of your grain and vintage and give it to his eunuchs and courtiers . . .

---

7. Hobbes, *Leviathan*, i. xiii. 9.
8. Pirkei Avot 3:2.
9. Judges 17:6, Also see Judges 21:25.

The day will come when you cry out because of the king whom you yourselves have chosen; and the LORD will not answer you on that day."[10]

Furthermore, Samuel emphasizes that by appointing a king and showing obedience to a human sovereign, the Jewish people risk turning away from God and engaging in an act tantamount to idolatry. In the Bible's perspective, the king is sovereign, but he must share that sovereignty with others, particularly the prophets who have a responsibility to rebuke the king if he violates God's law. For Hobbes' the human sovereign is above the law, makes the law, and enforces it as they see fit. In the Torah, the king is neither above the law nor its source. Rather, he must carry around a Torah scroll at all times as a reminder that God is the one true sovereign to whom even he must show obedience.

What do we make of Hobbes as Jews? To me, his reduction of the human being to their physical nature strikes me as a very flawed and simplistic understanding of human nature and human experience. To be sure, Hobbes was less concerned with human nature (which he seems to view with some plasticity) but with creating the right political and social conditions where people aren't fighting over limited resources and creating a violent unstable society.

Hobbes was also not a strong defender of religious liberty. He believed that, regardless of our personal views, we should obey the sovereign's view of religion to avoid conflict. Even though Hobbes goal was to remove political instability, we can see the harm done to minorities. This lack of separation between religion and state has historically been destructive for Jews and other minorities as well. There is, however, an alignment with Jewish values in how Hobbes believed that those who could not survive on their own labor deserved public support.

All of Hobbes' philosophy, though, stems from a view of human nature that denies the complexity of the human being, the place of a soul, and any recognizable concept of transcendent God who demands justice and to whom we are all accountable. There appears to be no place in his thought for any kind of spiritual relationship or engagement. His view of the human being was a low one: We're not only merely physical, but we're also selfish—as opposed to a more Jewish view, that we're bearers of the Image of God yet carrying a freedom, with inclinations to do both good and bad. However, we can recognize the value of being realistic about the need to reign in the worst human behavior to maintain moral order.

---

10. Book 1 of Samuel, 8:13-18.

The Jewish approach, though, might have a different solution for how to keep people moral without depending solely on the authority of the sovereign. We can largely accept Hobbes' premise that, without law, life is "solitary, poor, nasty, brutish, and short."[11] But we can also take the view of the Jewish legal tradition, that in addition to earthly sovereignty we also need halacha, God's law, as a set path, to guide and govern us.

Further, we have a complicated relationship to Hobbes' notion of supporting the sovereign. Given the history of monarchies as systems of exploitation with largely no concern for the poor common person, the idea of the social contract, that the government has responsibilities to the people, is potentially an improvement on previous systems. It was a crucial advancement that Hobbes was not merely pushing people to merely submit to the monarchy, but to also see the value in our social contract. By offering a justification for sovereign authority, Hobbes implicitly acknowledges that sovereignty is not absolute and rather is dependent on the will of the people.

So too, ancient Judaism definitely did embrace a form of monarchy, and it certainly also supports the need of some governmental authorities to regulate violence and maintain order. Nonetheless, aspirationally, we should seek to amplify the individual's greater moral potential for compassion and care and reason, rather than diminish them altogether. We should also recognize that the more that sovereign authority is invested in a small number of individuals, the greater likelihood for its abuse. Participatory government has long been a hallmark of modern democracies, and it is an essential safeguard against the abuse of power.

For us, though, the social contract goes beyond the government, as we also have a covenant with God. The human side of this contract is demonstrated in the Book of Exodus, when the Israelites say upon receiving the Torah, "'All that the Lord has spoken we will faithfully do!'"[12]

While traditional Jews have little problem giving up some freedom to act according to the will of God, Hobbes applies this kind of submission to the state, which is not something we should readily support. While we can make a king out of God, we know that no human authority can truly live up to that standard. Democracy, rather than a monarchy or oligarchy, is the least damaging form of earthly authority.

Of course, as Jews we also know all too well the history of powerful governments turning against the people they rule over. The ideal image of government we imagine should probably not be a terrifying Biblical seamonster, which indeed Tanakh describes as something God will defeat.

---

11. Hobbes, *Leviathan*, i. xiii. 9.
12. Exodus 24:7.

Instead, we might want to imagine society as described in the Torah, in which the community has a special responsibility to make sure everyone's needs are met,[13] and everyone is their brother's keeper.

---

13. Deuteronomy 15:4: "There shall be no needy among you."

10

René Descartes (1596–1650)

Is there anything we can be sure that we know? How can we know that we know anything at all? In a world in which there is misinformation and intentional lying in so many places that we look, is there anyone we can trust? Can we even trust ourselves?

René Descartes was born in France at a transformative time at the height of the scientific revolution. As a child, he was a meditator; he was ill, so he'd stay in bed late into the morning thinking. In his teenage years, he was immersed in math. He then served as a soldier in the Dutch States Army and resided in the Netherlands for the rest of his life.

Living in a scientific intellectual landscape, where there was a strong belief in attaining knowledge through verifiable methods, he dedicated his philosophical project to ensuring that truth and knowledge must have firm foundations. Rather than simply accept the metaphysical assumptions of the past, Descartes was convinced that one must begin philosophizing by starting with doubt. One must be skeptical of all that one knows until one finds those points of truth that cannot be questioned and then build on top of them.

Descartes' methodological skepticism begins in his *Meditations of First Philosophy,* by arguing that one cannot rely on their senses alone to determine whether or not something exists. Our senses can often deceive us. Just because we hear someone's voice doesn't mean they are actually present with us, for it could just be an audio recording. Furthermore, every time we dream, we experience a world that looks and feels like our own, but in the end, is only an illusion. While these examples may seem trivial to us, Descartes is committed to finding truth and knowledge that cannot be doubted under any circumstance. He goes so far as to raise the possibility that perhaps an "evil demon" has deceived him into believing everything he thinks is true. He writes:

> I will suppose, then, not that Deity, who is sovereignly good and the fountain of truth, but that some malignant demon, who is at once exceedingly potent and deceitful, has employed all his artifice to deceive me; I will suppose that the sky, the air, the earth, colors, figures, sounds, and all external things, are nothing better than the illusions of dreams, by means of which this being has laid snares for my credulity; I will consider myself as without hands, eyes, flesh, blood, or any of the senses, and as falsely believing that I am possessed of these.[1]

In a sense, Descartes is raising a question we hear even today: "How do we know that we don't live in a computer simulation? Isn't it possible that everything we experience is an illusion produced by something we do not see or know?" However, even if this were to be true, Descartes argues in his second meditation that there is at least one fact we can be certain about: our very existence. In Mediation II, he writes:

> But how do I know that there is not something ... of which it is impossible to entertain the slightest doubt? Is there not a God, or some being ... who causes these thoughts to arise in my mind? But why suppose such a being, for it may be I myself am capable of producing them? Am I, then, at least not something? ... Doubtless, then, I exist, since I am deceived; and, let him deceive me as he may, he can never bring it about that I am nothing, so long as I shall be conscious that I am something ... This proposition ... "I am, I exist," is necessarily true each time it is expressed by me, or conceived in my mind.[2]

Even if he is being deceived by an evil demon, Descartes concludes, there must be a *him* for the demon to deceive. The self must surely exist, even if nothing else does. This idea is central to much of Descartes' work, and he famously expresses it with the Latin phrase *Cogito, ergo sum* (I think therefore I am), published after his death in *The Search for Truth by Natural Light*. He explains it in the following fashion:

> It is necessary to know what doubt is, and what thought is, before we can be fully persuaded of this reasoning — I doubt, therefore I am — or what is the same — I think, therefore I am.[3]

1. Descartes, *Meditations On First Philosophy*, 13-16.
2. Descartes, *Meditations On First Philosophy*, 17-24.
3. Hallam, *Introduction to the Literature of Europe in the 15th, 16th, and 17th*

Descartes' emphasis on the act of thinking as indubitably proving our existence leads to what is known as Cartesian dualism, the notion that the mind exists independently of the body. Because there are times when our senses deceive us, our mind must exist apart from the body if it is to correct them. This idea serves to buttress his premise that our epistemic foundation cannot be built only by accepting truth and knowledge because we have been told so by others. We have to know things through reason, and not simply because a figure of authority has stated them to be true.

In Descartes' worldview, we can't take anything as a given. We have to actively remove our preconceptions and recognize that nothing is beyond doubt. Descartes wants us to embrace skepticism—not because the world is ultimately unknowable, as a postmodernist might suggest, but in order to build a stronger foundation for reason.

For me, I find this approach to be unreasonable, though not entirely alien to the Jewish tradition. Judaism's truth is dependent not on philosophical proofs but on accepting the testimony of those who came before us. To give just one example, we believe the Torah to be divine revelation not because it can be logically deduced but because our ancestors believed so. Judaism, at its core, is a tradition passed down from one generation to the next, a fact Moses emphasizes in his final speech to the Jewish people before his death:

> "Remember the days of old,
> Consider the years of ages past;
> Ask your parent, who will inform you,
> Your elders, who will tell you.[4]

That being said, the Jewish tradition does encourage a certain amount of skepticism, especially when it comes to religious authority. It was known that, when a student would ask the influential Modern Orthodox Rabbi Joseph Soloveitchik a question of *halachah*, Jewish law and practice he would reply, "And what would you say if I were not here for you to ask me?"[5] As religious people, we should not just accept what others, even figures of religious authority, tell us to do. Rather, a major part of being religious means thinking through issues for ourselves. Yes, there should be support and an appreciation for expertise, but in the end, the intellectual and moral burden is upon us.

Centuries, 451.

4. Deuteronomy 31:7.

5. This is a story told to me by Rabbi Dr. Eliezer Finkelman, among others.

We don't want to uncritically accept everything that is told to us. This is much different, though, than saying everything is assumed false until it can unequivocally be shown otherwise. While Judaism is based on reason, debate, and study as an intellectual tradition, there is not such a distrust of experience and foundational truth, or even of religious authority.

We also see in the Torah that the world contains misinformation which must be carefully evaluated. When God asks Adam why he ate the forbidden fruit, he answers by pawning off responsibility: "The woman You put at my side—she gave me of the tree, and I ate."[6] And then when God asked the woman, "What is this you have done!" The woman replied, "The serpent duped me, and I ate."[7] Of course, this does not go over well. The Torah knows that we have a tendency to attribute our failures to obedience, but we ultimately retain responsibility for our own decisions.

The midrash teaches that Adam added to God's prohibition that one was not only forbidden to eat from the tree but touch it as well. He told Eve that this is what God said. This as an example of how human beings distort what God says and wants (even when done with good intentions), and therefore some skepticism is always needed.

In Judaism, by and large, we *do* trust our senses. We don't wonder whether the entirety of the world, or the entirety of our mind, deceives us. Of course, we must be skeptical of who is speaking the truth, and we are told explicitly to beware of the false prophet.[8] We are also taught to be cautious of our *yetzer hara* (internal evil inclination trying to deceive us).

We must do the often-difficult work of fighting for truth and justice as things we can know. To be sure, we recognize that even God's word is not to be mindlessly accepted without question. Avraham challenges God when God threatens to destroy Sodom. And, in more current times, Elie Wiesel, after surviving the Holocaust, put God on trial in his play *The Trial of God*.

Descartes' challenge is very appropriate for the 21st-century religious person. A premodern person rejects skepticism and embraces the absolute, while the postmodern person doubts so much it undermines reason entirely. But Descartes, despite his unusual methods, seeks to land in a place where reason can be trusted. He just needs a deep intellectual journey to get there.

While, in my worldview, I'm willing to pre-accept a lot more as given to us, I believe Descartes demonstrated the integrity and courage we need today: to know what we truly know and to be humble about what we don't.

---

6. Genesis 3:12.
7. Genesis 3:13.
8. Deuteronomy 13:2–4.

11

John Locke (1632–1704)

Do we learn things from nature, or from nurture? Are ideas such as love, justice, truth, and beauty held instinctively in all humans, or must they be acquired? Is morality universal, or cultural?

John Locke was one of the most influential thinkers of the Enlightenment and is even considered by many to be the father of liberalism[1]. He was a British empiricist along with George Berkeley and David Hume[2]. He influenced Voltaire and Jean-Jacques Rousseau, as well as American Revolutionaries; his concept of "Natural Rights" was adopted most famously by Thomas Jefferson in the Declaration of Independence.[3]

The period he helped initiate was called the Enlightenment because it was a time when a new light source was found through reason. However, the commitment to a reason also led to a rejection of previous places where the light of knowledge was previously thought to be found, such as tradition, authority, and revelation. Further, the goal of the Enlightenment was not just to expand human knowledge but also to affirm the belief that knowledge founded on reason enables human freedom. Reason was not limited only to intellectual matters, but could best guide how human beings should live each day. The Enlightenment intended to free humanity from all forms of compulsion, so that human beings could reach their full potential. In the realm of ethics, the Enlightenment was no longer focused on an objective ideal good, as we saw with the Greeks, but rather saw the good as linked to individual happiness, something that could vary from person to person.

1. Hirschmann, *Gender, Class, and Freedom in Modern Political Theory*, 79.
2. Sharma, *Western Political Thought*, 440.
3. Korab-Karpowicz, *A History of Political Philosophy*, 291.

JOHN LOCKE (1632–1704)

For Locke, like other significant figures in the Enlightenment, science was central, and he believed we needed to demonstrate our truths with scientific proof. Consequently, Locke used an atomistic model of knowledge, not only for the hard sciences, but also for how he understood human behavior and society at large. All things, in Locke's thinking, could be broken down and analyzed. This was known as the "corpuscular theory," that everything in the world is made of particles called corpuscles. The qualities that we might observe in objects, such as color, were understood to be a feature of these corpuscles.

What made Locke a revolutionary thinker was that he rejected Platonism by arguing that humans have no innate knowledge. Instead, Locke was a committed empiricist and believed all that we know comes through our senses. Locke was skeptical of any kind of metaphysical knowledge at all because he believed that all we could know must emerge from our perception the world. Any abstract ideas we might conceive of were ultimately derived from the sensory input we receive from our experience of the world. In this kind of philosophy, there are no universal ideas, such as love, justice, truth, and beauty.[4] Locke's position was informed by the fact he lived in a time when Europeans began to have knowledge of other cultures around the world. With this came the awareness that certain features of morality Europeans assumed to be innate were in fact lacking in some parts of the world. For example, some cultures don't even believe in God at all.

While Descartes, along with Gottfried Wilhelm Leibniz, trusted only the *mind* because it was God-given, Locke believed the actual God-given source of knowledge was the *senses*.[5] Knowledge wasn't innate or deduced by reason but something that could only be learned from experience. The mind, for Locke, began as a *tabula rasa*, a blank slate, which would later be filled with empirical knowledge. The process of reasoning that Locke advocated for would come to be known as "abduction," meaning that we infer judgements based upon available evidence gathered by sensory experience. Although it might seem far-fetched to us, Locke believed we can't know what we haven't experienced.

---

4. It was commonly believed in Locke's time that, because God is good, it would be unfair for God to give innate ideas to only a few and not to all. If God is just, everyone must be given at least the simplest knowledge, of God's existence and of what is basically good.

5. Noam Chomsky would later build on the thought of Descartes with the idea of "Cartesian linguistics," a theory that grammar is innate rather than learned. Chomsky believes that there is an innate way of thinking in every human that generates a universal "deep structure" of language.

What do we make of Locke's thought as Jews? For one thing, it is positive that he embraced some notion of religious tolerance[6]. He felt that individuals should be free to pursue the truth of their beliefs as best as they are able without any coercion by the state. In his eyes, religious coercion was counter-productive because it would eventually lead to rebellion by those who held different beliefs. Locke also questioned whether religious beliefs could be coerced at all. Since belief is something that is internal to a person, how could the state force individuals to affirm one belief over another? While Locke's religious tolerance is to be praised, it is important to note that it did not extend to those who did not believe in God at all. He feared that the denial of Divine existence would lead society into chaos[7].

Mysticism in general and Jewish mysticism in particular is also foreign to Locke's method of philosophy. Locke's scientific worldview ruled out the possibility, as mysticism suggests that, through our inner lives, we can transcend, we can know God, we can cleave to the Divine, and we can travel, so to speak, spiritually and intellectually. For Locke, the only way to gain knowledge is through real-world experience, and there is no such thing as knowledge that transcends our physical experience of the world. Locke *did* believe in internal senses in addition to our external ones; while Locke did reject innate ideas, he did not reject the notion that humans have innate capacities, such as abilities for reason and perception. But this was still all based on experience, not revelation or Divine gifts given to our consciousness.

And, while Locke's main source of knowledge was human experience, Jews of course rely heavily on revelation and tradition. So how might the notion of Torah fit into his thought? I'd say that people around the world, by and large, have some sense of right from wrong without the clear text of the Torah; there *is* some basic level of innate universal morality. Torah, then, reinforces and deepens our already-ingrained sense of right and wrong. To be sure, there are many facets to morality and humans around the world disagree greatly about complex moral issues. Nonetheless, our psychological reactions of guilt, shame, and pride (to name just a few) are commonly predictable emotions based upon human experiences in moral dilemmas.

Locke's emphasis on empiricism and reason is similar to Maimonides and other proponents of rationalism within the Jewish tradition. As Maimonides makes clear, the Torah cannot contradict reason or contradict what our senses tell us to be true. And so, revelation does not undermine

---

6. McGrath, *Historical Theology, An Introduction to the History of Christian Thought*, 214–15.

7. Thoreau, *Waldron*, 217.

reason or empiricism, but rather provide a spiritual underpinning and ethical reinforcement for what can already be ascertained through reason. Additionally, Torah provides a comprehensive system and way of life that encompasses all that we do. We know rest is important, so the tradition gives us Shabbat. We know food is important, so the Torah gives us *kashrut*. We know families are indispensable, so the Torah gives us laws around how to maintain a family.

However, there are voices in the Jewish tradition that would disagree with Locke's belief that human beings are born as a blank slate and there is a great Jewish debate around the nature of a child. Is a child a wild beast that needs to be tamed? Or does a child have inherent gifts for parents and teachers to discover? This raises fascinating questions around theories of education. Should innate knowledge be harnessed, and innate goodness be strengthened? Or must we embrace rigidity to cultivate good behavior when there is no strong natural inclination for it? According to the midrash, while still in the womb, a child does acquire knowledge only to lose it upon birth.

When at last the time arrives for its entrance into the world, the angel comes to it [the child in the womb] and says: "At a certain hour your time will come to enter the light of the world." The child pleads with him, saying: "Why do you wish me to go out into the light of the world?" The angel replies: "You know, my child, that you were formed against your will; against your will you will be born; against your will you will die; and against your will you are destined to give an accounting before the King of Kings, the Holy One be Blessed." Nevertheless, the child remained unwilling to leave, and so the angel struck it with the candle that was burning at its head. Thereupon it went out into the light of the world, though against his will. Upon going out the infant forgot everything he had witnessed and everything he knew. Why does the child cry out on leaving his mother's womb? Because the place wherein he had been at rest and at ease was irretrievable and because of the condition of the world into which he must enter.[8]

The Talmud goes so far as to say that not only is the child aware while still in the womb, but it learns Torah[9]:

> And a candle is lit for it above its head (the fetus in his mother's womb), and it gazes from one end of the world to the other, as it is stated: "When His lamp shined above my head, and by His light I walked through darkness."[10] And do not wonder how one can see from one end of the world to the other, as a person

---

8. Midrash *Tanchuma, Pekudei* 3, translated by Samuel A. Berman.
9. Babylonian Talmud, Niddah 30b.
10. Job 29:3.

can sleep here, in this location, and see a dream that takes place in a place as distant as Spain. . . .And a fetus is taught the entire Torah while in the womb, as it is stated: "And He taught me and said to me: Let your heart hold fast My words; keep My commandments, and live."[11] And it also states: "As I was in the days of my youth, when the converse of God was upon my tent."[12]

It has been noted by Rabbi Joseph Soloveitchik and others that this rabbinic tale bears a striking resemblance to Plato's idea of anamnesis as found in the dialogue Meno (Meno's paradox). According to Plato, the soul is eternal and therefore can serve as a source of innate knowledge for a person. Therefore, when one is learning, one in fact rediscovering knowledge one already knows. Rabbi Soloveitchik takes this idea and applies it to the act of Torah study:

> The Jew studying Torah is like the amnesia victim who tries to reconstruct from fragments the beautiful world he once experienced. In other words, by learning Torah man returns to his own self; man finds himself, and advances toward a charted, illuminated and speaking I - existence. Once he finds himself, he finds redemption.[13]

Not only is Torah study an act of rediscovering oneself, the Baal Shem Tov, the founder of the Hasidic movement, went so far as to argue that "A person's soul will teach them."[14] We're not just blank slates. Instead, there is Divine knowledge within all people that we know only unconsciously and are tasked with re-discovering fully.

Overall, Locke did a service to the Jews; untested accepted knowledge can lead to fundamentalism. If there is no marketplace of ideas, there is no ability to offer proofs or counterproofs. Locke's skepticism of what we take for granted provides room for discovering what is not already known. Of course, Locke's own hypocrisy of speaking out against slavery and child labor but benefiting from them should give us pause and challenge us to reflect on our own moral hypocrisies, which we all have.

Judaism has always embraced a humility around what we know, and while the tradition would reject the idea that science is the source of absolutely all knowledge, it would reject even more the idea that innate

---

11. Proverbs 4:4.
12. Job 29:4.
13. Soloveitchik, *Redemption, Prayer, Talmud Torah*, 81.
14. Steinsaltz: *The Soul*, 27.

knowledge gives us all we need to know. Locke gave the world a framework for accepting debate and disagreement.

Judaism, as a pluralistic tradition, can embrace Plato and the idea of the objective good, and we say there are some things we know innately. At the same time, it can embrace Locke and say there are many of things we can't know innately but only through science. Judaism has room for both the transcendent or absolute and the cumulative development of knowledge. There is space in Judaism for inherent knowledge, learned knowledge, *and* knowledge that comes from revelation and tradition. How fortunate we are to not need to choose.

12

Baruch Spinoza (1632–1677)

How separate are our minds from our bodies? How separate is God from the world? Who wrote the Bible? Does God exist at all?

Baruch Spinoza is one of the most important Jewish philosophers of all time, but it is fair to say that his influence has been felt more strongly outside of Judaism than inside it. He was willing to go against the accepted beliefs of the Jewish community, which led him to an understanding of God and the Torah that differed vastly from the existing tradition, and eventually caused him to be excommunicated from the Jewish world.

Spinoza lived in the 17th century, but his impact on philosophy extends far beyond his time and would serve as the link to the emergence of pantheism in the 19th century. In some ways, it was Spinoza's biggest idea. In pantheism, God and nature are one and the same, and nothing exists beyond them. All of existence, including our thoughts, must be understood as merely part of the physical world, the result of natural processes.

This was a radical departure from the relatively common belief in Spinoza's time that God was distinct from nature and that a spiritual reality existed apart from the world. Before Spinoza, God's relationship to the world was conceived in the same way as the soul's relationship to the body. The two were separate and distinct even as one serves to animate the other.

This made Spinoza's pantheism hard for religious people to swallow; if God is simply existence as we know it, is there really a God at all? If God is the world, and the world is God, what is to distinguish this from atheism? Certainly, Spinoza's pantheism denies the possibility of a personal God who cares about us and to whom we can pray. According to the scholar Steven M.

Nadler, pantheism might sound like a religious position, but Spinoza's view doesn't contain reverence for God, just study of God as nature.[1]

Spinoza was also one of the originators of Biblical criticism and believed that the Bible can be studied as written by human authors. Spinoza wrote:

> All these details, the manner of narration, the testimony, and the context of the whole story lead to the plain conclusion that these books were written by another, and not by Moses in person.[2]

Challenging the authorship of the Torah, at that time, was a revolutionary act in the world of Jewish thought.

Because of his radical beliefs, Spinoza was famously excommunicated by his Jewish community in Amsterdam for unspecified "abominable heresies."[3] This was no small act for it was done at a time when kicking someone out of the Jewish community meant forcing them into an outside world that was hostile to Jews. Since he didn't become a Christian, where was he to go? The very idea one could live without religion was almost completely foreign in Spinoza's time.

As a younger contemporary of Renee Descartes, Spinoza was deeply influenced by him, but also differed from him in significant ways. He rejected Descartes' idea that the mind is separate from the body and that God is separate from nature. Instead, Spinoza was a metaphysical monist, who believed that one substance was the source of all existence. However, he did recognize that the physical world and human thought are not identical. Each one does offer a different perspective on the world, thus making him an "attribute dualist." But he did believe that the mental and physical were both the product of a single substance. For example, according to Spinoza, a rock is in essence no different from a human being. They are both made of the same matter. And so Spinoza was still in the realm of metaphysics, but he rejected a theistic metaphysic in favor, instead, in a pantheistic metaphysic.

While it's difficult to find sources for Spinoza's pantheism in the Jewish tradition, it's not enormously far off from the idea of God as understood by the Kabbalists and Hasidic masters. It says in Deuteronomy chapter 34:

> Know therefore this day and keep in mind that the Lord alone is God in heaven above and on earth below; there is no other.[4]

---

1. Nadler, *Baruch Spinoza*.
2. *The Chief Works of Benedict de Spinoza*, Translated by Robert Harvey Monro Elwes, G. Bell and sons, 123–124.
3. Nadler, *Spinoza: A Life*, 120.
4. Deuteronomy 34:9.

On its surface, this verse seems to mean that there is only one God, and not any others. However, a closer reading reveals a deeper interpretation: that the totality of existence, the heaven above and the earth below, is nothing other than God. This contention is similar to Spinoza's monism, the notion that everything in the world is simply a different aspect of the same divine substance.[5]

Based on this idea, the Kabbalists would come to a similar conclusion to Spinoza, and conclude that even a rock is of Divine substance. Born 110 years before Spinoza, the Kabbalist Moshe Cordovero taught:

> Realize that the Ein Sof [the Infinite] exists in each existent. Do not say, "This is a
> stone and not God." Rather, all Existence is God, and the stone is a thing
> pervaded by Divinity.[6]

What separates Spinoza is that the world is God and there is nothing more. The Kabbalistic perspective, however, maintains that God is within everything, but also beyond, a concept described as pan*en*theism.

To understand what this means, we can imagine that, in the beginning, God was eternally vast, like an infinite sheet of paper. But God's infinite being left no space for finite creation. Therefore, God contracted Godself (tzimtzum) and created an empty space into which to create—we can picture the paper having a hole in it. And into this hole, God created the world, like a big bang of God's substance. And so, while the infinite is *in* the creation, the infinite also remains outside of it. This is what makes possible to have a relationship with God as something that is not just myself or the sum total of existence. God can reveal Godself to us, what we call revelation, and we can cry out to God in prayer. In Spinoza's model, neither revelation nor prayer can exist in any traditional sense, because God is the world and the world is God, but there is no more.

For me, it's difficult to understand why Spinoza's monism would be appealing or sensible as a complete theory of reality for any religious person, but for a secular person, it may be very appealing.

I think we need to reject much of Spinoza's thought as Jews—as he undermines almost the entirety of Judaism. Firstly, his theology essentially eliminates the creation story as we traditionally understand it. If God is the world, then there can't be a cause to creation that is external to it.

---

5. This would be distinguished from substance dualism, which proposes a separation between mind and matter. For Spinoza, however, everything is ultimately matter.

6. Moshe Cordovero, Shi'ur Qomah 206b. Translation from Daniel Matt's *The Essential Kabbalah*.

Second, revelation is a key element of the Jewish religion, yet for Spinoza there is no being outside of nature that can communicate with us. Without revelation, the Torah is no longer divine. Third, prayer and Divine intervention are irrelevant if there is no transcendent God. Why should one pray if there is no one to listen? Accepting the ideas of Spinoza would require changing Judaism into a dramatically different religion.

So, what can we like about Spinoza? One possibility is his courage and willingness to go against the accepted wisdom of the community.[7] We can admire his fidelity to philosophy and the world of ideas, even if it meant being outside both the Christian and Jewish worlds.

We can also see Spinoza's pantheism as helping move one towards a more mystical view of God. Rather than view God as cold, abstract and distant, as is common for rationalism, Spinoza helps us realize that God is everywhere and found in everything. Understanding this can perhaps inspire us to move toward a mystical spirituality that can enable a closer and more intimate relationship with God.

Spinoza's pantheism may also be helpful for creating a sense of a global community by reminding us that we are all one. Maybe there is even some truth to monism, and by recognizing this, we can extend it to the ethical realm by seeing value in all people, animals, and the natural world.

To be sure, Spinoza's work was radical and revolutionary. But it was bold, smart and perhaps not irredeemable.

---

7. Though perhaps Spinoza actually wanted to be expelled.

13

Gottfried Wilhelm Leibniz (1646–1716)

WHY DO BAD THINGS happen to good people? Why doesn't God make everything perfect for everyone at all times? Do we have free will?

During the Enlightenment, the questions of philosophy and theology were seen as two separate domains, but newfound knowledge also caused thinkers to approach the realm of theology differently, as we see with Gottfried Wilhelm Leibniz.

Leibniz was a German mathematician, scientist, and philosopher, who developed his own unique way of understanding the makeup of reality. Leibniz was also a philosophical optimist, meaning he believed that God created the best of all possible worlds.

For most of us though, the world often doesn't feel that way. Whether consciously or not, we're all aware of the problem of theodicy: Why is there so much suffering in a world created by a purportedly good God?

The problem of theodicy rests on three theological commitments that monotheists typically hold:

1. God's benevolence: that God is good.
2. God's omnipotence: that God has the power to control all things.
3. Evil is real: that we know undue suffering is bad.

The most common move by religious people throughout the eras has been to give way on the third point—to say that, of course, God is good, and, of course, God is all-powerful, so there must be a fault in human understanding. What appears to us as evil from our perspective must in fact be good from God's perspective. Perhaps God's understanding of morality is better than ours in a way that to us is incomprehensible.

Or perhaps suffering is necessary and plays a constructive role in being a human being. This is particularly popular in Christian theology, wherein Jesus, the son of God, must reconcile an unjust world with the perfection of God by undergoing great suffering and even his own death.

The least appealing way of handling the theological problem is to deny God's benevolence. What would be the value of worshipping a God who is not good? However, it could be argued that this notion is represented briefly in the Hebrew Bible when God is described as the source of both good and evil. It says in the Book of Isaiah:

> I am the Lord and there is none else,
> I form light and create darkness,
> I make peace and create evil—
> I the Lord do all these things.[1]

A liberal theologian might address the problem of evil by arguing that even though God may be omnipotent, God chooses not to intervene to prevent unnecessary suffering. This is done to ensure humans have free will to act good or evil. The outcome of this is that people can do horrible things to each other, but what possible value is there to being human, one might ask, if humans are not free?

While I believe the answer to the question of theodicy is hidden from us in this life, I think one must recognize that suffering emerges independently of human decision. Famines, natural disasters, and terminal illnesses arise all the time without necessarily being caused by human failings or being necessary to preserve human freedom. However, Leibniz, in his position of optimism, argues that if an all-powerful and all-knowing God created this world, it must be the best possible world that could have been created. Therefore, what appears to be a flaw in the world must be a part of the intentional and benevolent plan.

With his rational defense of God's goodness, Leibniz seeks to bring together philosophy and theology, thereby reconciling faith and reason. This is a profoundly modern project of the Enlightenment. His understanding that this world is the best possible world *and* that humanity has much to gain through the use of reason both emerge in the Enlightenment.

As Jews, we should commend Leibniz for engaging in the struggle of theodicy. His work was significant in its time for having the intellectual courage to embrace such important challenges, and it is for good reason that it is continued to be studied.

---

1. Isaiah 45:6–7.

While there is much in Jewish thought that resonates with Leibniz's approach to the problem of evil, I don't think we can agree with his conclusion, that the suffering we encounter and witness reflects the best that the world can be.

We do find some examples in the Talmud[2] that suffering can be seen as a kind of divine punishment which should lead us to examine our actions. But modern Judaism has largely rejected that approach. A very liberal theologian like Rabbi Harold Kushner[3] solves the problem of theodicy by arguing that God is not omnipotent. He also rejects the optimism of believing we're in the best possible world, seeing it as a childish theology. How could we worship a God who has the power to stop evil and doesn't?

In Orthodoxy, Rabbi Dr. Yitz Greenberg has expressed similar sentiments in his post-Holocaust theology. Both he and Kushner agree that God engages in an act of *tzimtzum*, a contraction of God's presence in the world. According to Greenberg, one should view the Bible as true and believe that God intervened in history and performed the miracles of Tanakh. But at the same time, one must understand that as history progresses and humanity matures, God steps back further, and Judaism embraces that maturation[4]. This is similar to how a parent lets go of control of their child more and more as the child grows in their own responsibility.

As God intervenes less in history, we must maximize human responsibility much more than in ancient generations. For example, the problem of the Holocaust is not the question of "Where was God?" but "Where was humanity?" So too, the problems of cancer and natural disasters are not to be resolved by God, but through advancements in human knowledge.

A different Orthodox response is taken by Rabbi Joseph B. Soloveitchik. Although he was modern and rationalist, he sought to reframe the problem of theology. Unlike Leibniz, who thought that reason could help us answer the questions it raised, Soloveitchik argued that we must not focus on the question of evil but rather our active response to it (an idea later echoed by his student, Greenberg). Don't ask why bad things happen or why suffering exists. Rather, ask oneself what one's response to them should be.

---

2. Babylonian Talmud, Berachot 5a.

3. Rabbi Harold Kushner's book "When Bad Things Happen to Good People" is all about this approach.

4. It is, of course, unclear that humanity matures. On the level of human nature, its unlikely that humans are essentially more advanced than we were millennia ago. However, a stronger, albeit uncertain, case can be made that human maturation is experienced through more complex societal structures that we learn to live with and adapt to. Further, with deeper human empowerment through democracy and layers of capitalism, we have other life choices that didn't exist in prior millennia, and we must now attempt to live with more responsibility.

The lack of an answer to the problem of evil should be viewed as a call to our responsibility, Greenberg teaches.

On this problem, Soloveitchik felt the proper response is action, not thought. What makes us religious, for Soloveitchik, is not finding a perfect answer to our questions, but the actions of healing we're called to take. He doesn't reject the problems brought up by philosophy; he sees the integrity of them and sees the complexity of it all. But he also recognizes that theodicy is not resolvable. In a sense, he's not dismissing the philosophical project, but reorienting it and elevating it.

In addition to the problem of evil, Leibniz also explored another paradox, the belief in both free will and God's omnipotence. Though these two truths appear to contradict each other, both Leibniz and Jewish texts affirm they can live side by side, as it says in *Pirkei Avot*, the Ethics of the Fathers: "Everything is foreseen yet freedom of choice is granted."[5] According to Leibniz, God knows the future, and yet we're still free to act. The reason this is true is due to our limitations as humans. Though God knows what we will choose, and that may seem unfree, we don't know what we will choose, so we experience this as freedom. To address this paradox, one might also suggest that God sees all possible choices that could be made but not the specific one that we will make.

In the end, we must recognize that Leibniz does not deny the existence of suffering. So then why, in his view, does God allow this seeming imperfection? For Leibniz it exists so that humans can learn, repair their false notions and attain a higher good.

This is not too far off from the Jewish belief in *tikkun olam*, that bad things happen because the world is imperfect, and that it consequently must be repaired by humans. And so, I think, ultimately, we have to side with Rabbi Greenberg and Rabbi Soloveitchik. Regardless of God's role in the existence of evil, we have the moral power to know injustice when we see it. What matters is what we do about it.

---

5. Pirkei Avot 3:15.

14

Voltaire (1694–1798)

DOES GOD INTERVENE IN the world? Can we actually change the world for the better? Do we have any source of unimpeachable knowledge?

Born as François-Marie Arouet, Voltaire was a standout figure of the 18th-century French Enlightenment, known for being highly critical of both religion and slavery, as well as a major advocate for freedom of religion, freedom of speech, and separation of church and state.

He was born in Paris, and in his younger years he studied law, before coming to prefer writing, which made Voltaire famous for his literary wit. However, his satires got him into trouble, and he was imprisoned multiple times and ultimately exiled from France. After this initial fleeing, Voltaire stayed in England, where he was influenced by English philosophy and science. He eventually made his home elsewhere in France, in Chateau de Cirey, with his partner, the philosopher Émilie du Châtelet.

Incredibly prolific, Voltaire wrote in numerous different formats, including poems, novels, and plays. His most famous work, though, is a novella called *Candide*, which is full of ridicule of prominent thinkers and ideas, as well as being the venue where he'd wage his war against slavery[1]. Unfortunately, the nature of Voltaire's antisemitism has been debated for decades[2].

Voltaire was bold and often bordered on offensive, saying what he thought even when it was *avant-garde* or would be seen as provocative. He is the originator of the saying translated, "Truly, whoever can make you

---

1. Although, of course, all people have their own contradictions and complicity.
2. Hertzberg Hanover, *Voltaire and the Jews*.

believe absurdities can make you commit atrocities."[3] Voltaire was an advocate for religious pluralism, and personally he was a deist. The Stanford Encyclopedia of Philosophy explains Deism and its centrality during the Enlightenment:

> Deism is the form of religion most associated with the Enlightenment. According to deism, we can know by the natural light of reason that the universe is created and governed by a supreme intelligence; however, although this supreme being has a plan for creation from the beginning, the being does not interfere with creation; the deist typically rejects miracles and reliance on special revelation as a source of religious doctrine and belief, in favor of the natural light of reason.[4]

And so, Voltaire believed in a creator, but not one who supernaturally intervenes in the world or in history. This made him a major critic of all religions—not just the dominant Christianity—as he wanted to remove from society all of what he believed to be superstition. And still, Voltaire argued for tolerance toward all sides.

Though it's not an exact quote, the historian Evelyn Beatrice Hall paraphrased Voltaire's position on free expression as, "I disapprove of what you say, but I will defend to the death your right to say it."[5] For Voltaire, the government needs to be limited and speech needs to be free.

Taking his work seriously, he measured the value of a philosophy not just by its logical soundness, but also by whether it could incite practical social and political change. For Voltaire, this meant eradicating the "hope" as a response to societal problems. For him, hope was a disease that prevented human beings from taking responsibility for their circumstances. He was skeptical that Enlightenment advancements in science[6] could solve most of our problems and could even be usurped by tyrants. However, he did emphasize that each person must try their best to better their little corner of the world.

In his novella *Candide*, the title character says to a Muslim man, "You must have a vast and magnificent estate."

---

3. CATO Institute, *The Origins of a Warning from Voltaire*.

4. Bristow, *Enlightenment*.

5. Quote Investigator: "I Disapprove of What You Say, But I Will Defend to the Death Your Right to Say It."

6. A later philosopher of science, Thomas Kuhn, argued that scientific progress is not linear but involves major paradigm shifts. This understanding can leave us humbled by the scientific understanding of our day knowing that it too will be radically, and perhaps suddenly, eclipsed.

The man answers, "I have only twenty acres. I and my children cultivate them; and our labour preserves us from three great evils: weariness, vice, and want."

Contemplating this, Candide later says, "This honest Turk seems to be in a far better place than kings ... I also know that we must cultivate our garden."[7]

We're going to be much happier and our lives more stable, Voltaire believed, if we focus on our own corner and our own life. He advocated for a kind of isolationism; we cannot trust humans, and engaging in collective political and social matters will lead only to aggravation and disappointment. Because he did not believe large scale change to be truly possible, he argued we should just tend to our own "garden."

Voltaire held a radical faith in the idea of doubt. He agreed with John Locke that a person is born a *tabula rasa*, a blank slate that learns all it knows from its surroundings. Doubt also caused him to hold that many of the axiomatic truths of math and logic were in fact little more than mere hypotheses and should not be taken for granted. Voltaire saw that ideas are always shifting in different eras and different cultures, so, he thought, why should we believe that our knowledge of math and logic is eternal? With this in mind, Voltaire argued that we cannot grasp logical truth, which makes doubt our only reasonable ending place.

So what do we make of Voltaire as Jews? Of course, his tolerance for religious minorities is a value we must continue to uphold even though it must be noted that his writings often singled out Judaism as a religion deserving of criticism.

However, his extensive emphasis on cynicism runs counter to the Jewish values that spur us to bring change in the world. The idea that each person must simply cultivate their own garden is not entirely immoral or a bad way to live. But it does not enable us to uphold the Torah commandment, "Justice, justice, shall you pursue, that you may thrive and occupy the land that the Lord your God is giving you."[8]

Still, we can value Voltaire's skepticism and commitment to questioning in search of the truth. While we have a duty to do good in the world, the task involves first coming to an understanding of life's absurdity and systemic injustice. As the Hebrew Bible says in the Book of Ecclesiastes:

> If you see in a province oppression of the poor and suppression
> of right and justice, don't wonder at the fact; for one high official

---

7. See YouTube: The School of Life, *What Voltaire Meant By 'One Must Cultivate One's Own Garden.'*

8. Deuteronomy 16:20.

is protected by a higher one, and both of them by still higher ones.[9]

Skepticism is not wholly bad. The difference is that Jews see the seeming insurmountable-ness of the challenge and choose to fight anyway. We take seriously what's attributed to Rabbi Tarfon in *Pirkei Avot*:

> It is not your duty to finish the work, but neither are you at liberty to neglect it; If you have studied much Torah, you shall be given much reward. Faithful is your employer to pay you the reward of your labor; And know that the grant of reward unto the righteous is in the age to come.[10]

The first part of Rabbi Tarfon's teaching reminds us not to feel guilty if we cannot succeed in changing the world. In truth, no one can do so alone, and we must learn to accept the fact that the world will most likely remain broken even when we depart from it. The second part reminds us of the value of faith in fighting off cynicism. Our efforts always matter. If not in the here and now then most certainly in the world to come.

The Midrash further emphasizes the point that we must be involved in the world and take responsibility for it:

> If a person of learning participates in public affairs and serves as judge or arbiter, he gives stability to the land ... But if he sits in his home and says to himself, "What have the affairs of society to do with me? ... Why should I trouble myself with the people's voices of protest? Let my soul dwell in peace!"—if he does this, he overthrows the world.[11]

Lastly, it says in the Talmud that it is not sufficient for us to tend only to our little garden and ignore the world around us. If we do not act to protest injustice, even if we are unsure whether we can correct it, we will ultimately be held responsible for it.

> Everyone who can protest the wrongs of his household and does not, is responsible for the people of his household. For the people of his city, he is responsible for the people of his city. For the whole world, he is responsible for the whole world.[12]

---

9. Ecclesiastes 5:12.
10. Pirkei Avot 2:16.
11. Midrash *Tanchuma, Mishpatim* 2.
12. Babylonian Talmud, Shabbat 54b.

In Judaism, yes, we can accept doubt—of knowledge and of justice—but we must also strive toward a higher, divine truth. As Leonard Cohen put it, from the perspective to God, our task is to:

> Gather up the brokenness
> And bring it to me now
> The fragrance of those promises
> You never dared to vow.

We can accept that, as Voltaire says, we can't grasp absolute truth or justice. But we can and must work with what we have. We can therefore reject Voltaire as irresponsible for thinking the logical answer to the world's problems is only doubt and skepticism and tending to oneself.

Today we can imagine a disciple of Voltaire as an opinion columnist who has a tendency to cynically tear things down without necessarily offering anything constructive to replace them. As inheritors of a moral tradition, we need to instead affirm truths that add some moral texture to our lives. However, we can also admire Voltaire's fearlessness in pursuing his convictions, his dedication to freedom, and his ability to see contradictions most others ignored.

And so, Voltaire sets important foundations for us of pluralism and skepticism, but that is not sufficient on its own for us to live our fullest lives.

15

David Hume (1711–1776)

DO WE KNOW FOR sure that the sun will rise and we'll wake up in the morning? Can abstract reason alone bring us to knowledge, or do we need experience as well? How useful is it to know what will *probably* happen versus knowing something with absolute certainty?

David Hume was a Scottish Enlightenment-era philosopher and a proponent of empiricism and skepticism, in the camp of Thomas Hobbes and John Locke. He attended the University of Edinburgh at the age of 12, but, based on the deep skepticism he'd acquired, he worked himself into a nervous breakdown, seeing how difficult it is for truth to be established. He moved to France, where he wrote his famous *Treatise of Human Nature* before returning to Scotland. He later was appointed to work at the British embassy in Paris, where he became friends with the great French philosopher Jean-Jacques Rousseau.

At the root of Hume's skepticism was the idea that causality cannot definitively be proven; instead of proving our ideas in some absolute fashion, we rely lazily upon habit, custom, and prior assumptions about how things work. For Hume, the mere fact that we've seen the sun come up every day of our lives does not mean we know the sun will rise tomorrow.

Hume argued that we never actually witness the causal power, the actual force that causes things to happen, and so we merely make generalizations based on what we see in nature. For Hume, we can think about the finite and concrete that is visible to us, but we have no real impression of infinity—in the expansive sense, of how large things can get, or of how small things can get. We can hold no abstract ideas about time, space, or substance; only that which we can experience in the here and now.

Hume's empiricism led him to what is called the Is-Ought Problem, making the point that one cannot derive an "ought" from a set of facts about what "is." That is to say: There are descriptive statements and prescriptive statements, and you can't reach the prescriptive from the descriptive.

This also led Hume to distinguish between demonstrative statements and probable statements. A demonstrative statement can be upheld in logic; 2+2 equals 4, and you don't need experience to prove it. Probable statements are such that they're not found in the realm of logic but in the realm of empirical fact. For example, "Bob is in the house." You can walk in the house and see if Bob is there. For any statement we may propose to be meaningful, it first must be determined whether it's probable or demonstrative. If it's neither, we can't prove it, and it's unhelpful for finding truth.

For example, "The sun will rise tomorrow" is not a demonstrative statement, because it inevitability cannot be proven in any absolute logical sense. But it's also not a probable statement because we cannot observe the outcome of a future even before it has occurred. At best, experience teaches us that its likely, but we have no absolute rational grounds for such a belief. What Hume rejected was inductive inference: deducing things about the future based on past evidence.

Hume does say that statements like "The sun will rise tomorrow" can be useful, but they are not provable. Relying on custom or what Hume called mental habits to make sense of the world may be helpful when we don't have a rational justification for this, but it must be done with great caution.

One sees a similar inclination in the words of the prophet Isaiah:

> My Lord said:
> Because that people has approached [Me] with its mouth
> And honored Me with its lips,
> But has kept its heart far from Me,
> And its worship of Me has been
> A commandment of men, learned by rote.
> Truly, I shall further baffle that people
> With bafflement upon bafflement;
> And the wisdom of its wise shall fail,
> And the prudence of its prudent shall vanish.[1]

Here he cautions against "rote" religious worship and also reminds us the that there will always come a time when the "wisdom of the wise shall fail." This is very aligned with Hume who wants to break our reliance upon rote thinking and wants to challenge those fully invested in the perceived unbreakable power of reason. We will later see Immanuel Kant have

---

1. Isaiah 29:13-14.

disagreements with Hume, and yet Kant credited Hume with waking him up from "dogmatic slumbers" by challenging him to rethink his basic understanding of the world.[2]

On the issue of free will, Hume embraced "compatibilism," which is the belief that necessity and free will are ultimately compatible and can be reconciled with one another. He was generally skeptical of religious claims and criticized the teleological argument for the existence of God, which says that the complexity of the world indicated that someone must have created it.

Hume argued against the philosophical rationalists, ultimately suggesting that human behavior is led by the passions rather than by reason. "Reason is, and ought only to be the slave of the passions,"[3] [4] he wrote.

Hume held that our feelings, rather than moral reasoning, guides us in our decision-making and behaviors. It is the realm of the affective, not the cognitive, that sheds light on human action. As opposed to most Enlightenment thinkers, who were committed to reason, Hume believed that it is not thinking with clarity but rather feeling with forcefulness that leads to fulfillment. Hume's idea that ethics are primarily based on emotion rather than abstract moral principle is called sentimentalism.

In the history of philosophy, Hume is thought of as one of the three great British Empiricists, alongside John Locke and George Berkeley. For Locke, who came before Hume, the ideas that humans receive from the outside world should be seen as inputs, like a computer perhaps. Hume, by contrast, viewed these as impressions. Even as adults, Hume believed, our first reactions are physical and physiological, not conceptual. Here, once again, he makes the case for the primacy of the affect.

With empiricism, the criticisms levied by the Enlightenment against religion and tradition now become turned upon themselves and critique philosophy from the inside. We've seen the Enlightenment give birth to affirming reason over authority and dogma, and now, with Hume, reason undermined. By challenging someone like Descartes, who famously said "I think, therefore I am," Hume, not only questioned the superiority of the mind, but also undermined the prevalent conception of the self. Instead of a self that can be identified through reason, Hume believed all we really have is a "bundle of sensations" set in motion by the world around us.

---

2. Kant was indeed transformed as he went on to write the Critique of Pure Reason and develop a new notion of causality which he believed could withstand Hume's critique.

3. Atherton, *The Empiricists: Critical Essays on Locke, Berkeley, and Hume.*

4. Hume, *A Treatise of Human Nature: Being an Attempt to introduce the experimental Method of Reasoning into Moral Subjects*, 415.

For Descartes, humans are rational beings, and all one needs to do to find truth is sit in a room and think. However, with the birth of empiricism, Locke held that one needs experience in addition to reason. With Hume, not only is experience affirmed as a necessary addition to reason but it is shown how abstract reason can deceive itself.

So what do we make of Hume as Jews? First, we can see the undeniable value of empiricism and skepticism. In our lives, we don't know what causes impact us, and therefore we can't prove when something is *hashgacha pratit*, Divine providence. No matter how hard we might try, it is impossible to discern whether an event is based on the laws of nature that God put in place, or whether it is truly anomalous. Hume's emphasis on recognizing that tomorrow is not guaranteed can cause us to live with a sense of awe, with *yirah*, that what happens in the world must not to be taken for granted as necessary.

When we wake up in the morning, we traditionally say, "Thank you, living and eternal King, for giving my soul back in mercy. Great is your faithfulness."[5] What these words express is a sense of surprise out of the recognition that it was not guaranteed that we will wake up tomorrow. Rather, doing so should be seen as an act of divine mercy. We ascribe our waking to God's faithfulness, to what God does for us day after day.

There might be two types of faith as it relates to what we expect to happen in the future. One version of faith is where one sees things positively and sees and feels God in the world and believes in that God. A different form of faith however is where one sees a messy reality and doesn't experience God in any way but holds a faith in God's existence. It is a faith that holds a contradiction between a reality and a vision.

And indeed, while the Enlightenment's return to reason was an important development for Judaism, because it's a religion heavily reliant upon reason, Hume's skepticism was also deeply beneficial, because it shows that reason is never enough on its own. Furthermore, the modern Jewish movements toward Musar (ethics) and *Chasidut* (spirituality) both recognized that Jewish religious life cannot be sustained merely through the intellectual study of Talmud and strict adherence to *halacha*. We have to focus in on our inner life of desires and passions and emotions. It is the *yetzer tov* and the *yetzer hara*, these inclinations inside us toward good and bad and so much more happening within us and interconnected with the cosmos, that we must attend to, not logic alone.

Reason and emotion may not be a binary but often overlapping and often complimentary. However, there are times when reason can get in the

---

5. *Modeh Ani* prayer.

way of thinking clearly through the emotional realm. And the opposite is true as well where we can be emotionally overloaded and unable to analyze a situation clearly. There are often inconsistencies to explore too. Take desire for example, as it relates to probabilities. One might hear that the risk of death for a surgery is 3/10,000 and feel that is a very minor risk and proceed with the surgery. One might, also, however, feel that they really do have a chance to be the one out of 500 million to win the lottery even feeling disappointed when not winning. Our sense reason can become confused when we deeply desire a positive outcome in all situations.

In Tradition magazine, Rabbi Dr. Alan Brill pointed out that Hume's Is-Ought Problem has been used by Rabbi Walter Wurzburger[6] to argue against historicist and sociological understandings of halacha. Rather than assuming halacha can be determined by identifying the historical context that influenced its formation, it must rather represent higher principles that guide it. Halacha must challenge us, rather than meeting us where we currently are. Brill summarizes Wurzburger's argument by saying "empirical reality cannot create norms" and therefore Jews must turn to the norms of the Torah.[7] That being said, Rabbi Jonathan Sacks regularly pushed back against Hume's notion that we can find truth in feelings. He argued that, for Jews, truth must come from an objective source, from God. Hume became a foil for Rabbi Sacks to show that true morality needed to be grounded in revelation not sentimentalism.

Rabbi Eliezer Berkovits, on the other hand, posited in his PhD dissertation that Torah is compatible with Hume's approach to knowledge because it is indeed grounded in empirical truths about the world. The Torah has an empirical bend, in one sense, since laws have goals and certain actions (mitzvot) are meant to produce certain good outcomes, and this can be tested against reality. However, he added that Torah comes with further objective knowledge from God. Torah, then, is empiricism plus revelation.[8]

To be sure, the problem of induction, for Hume, is not just about morality but about rationality as a whole. With induction, we risk coming to worship the status quo. It is too easy to come to believe that the way things are is the way things have always been and will always be. This is a crucial argument and important for religion to help us challenge the status quo rather than simply and blindly reaffirm it. If we can question whether the sun will rise tomorrow, all the more so we can remain skeptical that oppression and injustice are built into the fabric of human existence and cannot be changed.

6. Wurzburger, *Is Sociology Integral to the Halakhah?*
7. Brill, *A Tiny but Articulate Minority.*
8. Berkovits, *Hume and Deism.*

While skepticism and empiricism aren't the only tools Jews have for acquiring knowledge about the world, they are certainly ones worth using.

16

Jean-Jacques Rousseau (1712–1778)

ARE PUBLIC EDUCATION AND socialization making our children worse? Are our laws as beneficial as society tells us they are?

While lots of philosophers have had few reservations about defending elements of the status quo, Jean-Jacques Rousseau was unafraid of questioning everything about the way society was run and the impact it had on the people.

Born in Geneva, Rousseau lost his mother when he was just a few days old, and his father subsequently fled their home, leaving him with his uncle. When he was young, Rousseau and his family had to flee Geneva due to a legal dispute. That set him on a course of instability and isolation for the rest of his life.

He tried to become a composer, and shortly after entering the world of philosophy, his books were banned in Switzerland and France, and a warrant for his arrest was issued. Rousseau accepted an invitation from David Hume to live in England, but the two of them could not get along, and he returned to France, where he died at age 66, less than a year before the French Revolution.

In his lifetime, Rousseau challenged the prevailing view of his day on human nature. While others believed humans were naturally malicious, or at best a blank slate, Rousseau argued that humans were fundamentally decent, and that it was society that was corrupting them toward vices and sins.

Rousseau believed that in the natural state, one lives simply, with a tendency toward the positive qualities of human character. Socialization, however, leads to moral degeneration. Why is this? Because society teaches us a pernicious form of self-love, what Rousseau called *amour-propre*, that causes jealousy, pride, and unhealthy social dynamics. Rather than view ourselves objectively, society teaches us to constantly search out the approval of others. In doing so, we compare ourselves to those around us and inevitably feel great resentment when we don't receive the recognition we feel that we deserve. To prove the corrupting influence of modern society, Rousseau looked at examples of indigenous populations, who appeared to be living happier and healthier lives until guns, alcohol, and the like were introduced to their communities.

Rousseau's book *Emile*, or *On Education*, would become one of the most influential books on education and parenting in history. In it, he argues that children are inherently good—with a natural capacity for compassion and empathy—and their education should build on their innate goodness, rather than seek to impose social norms on them. Education, he held, should be focused on the child, not on societal needs. Rather than be forced into becoming something she is not, the child is to be encouraged to have a sense of agency, to explore the world and themselves within it.

Rousseau advocated for children being given time to play, especially by spending time in nature and in the woods and near lakes. He wanted a holistic return to nature, which led him to advocate for breastfeeding. In addition to his fallout with Hume, he had a fallout with another reformer, Voltaire, because of his radical insistence on a state of nature being better than civilization.

With his appreciation for the natural self and his valuing of the inner life, Rousseau can be seen as a founder of Romanticism.

> Romanticism can be seen as a rejection of the precepts of order, calm, harmony, balance, idealization, and rationality that typified Classicism in general and late 18th-century Neoclassicism in particular ... Romanticism emphasized the individual, the subjective, the irrational, the imaginative, the personal, the spontaneous, the emotional, the visionary, and the transcendental.[1]

By rejecting the conventional wisdom regarding how society ought to run, Rousseau sought to bring out better qualities in human beings that were otherwise being suppressed.

Politics was at the center of Rousseau's philosophy. He argued strongly against the inequalities created by a feudalist monarchy, and his critique of the status quo made him a major influence on the French Revolution, which began shortly after his death. Revolutionaries took inspiration from the following quote:

---

1. Encyclopedia Britannica, *Romanticism*.

JEAN-JACQUES ROUSSEAU (1712-1778)

> It is manifestly against the law of nature ... that a child should command an aged man, that an imbecile should lead a sage, and that a handful of people should gorge themselves on superfluities while the hungry multitude lacks even necessities.[2]

Rousseau was influenced by English political thinkers, such as Hobbes and Locke; similar to them, Rousseau wanted to bring humanity back to a hypothetical natural state, in contrast to what society looked like in his time.

However, Rousseau differed from them in important ways. While Enlightenment thinkers believed it was possible to use reason to shape culture and better the world, Rousseau believed human potential was found in isolation and nature. Rather than see humans as selfish, like Hobbes, and therefore require civilization to tame our bad instincts, Rousseau goes in the total opposite direction. He viewed human nature on its own as profound and beautiful, only to then be polluted by social engineering. In particular, Rousseau believed that modern arts and sciences disrupt our morals and decrease our happiness.

For Rousseau, it was not just society that was the problem, but the culture's overreliance on reason. An education based solely on reason, he believed, was bound to crowd out a person's other natural qualities. He believed that, instead of educating our minds, we need to educate our senses. So too, he believed that religious engagement should be led by the heart, not the head. In his eyes, the role of religion was less about imparting correct beliefs and more about fostering bonds of love between citizens. Therefore, it plays an important role in nurturing and sustaining a political community.

Rousseau opens his important work *The Social Contract* with his impactful line:

> Man is born free, and everywhere he is in chains. Here's one who thinks he is the master of others, yet he is more enslaved than they are.[3]

While it's argued that structures such as the law make us better people, Rousseau believed laws are ultimately driven by selfish motives, such as protecting property and imposing the will of the rich on the poor. With how much social upheaval and unrest was occurring in mid-18th century France, Rousseau found himself at the epicenter of the era's class conflict. Siding against those in power, he rejected the notion of society being run by the church, by the monarchy, and by the aristocrats when the power needed to belong to the citizens.

2. Haraszti, *John Adams and Rousseau*.
3. Rousseau, *The Social Contract*.

In addition to giving a great deal of intellectual fuel to the French revolutionaries, he was later an influence on Karl Marx's ideas about the revolutionary overthrow of capitalism to create a more just and ideal society. In fact, Marx concludes the *Communist Manifesto* with a reference to Rousseau, when he writes:

> The proletarians have nothing to lose but their chains. They have a world to win. Working men of all countries, unite![4]

For those of us influenced by Jewish values, we can see many admirable ideas in Rousseau's work. However, we don't sign on wholeheartedly. For one thing, Judaism generally rejects the idea that society only influences us for the worst. For example, Maimonides explains that those we live beside impact us for better and for worse.

> It is natural for a man's character and actions to be influenced by his friends and associates and for him to follow the local norms of behavior. Therefore, he should associate with the righteous and be constantly in the company of the wise, so as to learn from their deeds. Conversely, he should keep away from the wicked who walk in darkness, so as not to learn from their deeds.[5]

It is also the case that Judaism does not conceive of education only as a form of socialization. While much of religious education is intended to teach the child how to be a Jew, the act of Torah study is meant to provide tools that will guide one toward living a better life.

At the same time, though, we can embrace the idea that humans, at the deepest level of the soul, are inherently good even if their actions don't always demonstrate this. We say in the traditional morning blessings:

> My God, the soul You placed within me is pure. You created it, You fashioned it, You breathed it into me, You safeguard it within me.[6]

So too, we can recognize that traditional classroom education in an institutional setting is not the only way to acquire wisdom. Some of the greatest Torah scholars learned in the home. Rabbi Moshe Feinstein, one of the most important rabbis of the 20th century, learned from his father. We affirm the huge Jewish commitment to formal schooling, but we can also confirm Rousseau's position that other methods of education are valid pathways. This diversity can be seen in the vastly different approaches taken by

---

4. Marx and Engels, *The Communist Manifesto*.
5. Hilkhot Deot 6:1.
6. Morning Blessings, Artscroll Siddur.

the Litvaks, the Lithuanian rationalists who valued (and continue to value) book learning in the *beit midrash* above all else, versus the Hasidim, who traditionally emphasized a more organic spiritual growth through prayer, preaching, and spiritual practice.

We also find a more complex notion of Rousseau's idea that civilization can be damaging. On the one hand, Jews see it as important to embrace civilization, because it is our chance to influence the world for the better. However, through Shabbat, we also practice restraint of that impulse, returning to our natural state of being, much like Rousseau wanted. As Abraham Joshua Heschel stated in his iconic work *The Sabbath*:

> Six days a week we wrestle with the world, wringing profit from the earth; on the Sabbath we especially care for the seed of eternity planted in the soul. The world has our hands, but our soul belongs to Someone Else. Six days a week we seek to dominate the world, on the seventh day we try to dominate the self.[7]

As Jews, we don't isolate from society, but we don't want to become owned by it either. We engage deeply with society and government and workplace six days a week, but on Shabbat we find our freedom, removing ourselves completely, though temporarily.

Rousseau's desire to return humanity to its natural, dare I say, Godly state is highly commendable. His disruptive and revolutionary tendencies were an example of, if not messianism, a desire to radically change the world for the better.

---

7. Heschel, *The Sabbath*.

17

Immanuel Kant (1724–1804)

WHAT IS THE MOST important rule for humans to live by? Is it ever okay to lie? Which is more moral: a big government or a small one?

Born in Königsberg, Prussia, Immanuel Kant was raised under the influence of Pietistic Lutheranism. But, when he grew up, he witnessed the world's increasing secularism, and he saw a need to replace the authority of religion with an authority of reason.

In his personal life, he lived as somewhat of a hermit. Though he was on occasion sociable, he never left his hometown, and he was never married. We've looked at lots of philosophers who've had to flee and travel all over, but Kant was an anomaly in that he always studied and always taught in the same place. Even when the Prussian king banned him from teaching, he waited and returned to his post when the king died.

Seeing the changing tides around religion, Kant made epistemology—the study of how we know what we know—and morality the primary focuses of his work. Religions, Kant believed, were flawed, but they did the important work of promoting ethics. As such, Kant sought to somehow salvage the ethical emptiness of the Enlightenment's emphasis on reason by imbuing it with a moral philosophy.

Written on Kant's tombstone is his quote:

> Two things fill the mind with ever new and increasing admiration and awe, the more often and steadily we reflect upon them: the starry heavens above me and the moral law within me.[1]

Based on natural morality, one does not necessarily need revelation to know what is good. One can find the moral law within. Without people

---

1. Kant, *Critique of Practical Reason*, 5:161, translated. Guyer, 1.

paying as much attention to religion pushing moral living, Kant thought one could turn further inward to remain committed. Prior to Kant, one presumed they knew what was good and just needed to submit. But now one knew that the objective passes through the subjective filter of the mind and thus we must all now determine what the good actually is. In a new era of autonomy, we are now co-authors of the good. But this does not mean everything goes, of course. For Kant, obeying God can never fully lead to moral actualization since its heteronomy (embraced a law given by someone else). To be moral, for Kant, one must live with autonomy and become a creator of moral law.

Kant's attempt to fill the ethical void caused by the devaluing of religion was called the "categorical imperative." Kant wrote in his *Groundwork for the Metaphysic of Morals*:

> So there is only one categorical imperative, and this is it: Act only on that maxim through which you can at the same time will that it should become a universal law.[2]

When deciding how to live your life, Kant was saying, you should imagine what the world would be like if *everyone* were to live that way.

For Jews, this is nothing new. Hillel is recorded as saying over 2,000 years ago, when a convert asks for a quick summary of the Torah:

> That which is hateful to you do not do to another; that is the entire Torah, and the rest is its interpretation. Go study.[3]

Similarly, Rabbi Akiva identifies Leviticus 19:18, "Love your fellow as yourself," as the "fundamental principle of the Torah."[4]

Rabbi Akiva says this in response to a metaphor presented in the Jerusalem Talmud: If a person is cutting food and accidentally cuts their own hand, would it make sense for one hand to take revenge on the other?[5] It is no different with people, the Jerusalem Talmud teaches, once we realize that we're all just parts of the same body.

In the Middle Ages, Maimonides expressed a similar sentiment when he wrote, in his Laws of Repentance:

> Throughout the entire year, a person should always look at themselves as equally balanced between merit and sin and the world as equally balanced between merit and sin. If they perform one

2. Kant, *Groundwork for the Metaphysic of Morals*.
3. Babylonian Talmud, Shabbat 31a.
4. Rashi on Leviticus 19:18:2.
5. Jerusalem Talmud, Nedarim 9:4.

sin, they tip the balance and that of the entire world to the side of guilt and brings destruction upon themselves.

[On the other hand,] if one performs one mitzvah, they tip their balance and that of the entire world to the side of merit and bring deliverance and salvation to themselves and others.[6]

Kant and the Jewish tradition would agree that, while we tend to think of our actions as significant, there is so much good and bad done all throughout that world, and if we were to collectively consider the impact of our behavior, we could make the world vastly better.

In this respect, Kant rejected libertarianism, which tends to emphasize the importance of human freedom over and above all else. While there is a powerful appeal to seeking a kind of radical liberty from government and communal responsibility, the categorical imperative implies that we all have a duty to one another.

Kant was the innovator of deontological ethics, or ethics based in the notion of duty.

> In deontological ethics an action is considered morally good because of some characteristic of the action itself, not because the product of the action is good. Deontological ethics holds that at least some acts are morally obligatory regardless of their consequences for human welfare. Descriptive of such ethics are such expressions as "Duty for duty's sake," "Virtue is its own reward," and "Let justice be done though the heavens fall."[7]

In short, we must do the right thing not because it is bound to have a positive impact (utilitarianism), but because doing the right thing is what we need to do (deontology).

What a powerful tool this can be against despair. So often, we worry about what the point of trying to do a mitzvah even is, and here Kant shares the Jewish value that the good thing must be done out of obligation. We hope that the right results will follow, but we can worry about that after we do the right thing. Because of the similarity between Kant's notion of the categorical imperative and the Jewish notion of mitzvah, many Jews in Germany felt a kinship with Kant's thought. As a result, it would go on to have a great influence on Jewish thought in the 19th and early 20th century.

When Kant applies his ethics to politics, he argues against the idea that freedom is something that is guaranteed by the government. Rather, we are free when we embrace ethics. By submitting oneself to the categorical

---

6. Mishneh Torah, Repentance 3.
7. Encyclopedia Britannica, *Deontological Ethics*.

imperative, one is liberated from the selfish interests that so often determine how we act and how society functions. This is a new read on liberty and society. Freedom is not the absence of government, but the acceptance of obligations.

It should be unsurprising that those who have sought to use philosophy as a part of their traditional Jewish thought have been eager to use the work of Kant. Rabbi Joseph B. Soloveitchik, the quintessential Modern Orthodox thinker of the 20th century, had Kant at the center of his model of ethics[8]. Kant can be a hero for those who want to make our moral responsibilities more robust and want to build a religious ethos on reason.

While the Torah and ancient sages set an important groundwork for how Jews think about ethics today, Kant gives us a way to universalize ethical constructs. And Judaism is sympathetic to the notion that changing the world is going to happen from the human choices we make.

And Kant arrived at his morality by placing a value on the human being that in Judaism we can accept as a shared value. Kant wrote in his treatise on morals:

> Rational beings are called 'persons', because their nature already marks them out as ends in themselves (i.e., as not to be used merely as means)—which makes such a being an object of respect, and something that sets limits to what anyone can choose to do. Such beings are not merely subjective ends whose existence as a result of our action has value for us, but are objective ends, i.e., things ... whose existence is an end in itself. It is indeed an irreplaceable end: you can't substitute for it something else to which it would be merely a means. If there were no such ends in themselves, nothing of absolute value could be found, and if all value were conditional and thus contingent, no supreme practical principle for reason could be found anywhere.[9]

This idea that other people exist not be used by us, but for their own, irreplicable, inherent value, sounds like something straight from the more modern Hasidic-influenced philosopher Martin Buber, with his notion of "I and Thou." This is because Kant had a direct influence on Buber and all German philosophy after himself.[10]

---

8. Rabbi Soloveitchik drew upon Hermann Cohen's neo-Kantianism to develop his notion of halacha as math/science.

9. Kant, *Groundwork for the Metaphysic of Morals*.

10. Franz Rosenzweig directly cites this piece from Kant in his own writings developing the idea of I-Thou.

However, I don't think we, as Jews, should uncritically accept the black-and-white obligations of the categorical imperative, if only because Kant conceived of them as absolutes in a way that doesn't accord with the gray areas embraced by Jewish law. For instance, the categorical imperative would say that you can *never* lie, because, if everyone lied, the world would fall apart. According to Kant's thinking, if a murderer comes to one's door seeking to kill someone inside one's home, the homeowner is ethically obligated not to lie if they ask if they are there. However, Jewish law is clear that there are times when it is not only permissible but even required to lie. If someone in Nazi Germany is hiding a Jew in their home, we know that the value of saving a life in this case outweighs the value of truth.

And still, the goal of Jewish ethics remains to tip the scale of the world toward the good. When we consider, for example, our obligations to combat climate change, or to feed and house people, we can take inspiration from Kant by using the categorical imperative to give us hope in the face of seemingly insurmountable challenges. It doesn't necessarily matter whether we're able to complete the work of achieving justice. We must do good deeds because, if *everyone* were to do good deeds, the world would be much better off—and if everyone were to ignore the problems of the world, our societies would collapse.

18

Jeremy Bentham (1748–1832)

Is HAPPINESS THE MOST important thing in life? What should be our measure of success on our work to heal the world? Are we just as responsible for people on the other side of the world as we are to our own children?

The English thinker Jeremy Bentham arrived at what he believed to be an overarching answer to most questions of morality, as the father of utilitarianism, an idea so profound to him that it caused him to leave a promising career in law to pursue his philosophical work.

Utilitarianism is a philosophy in which "an action . . . is right if it tends to promote happiness or pleasure and wrong if it tends to produce unhappiness or pain —not just for the performer of the action but also for everyone else affected by it."[11]

That is to say that utilitarians seek to maximize happiness for the greatest number of people. According to Bentham, human behavior is motivated by the avoidance of pain and the pursuit of pleasure. This is the primary moral criterion for deciding moral issues: the utility of a pursuit to generate happiness and reduce suffering.

Bentham begins Chapter 1 of his work *Principles of Morals and Legislation* by writing:

> Nature has placed mankind under the governance of two sovereign masters, pain and pleasure. They alone point out what we ought to do and determine what we shall do; the standard of right and wrong, and the chain of causes and effects, are both

---

11. Encyclopedia Britannica, *Utilitarianism*.

fastened to their throne. They govern us in all we do, all we say, all we think.[12]

This rests on what philosophers would call a "hedonistic" approach—not hedonism referring to an amoral selfishness, but simply that pleasure is the measure of accounting for goodness in the world. In this respect, hedonism is rooted in equality; no one person's pleasure is more valuable than another's. The pleasure of a philosopher taking joy in lofty discourse is not privileged over that of someone in poverty finding pleasure in a satisfying meal.

With the egalitarian nature of utilitarianism, it follows that, while it would be best to make everyone happy, when not possible, it is preferable to make the many happy rather than just the few.

One of the main benefits to such a system is its simplicity. Instead of needing to make complex moral decisions based on a mastery of a particular religious tradition or expertise in philosophy, we can simply think of how to bring the most pleasure to the most people. This can enable us to avoid confusion in morality, which often leads to us giving up and accepting injustices. Bentham's system, on the other hand, equips everyone, including the government, to make moral calculations that generally benefit the masses. And so, in addition to being pro-equality, utilitarianism is pro-democracy, allowing people to hold legislators accountable to the overall public and not simply to a small group of elites.

One word that summarizes the ideas at play here is consequentialism. Bentham cares not about the intentions behind a person's actions but the consequences. Whether a person means well is irrelevant if the consequences themselves bring about greater suffering.

So what should a Jew make of utilitarianism? At its most basic level, it sounds like a great idea. What is *tikkun olam* if not an attempt to repair the world on a macro scale. Why would we not want to do the most good for the most people? We of course, by and large, want people to be happier and suffer less.

However, there are important ways in which Judaism rejects a utilitarian ethic. For example, there is the Jewish value that every human has infinite dignity—each life is an entire universe. Therefore, we cannot hold as a rule that two lives are more valuable than one. Infinity plus infinity still equals infinity. Further, there are religious and moral principles that prevent utilitarian calculations. For instance, the rabbis make clear that you cannot kill one innocent person to save two (assuming this is not an instance of self-defense).

---

12. Bentham, *An Introduction to the Principles of Morals and Legislation*.

Take the famous trolley problem. To review: A hypothetical trolley is heading down a track and bound to kill five people. You have the option to pull a lever to divert the trolley to a path on which it will run over and kill one person instead. Should you cause the trolley to kill one person in order to save the five?

For a utilitarian, the choice is not difficult: You send the trolley to kill the one. In Jewish morality, it's more complicated. In fact, a similar case is discussed by the Jerusalem Talmud:

> It was stated: "A group of people on the road were met by Gentiles who said to them, give us one of you that we may kill him, otherwise we shall kill all of you; even if all of them are killed they should not hand over a person.[13]

From this it appears that Jewish law would prohibit one from pulling the lever, thereby killing one person to save five. However, halachic authorities have debated this question, without clear agreement. Yet rather than focusing exclusively on the consequences, they tend to analyze the act itself and explore whether the consequences are inherent to the act or can be seen as separate from it.

The essential difference between Bentham and Judaism is that he more or less viewed people as represented by totals of happiness points in a game. In Judaism, we see that the root of a person goes deeper than the pleasures they accumulate. They are made in God's image, and they should be treated as such. Bentham, by contrast, famously said:

> Natural rights is simple nonsense: natural and imprescriptible rights, rhetorical nonsense—nonsense upon stilts.

Also recall the way utilitarianism cares more about consequences than intention. This isn't foreign to Judaism. We have the trope that Judaism is concerned primarily with actions. And yet, we should understand that Judaism cares very much about intentionality. Yes, we want to do the right thing regardless of thoughts and beliefs, but all things being equal, *kavanah* does matter, both religiously and ethically. For example, Jewish law does not treat intentional murder as the same as an unintentional killing even if both have the same consequences. The Torah specifies that one who killed another accidentally is not sentenced to death but rather allowed to take refuge in special cities designated for that purpose.[14] Utilitarianism and its focus on consequences does not always equal justice.

---

13. Jerusalem Talmud, Terumot 8:4.
14. Numbers 35:25.

So too, Maimonides posited that, when giving *tzedakah*, it is better to give just one coin every day than to give a massive sum of money all at once.[15] Why? Because it is not just about the practical consequences of the mitzvah, but also about the effect the mitzvah has on the human soul.

Still, these Jewish ideas are no excuse for not considering the impact of our actions. The Talmud famously asks, "Who is the one that is wise?" and answers, "the one who can foresee the consequences of their actions."[16] It is not sufficient to think that one's actions are justified in an abstract sense, but one must also strive to think through their impact on themselves and others. When discussing gun control, a contemporary rabbi has argued that Jewish values dictate that our laws should be based on utilitarian consequentialism (backed by statistics) rather than more acutely focused rules. He argued:

> Rabbenu Nissim (14th century Spain) writes that when evaluating the prohibition of whether to sell weapons, we need to look at the total result. If more harm than good will result from the sale of weapons, then we should not sell the weapons.[17]

At its core, the dissonance between Bentham and Jewish thought is that utilitarianism relies unwaveringly on the idea that the end purpose of life is pleasure. As Jews, we see a plurality of goals, such as being of service to God and others, improving one's character, fulfilling one's responsibilities, seeking meaning, and connecting to God by doing *mitzvot*.

According to some utilitarians, it is best to spend one's efforts helping those with the greatest need, even if they live far away from us. However, we do believe the world simply works better if we see ourselves as more responsible to our own children than we are to a stranger, and more responsible to a local community member than we are to someone across the world.

In the philosophy of Jeremy Bentham, we see goodness as a simple calculation. In Judaism, however, we know that the human soul goes so much deeper.

---

15. Maimonides' commentary to Pirkei Avot 3:15.
16. Babylonian Talmud, Tamid 32b.
17. Muskat, *A Torah Perspective on Gun Control*.

19

Mary Wollstonecraft (1759–1797)

THE HISTORY OF RECORDED philosophy is primarily a history of men. Only as we approach modernity do we begin to see women enter the record. Mary Wollstonecraft will be the first woman covered in this series. Her prescient feminism, self-taught brilliance, complex personal life, and untimely death all contribute to her mythology. Wollstonecraft also offers us an opportunity to think about how Jewish tradition overlaps, and departs from, early feminist thinking.

Born in 1759 in London, England, Mary Wollstonecraft was the daughter of a farmer. Like any girl of the era, her education was limited, though it was enough that she was able to work as a school teacher, governess, and even translator.[1] In her brief 38 years of life, Wollstonecraft—largely self-taught, being denied access to higher education as a woman—wrote several books concerning the education of women and girls, as well as a novel. Her most influential work was *A Vindication of the Rights of Women*, published in 1792, which calls for the men and women to be equally educated.[2]

Despite the power and almost prophetic nature of her writing, which I will get to shortly, it must be noted that Wollstonecraft is often talked about as a tragic and scandalous figure. Many people know more about her personal life than they do about her philosophical contributions. Much is made of the fact that she had a child out of wedlock. This was in 1794, when she lived with an American general during the French Revolution; when the love affair soured, she attempted suicide.[3] Others note that she was

---

1. Encyclopedia Britannica, *Mary Wollstonecraft*.
2. Encyclopedia Britannica, *Mary Wollstonecraft*.
3. Encyclopedia Britannica, *Mary Wollstonecraft*.

pregnant with another child when she married William Godwin.[4] In a true tragedy, she died just eleven days after giving birth. That child was Mary Shelley, whose fame would in time come to outstrip her mother's.[5]

And yet, the tragedies and so-called scandals of Wollstonecraft's life are only part of the story. Consider that, as a woman, she was barred from the university. In fact, it would not be until over seventy years after her death that the first women would be admitted to university in Britain, when nine women were admitted to the University of London.[6] So the fact is that Wollstonecraft, without access to the platforms of learning or scholarship that she so deserved, and without any kind of meaningful tradition of female scholarship to build on, managed to leave a lasting mark on Western philosophy. That her contributions are overshadowed by her personal life must be understood as misogynistic. After all, many male philosophers have had deeply scandalous personal lives, and yet their ideas are examined in their own right. We do not begin each discussion of Nietzsche or Schopenhauer, for example, by emphasizing that both men had syphilis; instead, we privilege their formidable philosophical contributions over their complicated personal lives. We can see, therefore that in life and in death, Wollstonecraft has not gotten a fair shake. Let's see what we can do about that.

Mary Wollstonecraft was a British philosopher, women's rights advocate, and one of the founders of modern feminism. She was deeply influenced by the work of Enlightenment thinker John Locke, which to say, she placed reason above all else.[7] In Locke's understanding, men have God-given rights discoverable by reason; in Wollstonecraft's view, women also have these rights, because reason is available to them. Simply put, because women like men have reason, they should have freedom. Today, we might feel uncomfortable with the idea of reason as a prerequisite for participating in civil life; we would never accept a society in which differently abled people were barred from basic rights, for example[8]. But at the time, Wollstonecraft's arguments that anyone other than men deserved rights were considered deeply radical.[9] That Wollstonecraft arrived at such revolutionary feminist ideas without any substantive history of women's rights to build on speaks to her irrepressible brilliance.

4. Encyclopedia Britannica, *Mary Wollstonecraft*.
5. Carr, *The Eerie Gravestone Where Frankenstein's Story Began*.
6. University of London, *Leading Women 1868-2018*.
7. Tomaselli, *Mary Wollstonecraft*.
8. There are many states where severe mental disabilities would cause one to lose the right to vote.
9. Carr, *The Eerie Gravestone Where Frankenstein's Story Began*.

Wollstonecraft did support voting rights for women in theory. In *A Vindication of the Rights of Women*, she wrote "... I really think that women ought to have representatives, instead of being arbitrarily governed without having any direct share allowed them in the deliberations of government."[10] However, she acknowledged that it made sense that women were denied basic freedoms—including the right to vote—because women's minds remained weak from a lack of education. Having the right to vote and participate in society, she reasoned, requires being informed, which is to say, educated. Therefore, it was the ways that women and girls were (and were not) educated that made them fit for little else but subjugation.

> "Women are told from their infancy, and taught by the example of their mothers, that a little knowledge of human weakness, justly termed cunning, softness of temper, outward obedience, and a scrupulous attention to a puerile kind of propriety, will obtain for them the protection of man; and should they be beautiful, everything else is needless, for at least twenty years of their lives."[11]

No wonder women are obsessed with their beauty: it is all they have been taught. In the societal structure that Wollstonecraft lived in, a woman's only source of power was to be in the gaze of men. For women, power cannot come from wisdom or even virtue. Her solution, most famously outlined in *A Vindication of the Rights of Women* but also visible in her earlier work, *Thoughts on the Education of Daughters* (1787), is a complete reform of the education such that boys and girls are educated equally.

In her writing, you can feel her passion, her frustration, and even her wit: "My own sex, I hope, will excuse me, if I treat them like rational creatures, instead of flattering their fascinating graces, and viewing them as if they were in a state of perpetual childhood, unable to stand alone."[12]

She notes that it's not just women who are enslaved to the limitations of the education system of the day, but also that many men are hurt by it.

> "... we may instance the example of military men, who are, like them, sent into the world before their minds have been stored with knowledge or fortified by principles. The consequences are similar; soldiers acquire a little superficial knowledge, snatched from the muddy current of conversation ..."[13]

10. Sottosanti, *A Vindication of the Rights of Woman*.
11. Wollstonecraft, *A Vindication of the Rights of Woman*, 84.
12. Wollstonecraft, *A Vindication of the Rights of Woman*.
13. Wollstonecraft, *A Vindication of the Rights of Woman*, 88-89.

Her observations seem to anticipate the centuries-later discussion of so-called "toxic masculinity," and the ways in which it is harmful not just to women but also to men.

For Wollstonecraft—as for Locke, by the way—education is the key to create active, informed citizens, and even morality.[14] Her suggested reforms were way ahead of their time, including the envisioning of a national educational system in which boys and girls learned in mixed classrooms.[15] Despite her incredible foresight, only recently has Wollstonecraft begun to get her due in terms of her influence on feminism. For two centuries, she was dismissed on account of her personal life. Even today, as she is getting the renewed attention and respect she deserves, there is no significant memorial to her anywhere in England or abroad.[16]

Someone who never doubted Wollstonecraft's legacy was her own daughter, Mary Shelley—the very same who went on to write the hugely influential book, *Frankenstein*. Profoundly affected by her mother's philosophy, the younger Mary wrote, "The memory of my mother has always been the pride and delight of my life."[17] It is said that Mary Shelley learned the alphabet by tracing the letters on her mother's grave. We know for a fact that Mary Shelley read all of her mother's work several times, and even wrote about the pressure she felt to rise to her mother's talent. In a way it's a comfort that in Mary Shelley, one of the great writers of the English language, we see some of Mary Wollstonecraft's vision for women's education coming to life.[18]

Some of Wollstonecraft's writings reflect a historical reality in Judaism. After all, from the time of the Talmud, Jewish leaders have been arguing against giving women a religious education comparable to that of men, as well as access to our sacred texts. In the Talmud, the rabbis expound on Deuteronomy 11:19 (*And you shall teach your sons*[19]) to conclude that we are commanded only to teach Torah to boys and men, not to girls and women.[20] Elsewhere, some rabbis go beyond stating that women are not obligated to learn Torah, and say they are in fact barred from it. From tractate Sotah: "Rabbi Eliezer says: Anyone who teaches his daughter Torah is teaching her

---

14. Tomaselli, *Mary Wollstonecraft*.
15. Wollstonecraft, *A Vindication of the Rights of Woman*.
16. Rowlatt, *The original suffragette: the extraordinary Mary Wollstonecraft*.
17. Carr, *The Eerie Gravestone Where Frankenstein's Story Began*.
18. Carr, *The Eerie Gravestone Where Frankenstein's Story Began*.
19. Deuteronomy 11:19.
20. Babylonian Talmud, Kiddushin 29b:8–10.

tiflut."[21] The word I have left untranslated here, *tiflut*, is a notable one. It is sometimes translated as "promiscuity" but a truer translation might be "frivolity" or "trivialness."[22] Some say this probation comes from the idea that teaching a daughter the halakhah on forbidden sexual acts might, in the words of Rabbi Marcus Jastrow, "excite her sensuality."[23] In the Talmud Yerushalmi version of Sotah, Rabbi Eliezer speaks even more shockingly: "Let the words of Torah be burnt, rather than handed over to women."[24]

In his commentary on Sotah, Rashi expounds that the fear is that women will learn "cunning" from Torah and pursue immoral matters.[25] The Rambam returns to the word *tiflut*, translating it as "worthless words."[26] The suggestion here seems to be that the so-called weakness of women's minds will actually distort the meaning of Torah itself.

Any feminist will find it painful and alienating to read these passages. We might also hear echoes of what Wollstonecraft described when she noted that a lack of education made women of her time unfit for political life: so too, in the time of the rabbis, barring women from the beit midrash became a kind of self-fulfilling prophecy. Women were considered weak minded so they were barred from Torah study, and being barred from Torah study made them unable to understand discussions of Torah, which justified them being barred from Torah study, and on and on.

Wollstonecraft would say that women of the time were not fundamentally inferior, but rather that the lack of a systematic pathway education limited the development of their abilities when it came to Torah and commentary. She would no doubt be heartened to learn that today, we are moving toward more equality when it comes to access to Jewish learning. A shining example comes from Rabba Sarah Hurwitz. (Rabba comes from her choice to feminize the word Rabbi.)[27] Ordained in 2009, she is the co-founder of Yeshivat Maharat, an open Orthodox institution and the first Orthodox yeshiva to ordain women as clergy.[28] Here, women have the opportunity to study Talmud and the depths of halakha as in any yeshiva of men.

21. Babylonian Talmud, Sotah 20a:7.
22. Jastrow Dictionary, *Tiflut*.
23. Jastrow Dictionary, *Tiflut*.
24. Jerusalem Talmud, Sotah, 3:4.
25. Rashi on Sotah 21b: 1:2.
26. Rambam on Mishnah Sotah 3:4:1.
27. Re, *Bronx rabbi ushers in the next generation of female rabbis.*
28. Maharat, *Rabba Sara Hurwitz.*

But examples of female Jewish sages go as far back in the Talmud, mostly famously, Beruriah, the wife of Rabbi Meir. She is cited in the Talmud as making fierce, incisive arguments. In Berakhot, for example, she corrects her husband by citing Psalms correctly.[29] Like Wollstonecraft, she was a woman-scholar without a model for what she was doing; and like Wollstonecraft, she had a tragic personal life. Rashi relates the uncomfortable story of her suicide in his commentary on Avodah Zarah.[30] But unlike Wollstonecraft, Beruriah was granted the respect she deserved. In the Talmud, she is quoted among the best.

In the twentieth and twenty-first centuries, women have increasingly breathed new life into Jewish tradition. Take for example, the liberal Jewish feminist Professor Judith Plaskow, who famously wrote a midrash on Genesis about Adam's two wives, Lilith and Eve. In her version, Eve and Lilith form a sisterly bond that exposes the patriarchal structures woven into Judaism.[31] This is someone whose Judaism and feminism are deeply intwined. In the introduction to *Standing Again at Sinai*, she wrote, "I am not a Jew in the synagogue and a feminist in the world. I am a Jewish feminist and a feminist Jew in every moment of my life."[32]

Plaskow certainly sees feminist Judaism as operating outside of rabbinic Judaism.[33] For a Jewish feminist who makes a place for herself within the context of traditional Jewish thought, we might look at the feminist biblical scholar Tamar Ross, a professor of Jewish theology at Bar-Ilan University in Israel. Dr. Ross has dedicated her life to correcting the invisibility of women in Jewish thought. She argues that women have unique experiences and frameworks that have often been overlooked by scholars:

> "In assuming that the prevailing division of gender roles is correct and natural, and basing research on questions that were originally formulated only by men, scholars often missed much of what was distinctive about women's experiences."[34]

Here, we see her pointing out a cycle of exclusion and invisibility that was so apparent to Wollstonecraft.

A place where Jewish thought might depart from Wollstonecraft is her emphasis on reason, namely, that political rights should primarily be

---

29. Babylonian Talmud, Berakhot 10a.
30. Rashi on Avodah Zarah 18b.
31. Adler, *Judith Plaskow*.
32. Plaskow, *Standing Against at Sinai*, ix-x.
33. Plaskow, *Standing Against at Sinai*, 71.
34. Ross, *Feminism Changes the Study of Jewish Thoughts*.

premised on the capacity to reason. Instead, we can agree that rights are inherent to every person—man or women. Nobody is subject to an entry fee of reason[35]. Indeed, *Tzelem Elokim*, the Jewish belief that we are all made in God's image, goes way deeper than the capacity to reason.[36] It is in our very souls.

Torah is very clear that when we stood at Sinai and accepted the *brit*, the covenant with God, it was not just men who were present but "men, women, and children."[37]

When we make Jewish discourse available to all Jews, we are all richer for it. It is not only women who benefit from inclusion. Men get access to new forms of wisdom. And individuals who do not identify as men or women, but who occupy space along the broad nonbinary spectrum of gender identity, are also free to bring their wisdom to our learning. In this way, we may be moving towards the future that Wollstonecraft dreamed of: one in which education is within anyone's reach.

---

35. To be sure, from a Jewish perspective, one who is mentally incompetent doesn't have "political" rights. Their actions don't have halachic significance, because they cannot be held responsible for them. Plus, children also don't have the kinds of political rights that Wollstonecraft is advocating for women and that is true in both halacha and modern law. This is assumed to be because they haven't advanced their capacity for reason yet.

36. Genesis 1:26-27.

37. Deuteronomy 31:10–13.

20

Georg Wilhelm Friedrich Hegel (1770–1831)

ARE POLARIZED ARGUMENTS INHERENTLY bad? How do human values advance? What is the relationship between the real and the ideal?

Georg Wilhelm Friedrich Hegel was engaged in numerous fields of philosophy, though he can be placed firmly in the camp of German Idealism, which emerged as a major response to the Enlightenment. Beginning with Immanuel Kant, German Idealism aspired to use reason to grasp the world and human beings place within it. Rather than rely only on science, it recognized that human history, culture, and religion were to play a major role alongside reason in making sense of human existence. Though famous for its difficulty, German Idealism sought to address the most pressing political and ethical questions about what it meant to be a human being in the modern world.

A major theme in nearly all of Hegel's writings is the question of freedom. Unlike earlier Enlightenment thinkers who thought of freedom as a natural right of human beings, Hegel asserted that reason and freedom are not given to us automatically, but are things that are achieved in history. One cannot find freedom simply by running off into the woods and meditating; it is something that must be reached through historical progress. People, according to Hegel were not created knowing how to be reasonable or free. Instead, the story of humanity is one of marching toward better ways to think and live.

For Hegel, progress in human history is achieved through "dialectics." "Dialectics," can be defined as "a term used to describe a method of philosophical argument that involves some sort of contradictory process between

GEORG WILHELM FRIEDRICH HEGEL (1770–1831)

opposing sides."[1] This is not only between ideas but also between people as Hegel explores the power dynamics within a "master-slave dialectic."

Our social, intellectual, and political world is constantly filled with contradictions and those clashes lead to the development of history. In this model, a dialectic consists of a thesis and an antithesis, and the clash between them results in a synthesis. Hegel uses the example of the state and the individual which appear to exist in conflict with one another. The tension between them, though, is what eventually leads political life from a monarchy to representative government. Conflicts such as these enable the development of human social and political life. And, as humanity progresses, the old syntheses become the new theses and antitheses, and the dialectical process continues to play out.

But dialectics can also work in the realm of the more abstract. Hegel examines the thesis of "pure being" and the antithesis of "nothingness." The synthesis, he finds, is "becoming."

This sounds very much like the Jewish idea of God as revealed in the Torah to Moses. At the burning bush, Moshe asks God for God's name, so he can tell the Israelites who spoke to him. God answers cryptically, "*Ehyeh-Asher-Ehyeh*," I Will Be What I Will Be.[2]

God, we see from both the Torah and a parallel in Hegel, is not strictly a "being," and God is not "nothing" either. But the product of the tensions between both, "becoming," describes God much better.

As an idealist, Hegel gave much thought to what he called "Spirit." For Hegel, everything from our inner depths of consciousness to our outward political battles is all part of a single Spirit, a single mind, a single dimension. Hegel seems to be a monist[3]—instead of recognizing a distinction between the physical and what lies beyond it, Hegel held that everything is Spirit. While, for Kant, consciousness and eternal truths were in another, unchanging realm, Hegel saw Spirit as existing in this world. Thus, it was not immovable, but dynamic.

And because everything in Spirit is interconnected, to Hegel we're not *creating* progress through dialectics, but revealing connections within the universe that, in a sense, already exist. But, at the same time, for Hegel, we cannot know the outcome of a dialectic until it has occurred. When one looks at human history, one sees Spirit undergoing a variety of forms and transformation, which Hegel believed to be different stages of human

---

1. Maybee, *Hegel's Dialectics*.
2. Exodus 3:14.
3. Although this is certainly a point of debate and he's certainly not a monist in the way that many Hasidic thinkers have traditionally been.

consciousness throughout history. Yes, we progress slowly, but there are also revolutionary moments in which we can have a "paradigm shift." That change can emerge from whole societies, but it can also occur as the result of an inspired individual—Hegel believed Napoleon was one of them—and such a person might not even be aware that the political changes they usher in may cause a historical leap of human consciousness.

Though Hegel was a German Lutheran, his dialectical approach to God and human history is similar to Kabbalah, a topic that was of interest to him. Like in Kabbalah, Hegel conceives of God as more of a dynamic process than as a static being. Kabbalistic thinkers who preceded Hegel, such as the Ramchal, saw this process taking place not with regards to the sefirot in the heavenly realm but in human history as well.

By putting human action at the center of history, Hegel is at the same time humbling us. Because the nature of consciousness evolves, we must know that we're by and large stuck in the consciousness of our time. As Hegel famously said, "The owl of Minerva only flies at dusk." By this he meant that we can only use reason to fully grasp a form of life and consciousness after it has ceased to be. As a result, humans are inevitably and essentially products of history.

The ultimate goal of history, for Hegel, is to bring human consciousness to a state of Absolute Spirit. That is the point at which our work is complete. Rather than feeling alienated from the world and from each other, Absolute Spirit means our use of reason combined with the right social and political structures will enable a form of consciousness that enables us to recognize the way we are bound to the state and those we live beside. Hegel writes about this in *Phenomenology of Spirit*:

> History is a conscious, self-mediating process— [it is] Spirit emptied out into time.

And so, reality itself is inextricably intertwined with history. This, like Judaism, implies that there is an extreme amount of importance to our actions.

Hegel is known as having set the intellectual roots for German social welfare. In this regard, there is a connection between him and Karl Marx. Marx, like Hegel, is not merely describing historical processes, but saying freedom needs to keep being actualized. Hegel wanted to set free the Spirit of the universe, and Marx sought to break the chains of the working class.

Beyond Hegel's view of the progress of humanity and the world, which Jews can just about wholeheartedly sign onto, we can see parallels between Hegel's thought and Judaism throughout.

Hegel sees human reason and freedom developing through dialectics, and all of rabbinic history shows Jewish law developing through *machloket*, through productive argument. Jews would agree with Hegel that new revelations are not a threat, but an indicator or movement toward a better world. The difference between them is that Hegel's analysis of history showed one form of life being replaced by another. Judaism, however, believes the Torah is eternal, and while the application of the law might change through dialectics, the essence of the Torah does not.

Rav Kook especially agreed with this. Like some rabbis in his time, he took a Hegelian approach to history, which held that conflict in new eras is good as it produces more enlightened truths. When tradition and modernity clash, that's not a problem. That's an opportunity. When Jewish theology rooted in diaspora living clashed with Zionism it was a chance to synthesize to something new and revitalize the Torah. Furthermore, when reason and revelation clash, you don't just choose a side, you allow them to bring you to a new place. For example, Rav Kook felt that even biblical criticism and even atheism can lead one to a more enlightened knowledge of the Torah and God.

Second, much like the way Hegel sees Spirit progressing and along with it, the human conception of God, we too recognize a progression of how God is revealed through different eras. In the Exodus story, we're virtually taken by the hand of a God who splits the Red Sea. For the Jews of that time, God exists as an absolute power to whom they must submit. However, by the time of the stories of Esther and of Hanukkah, God's presence was much more hidden. And now, in our time, responsibility for justice rests in human hands more than ever before.

And we cannot ignore that Hegel's thought feels closely related to Kabbalah. Yes, we experience light and darkness in the world, but we must see that they are all part of one whole. As with Hegel, dialectical opposites cannot exist without each other, and therefore both are necessary. Their unity is played out in a dynamic conflict that moves us toward an ideal world.

It is true, however, that in Judaism we *do* accept that there are some ideas and eternal truths that can be held outside the context of history. There are eternal truths—such as that of justice—that are accessible throughout time. On the other hand, there are certainly Jewish ideas about justice that evolve over time. Consider the notion that "an eye for an eye" is reengaged by the rabbis to only entail financial compensation. Consider the evolution of the status of women in Jewish law.

Whereas for Hegel Absolute Spirit can be reached only at the end of history, Jews believe God's oneness has always existed, and is available to us in every moment, if only we open ourselves up to its true reality.

21

John Stuart Mill (1806–1873)

WHAT IS THE MEANING of life? If it is happiness, what does "happiness" even mean? What type of society allows happiness to be found by the most people?

A British utilitarian, John Stuart Mill was less skeptical than David Hume, and less dogmatic than Jeremy Bentham—though those previous thinkers helped shape his thought. Mill, then, was more of a reformer and a refiner than a revolutionary.

Mill wrestled with Bentham's happiness principle, his idea that the ultimate goal of all of society is to maximize happiness of any kind. He generally agreed with the idea, but he wanted to figure out how to balance an individual's happiness with the welfare of society at large. Further, Mill wanted a way to motivate people to act not just for their own happiness, but for the happiness of everyone.

And so, Mill's innovation was the "harm principle," the idea that people should by and large be free to pursue their own happiness—with one exception, when it interferes with the welfare of others. One's own pursuit of happiness is not a license to harm someone else.

Later in his life, Mill became a member of British Parliament, which enabled him to put his philosophy into practice. As a public intellectual and practical philosopher, he was a strong advocate for free speech and for human rights. This included strong support for women's suffrage and opposition to slavery.

At the same time, Mill was what today we would think of as a classic libertarian. He wanted a free-market economy in which the government would rarely intervene. Although he cared about society's well-being, he believed that was best achieved by prioritizing the freedom of the individual. This made Mill and architect of Victorian liberalism.

However, unlike libertarians today, which we rightly or wrongly tend to think of as amoral[1], Mill gave great consideration to what constitutes a good life. Unlike Bentham, who valued merely the duration and intensity of pleasure, Mill held that we must consider the quality of the pleasure we're seeking. To Mill, sensual pleasures *were not* of equal value to the pleasure derived from higher intellectual endeavors. Indeed, he believed we should have a society that puts more emphasis on higher pleasures.

Mill distinguished between kinds of pleasure by recognizing two categories of desire. You can desire a thing for its own sake, such as a piece of cake that will be of no benefit to you beyond the minutes you spend eating it. Or you can be motivated by something beyond the immediate pleasure, such as a sense of duty or responsibility. For Mill, it was better to desire something as a means toward happiness than to desire something as an end in itself.

These notions of happiness have a complex relationship with the Jewish tradition. We know that happiness is not *the sole purpose* of life in Judaism, the way utilitarians would consider it to be the ultimate goal of society. However, happiness does occupy a central role.

The entire Book of Psalms begins with the word *Ashrei*, or "Happy":

> Happy is the one who has not followed the counsel of the
> wicked,
> or taken the path of sinners,
> or joined the company of the insolent;
> rather, the teaching of the Lord is their delight,
> and they study that teaching day and night.[2]

So too, we recite from the Psalms and daily prayers:

> Happy are those who dwell in Your house;
> they forever praise You. *Selah.*[3]

Happiness, we see, comes from living a good life in line with the will of God. This works well with Mill's critique of Bentham. We don't necessarily learn from Judaism, "Happy is the one who has a lot of cake." Instead, happiness comes from doing the right thing in service of a larger purpose.

Further, we learn from Pirkei Avot, the Ethics of the Fathers:

1. We rightly or wrongly tend to think of them as believing that the only moral principle which should guide politics is that of individual freedom.
2. Psalms 1:1–2.
3. Psalms 84:5.

Ben Zoma said . . . Who is rich? One who rejoices in their lot, as it is said[4]: "You shall enjoy the fruit of your labors, you shall be happy and you shall prosper."[5]

This is another example of how Judaism most certainly does not discount the importance of material survival and success. However, unlike modern notions of happiness which often assume one never has enough and therefore desires more, Judaism pushes us to recognize we can be happy with what we have and not just with what we wish we had. Even so, happiness through material survival and success is only the outer indication of something more profound. One of the great Jewish insights is that we *do* have the social-justice imperative of meeting people's basic human needs including basic physical securities and comforts, but then we also need to do the intellectual and spiritual work of finding fulfillment in something bigger.

Maimonides wrote in his *Guide for the Perplexed*:

> The general object of the Law is twofold: the well-being of the soul, and the well-being of the body. The well-being of the soul is promoted by correct opinions communicated to the people according to their capacity . . . The well-being of the body is established by a proper management of the relations in which we live one to another.[6]

Here the Rambam would be in agreement with the harm principle; ethics *are* tied to our happiness, because people don't exist on individual islands. We are all interconnected. The well-being of the "body" refers to the body politic and so for Maimonides, an overall purpose of Jewish practices is to improve the welfare of others in society.

Rabbis Jack Riemer and Elie Spitz expounded on the levels of happiness in the Hebrew word *ashrei*. They wrote in their *Duets on Psalms: Drawing Meaning From Ancient Words*:

> To delve deeper into defining happiness, let us look at the opening letter, which will reveal that happiness is an inner quality. In Hebrew, *ashrei* begins with an *alef* (א), the first letter of the alphabet. One other Hebrew consonant, *ayin* (ע), is silent, taking its sound from the vowel attached. These two letters at the start of a word repeatedly signify inner versus outer. When beginning with an *ayin*, "or" spells "skin"; with an *aleph*, it means

---

4. Psalms 128:2.
5. Pirkei Avot 4:1.
6. Maimonides, *Guide for the Perplexed*, 3:27, translated by Friedlander.

"light"; *asher* with an *ayin* means "wealth"; with an *aleph*, it means "happiness." This opening word, therefore, teaches that happiness is an inner experience, distinguished from externals such as wealth. Happiness is a lingering quiet mind and an open heart, a cultivated tendency.[7]

Happiness, we know from both Mill and Judaism, is not about immediate pleasure, but about uncovering something deeper and more hidden. As such, we can agree with Mill that, while utilitarianism was an important historical development, it went too far by valuing base emotions above all else. We can therefore appreciate Mill's nuancing from Bentham's less flexible approach.

We can also see utilitarianism as a movement toward universalizing philosophers' concerns. Utilitarians were among the first ones to think seriously about the good of all people. They moved ethical concern from the individual to the masses.

Nevertheless, happiness remains only one tool in the Jewish toolbox. As a rich tradition of law and lore, Judaism does not feel the need to find simplistic calculations for the good that utilitarians propose. Instead, the ethics, narratives, and larger richly layered systems of the Jewish canon allows us to embrace gray areas, tensions, and competing values.

And so, is Judaism all about happiness? Probably not. But focusing on a life of virtue is likely to do the incidental work of bringing you to a happier place. In Judaism, we follow not only Mill's harm principle, but also vast, intertwined sets of other principles to bring us to the higher happiness Mill hoped all people would find.

---

7. Riemer and Spitz, *Duets on Psalms: Drawing Meaning from Ancient Words.*

22

Søren Kierkegaard (1813–1855)

Is THE FATE OF a person determined by their surroundings? Or can we control our lives with the choices we make? In a world in which we seemingly always have a multitude of options to pick from, is so much choice even a good thing?

Søren Kierkegaard was born in Norway, and, living in 19th century Europe, he engaged in philosophy by responding to the German idealism that dominated the thinking of those around him, particularly the ideas promulgated by Hegel.

Hegel's idealism, as we've discussed, viewed human progress through the lens of paradigm-shifting human developments. As such, for Hegel, people had no choice but to be products of the eras in which they lived. Kierkegaard, however, rejected Hegel's approach which focused on human thought and society throughout history in favor of an approach that embraced the subjective position of the individual. According to Kierkegaard, each individual is free and self-determining. We can make real choices on how to act in the world, and it is our choices, not our surroundings, that determine who we are.

While, for both Hegel and Kierkegaard, we have a choice between hedonism and adherence to a higher sense of ethics, Hegel emphasized the impact of one's historical period and life conditions, how the political structures and religious ideas of one's time heavily guided one's life. Kierkegaard, however, proposed that we have total freedom—not in all things, but in the choices we make.

But this freedom to choose, Kierkegaard believed, does not necessarily make us happier. Instead, it can cause a subjective predicament and make us full of dread. Once one sees the enormity of the possibilities before us combined with our freedom to respond to them in any which way, a new anxiety is born. Kierkegaard calls this "the dizziness of freedom."

This "dizziness of freedom" is a huge part of the problem with being a modern person. Whatever job, life partner, or consumer acquisition you pick, you'll possibly regret it knowing you could have found something or somebody different. You will always feel inadequate by making the wrong choice. What this makes clear is that the apparent simplicity of premodern life can lead to more happiness than the modern condition to do anything one wants.

For me, Jewish practice can be an antidote to the paradox of freedom described by Kierkegaard. By limiting my life to the options within a set Jewish path, I and others find that there is a higher freedom in eliminating some of the overwhelming number of choices we can make.[1] By following Jewish practice, one makes themselves smaller. By limiting your options, you can be b'simcha.

The Jewish tradition often takes a counterintuitive position: that it is better to do a good deed out of a sense of obligation than it is to do a good deed voluntarily. We learn in Tractate Kiddushin, in the Talmud:

> As Rabbi Ḥanina says: Greater is one who is commanded to do a mitzva and performs it than one who is not commanded to do a mitzva and performs it.[2]

In Judaism, we understand that it is not truly satisfying to do whatever you want. Freedom, instead, is achieved by fulfilling our moral obligations and finding liberation in the next height[3]. This is because happiness cannot be sought out as the first step. There is greater joy, we know, in moving toward becoming an actualized moral being than there is in living in the uncertainty of unlimited choices.

Kierkegaard would not disagree with the priorities of Jewish living entirely. For him, there are three rungs on which a person could live their life. The lowest is all about aesthetics, senses of pleasures. If one makes the right

---

1. This can be true on three different levels. a) It is only by having set rules that one can gain self-mastery. Otherwise, one is constantly led by their passions and desires. b) By following rules, one is "freed" from the anxiety of having so many options. c) It is only by following rules that are not part of the dominant secular order that one can find a way to escape it.

2. Babylonia Talmud, Kiddushin 31a.

3. If we believe we are commanded by God, we believe in some sense that the Torah and mitzvot are divine. We don't have to make a choice that is filled with anxiety, because the act of mitzvah is a divine truth. Kierkegaard is struggling with the decision of faith that is fundamentally ungrounded. This is what makes him modern, but traditional Jewish thought doesn't really allow for that possibility.

choices to transcend that, they enter the world of ethics. Further up, one finds the truly religious life. Kierkegaard called such a person "the knight of faith." They find their freedom when transcending ethics into the religious.

While Judaism can be seen as offering a similar hierarchy of values, it is in fact fuzzier than that. Seeking pleasure isn't inherently *worse* than ethics or religious devotion and ritual unless it causes one to act unethically and violate the mitzvot. Instead, religion *informs* the ways in which we interact with aesthetics and ethics. These areas cannot be separated—they all touch upon one another. For Kierkegaard, your relationship to God is potentially more important than your relationship to other people, yet for us, they are entirely intertwined. We read in the Book of Leviticus:

> Love your fellow as yourself: I am the Lord.[4]

The religious and interpersonal are rendered *in the same sentence* — at least in a language with punctuation. For Kierkegaard, though, there are potentially moments when religion triumphs over all.

His principal example of this "knight of faith" was the first Jew: Abraham, though for reasons we might not all agree with. In the story of the Binding of Isaac, Kierkegaard took Abraham to be a hero. Why? Because, in Kierkegaard's thought, ethics is relegated to the human realm. One need not be religious to know how to act ethically. If religion is to truly mean to be an encounter with the divine, it must exist at a level that is in some sense beyond ethics. Therefore, Abraham becomes a knight of faith, when he confronts God's command to sacrifice his son. Because he recognizes this act is incomprehensible at the level of ethics, following it requires a leap of faith.

God's command to Abraham is described by Kierkegaard as a "teleological suspension of the ethical," a controversial idea that some in recent Jewish thought have embraced, including Rabbi Joseph B. Soloveitchik, who wasn't always Kierkegaardian, but became so in his later work. It reflects the notion that ethics, as conceived by human beings, may at times be suspended in order to actualize the divine will.

See, in his earlier philosophical writings, Soloveitchik, a foundational figure in Modern Orthodoxy, drew upon the thought of Hermann Cohen, a major proponent of neo-Kantianism. Cohen's emphasis on the way human beings construct the rules of math and physics was a large influence on his work *Halakhic Man*, which argues that halacha can be formalized in a way that is similar to how mathematicians deduce new equations and theorems.

In Soloveitchik's later writing, though, he famously portrays *The Lonely Man of Faith* as a figure who never feels fully comfortable in the

---

4. Leviticus 19:18.

social conventions and ethics of their time. Here, he embraces Kierkegaard's understanding that faith may not align directly or be comprehensible in the world one finds themselves.[5]

Kierkegaard is considered the father of existentialism. Existentialism can be identified by four key components:

1. Existence is always particular and individual—always *my* existence, *your* existence, *his* existence, *her* existence.
2. Existence is primarily the problem of existence . . . it is, therefore, also the investigation of the meaning of Being.
3. That investigation is continually faced with diverse possibilities, from among which the existent . . . must make a selection, to which he must then commit himself.
4. Because those possibilities are constituted by the individual's relationships with things and with other humans, existence is always a being-in-the-world.[6]

These were radical moves to make at the time: the idea that knowledge and truth moves from the objective to the subjective, from the collective to the individual. In existentialism, the world has no intrinsic or obvious meaning. Rather, individuals are responsible for coming up with meaning on their own. While, for Hegel, the meaning of our lives was limited by our respective historical periods in the march of human progress, Kierkegaard believed we could transcend that through the act of faith.

Even though Kierkegaard was willing to open all doors in the search of meaning and purpose, he in no way abandoned his faith in God, as his successors in existentialism do, most notably Jean-Paul Sartre.

It is notable that Kierkegaard never got married. He was once close to marriage, but ended up calling it off. Kierkegaard famously said:

> If you marry, you will regret it; if you do not marry, you will also regret it; if you marry or if you do not marry, you will regret both; whether you marry or you do not marry, you will regret both. Laugh at the world's follies, you will regret it; weep over them, you will also regret it; if you laugh at the world's follies or

---

5. While there is a bit of Kierkegaard in "The Lonely Man of Faith," (he even describes Abraham as a knight of faith in it) the Rav also goes out of his way to differentiate his approach in the book from Kierkegaard as you can see in this quote: "Our description of the "individuality" and autonomy of the faith gesture should not be associated with Tertullian's apothegm credo quia absurdum est. Neither should it be equated with Kierkegaard's "leap into the absurd." The Rav is most Kierkegaardian in his writings on the Akedah.

6. Encyclopedia Britannica, *Existentialism*.

> if you weep over them, you will regret both; whether you laugh at the world's follies or you weep over them, you will regret both. Believe a girl, you will regret it; if you do not believe her, you will also regret it; if you believe a girl or you do not believe her, you will regret both; whether you believe a girl or you do not believe her, you will regret both. If you hang yourself, you will regret it; if you do not hang yourself, you will regret it; if you hang yourself or you do not hang yourself, you will regret both; whether you hang yourself or you do not hang yourself, you will regret both. This, gentlemen, is the sum of all practical wisdom.[7]

The anxiety and discomfort induced by choice pervaded every aspect of his life. This is in stark contrast with the Jewish view of marriage being almost unambiguously positive, as well illustrated by the Lubavitcher Rebbe who reportedly told his doctor:

> The time I devote to have tea with my wife every day is as important to me as the obligation to put on Tefillin every day.[8]

And so, does Kierkegaard's philosophy blend right in with the wisdom that long has guided the Jewish people, like Kant's or Hegel's? Not really. But I think, in addition to learning from Kierkegaard, we can look to Rav Soloveitchik as a model. Like him, we too may identify with different philosophers at different points in our lives, even ones whose ideas differ radically from each other.

Kierkegaard, we learn, though his ideas don't scream "Judaism!" has a deeply religious fulcrum. He just moves religion from a place of dogma and authority to a place of individual experience and commitment. This is not at all out of step with the founders of the Hasidic movement, who encouraged their followers' not only to focus on the minute details of observance but also to recognize that one's inner, subjective experience was of great religious significance. And so, if you're in a stage of life right now in which you're drowning in anxiety and despair, it might be wise to turn to Kierkegaard.

We know from Judaism that there is absolutely a place for the objective and the communal. Still, Kierkegaard's existentialism can teach us not to ignore the subjective and the individual.

---

7. Popova, *Either/Or: Kierkegaard on Transcending the Tyranny of Binary Choice and Double Regret*.

8. Hodakov, *Wisdom from the Rebbe*.

23

Henry David Thoreau (1817–1862)

Is LIFE BETTER LIVED in the solitude of the woods, or by making change in the streets? How does one come to connect with eternal truths? How should a person respond to an unjust government?

This week our journey finally takes us to America, where we meet Henry David Thoreau, a 19th-century transcendentalist from Massachusetts. Transcendentalism was a modern philosophical movement inspired by the American writer Ralph Waldo Emerson.

> The transcendentalists operated with the sense that a new era was at hand. They were critics of their contemporary society for its unthinking conformity, and urged that each person find, in Emerson's words, "an original relation to the universe."[1] Emerson and Thoreau sought this relation in solitude amidst nature, and in their writing. By the 1840s they, along with other transcendentalists, were engaged in the social experiments of Brook Farm, Fruitlands, and Walden; and, by the 1850s in an increasingly urgent critique of American slavery.[2]

Thoreau's most famous book was *Walden; Or, Life in the Woods*, a memoir reflecting on what it means to live simply in nature, based on his experience living by the aforementioned Walden Pond. The poet Robert Frost would later say, "In one book . . . he surpasses everything we have had in America."[3]

---

1. Emerson, *Ralph Waldo Emerson* (The Oxford Authors), Richard Poirier (ed.).
2. Goodman, *Transcendentalism*.
3. Frost, *Letter to Wade Van Dore*.

In this work, Thoreau describes this life as the way out of the groupthink of society. He writes:

> I find it wholesome to be alone the greater part of the time. To be in company, even with the best, is soon wearisome and dissipating. I love to be alone. I never found the companion that was so companionable as solitude.[4]

While we tend to think of Thoreau as advocating for an isolated "life in the woods," he is also notable for his essay *Civil Disobedience*, about the obligation to disobey an unjust government. In this case, he was a staunch opponent of slavery and of the Spanish-American War. We see from the diversity of his interests that Thoreau both receded from society and sought to change it.

And, beyond writing and speaking, Thoreau backed up his thoughts with his actions. In one case, he refused to pay for six years of owed poll taxes, in protest of government policies, so he was jailed for a night, until somebody paid the taxes behind his back. Further, he was a "conductor" of the Underground Railroad, the effort to help Black people escape slavery and flee to places where they would be free and safe.

Thoreau was an early proponent of conscientious objection and nonviolent resistance, ideas that would be embraced by Mahatma Gandhi and Martin Luther King Jr. in the generations that followed him.

Mahatma Gandhi was deeply inspired by Civil Disobedience and, in his activism, took Thoreau's ideas in a more strictly pacifistic direction. In his autobiography, Dr. Martin Luther King Jr. wrote:

> Whether expressed in a sit-in at lunch counters, a freedom ride into Mississippi, a peaceful protest in Albany, Georgia, a bus boycott in Montgomery, Alabama, these are outgrowths of Thoreau's insistence that evil must be resisted and that no moral man can patiently adjust to injustice.[5]

The Jewish philosopher Martin Buber, in Man's Duty as Man, accepted Thoreau's idea that, when a law is unjust, a person is obligated to break it.[6]

These notions don't seem so radical today, but, in Thoreau's time, they were unheard of. This is a testament to Thoreau's bravery and the philosophy of self-reliance that transcendentalists espoused. While many philosophical schools remain primarily in the realm of theory, transcendentalism was one that directly enabled moral courage.

4. Thoreau, *Walden*, 212.
5. King, *The Autobiography of Martin Luther King, Jr.*
6. Buber, *Man's Duty as Man*.

Thoreau's principles of protest are something that should deeply inspire us as Jews. We can consider how the Jewish tradition, at its best, has embraced Thoreau's idea of conscientious objection. For instance, in the 1960s, the Boston Beit Din wrote a *teshuva* saying that refusal to serve in the Vietnam War was Jewishly permissible.[7] One could avoid the mandate of government based upon their personal conscience.

Thoreau, by speaking out against the injustices of his time and developing the social-change tool of nonviolent resistance, set into motion a historically impactful way of being in the world and a tradition of resistance we should seek to continue today—in addition to other means of action such as persuasion and political advocacy.

However, there are some Jewish nuances to the notion of civil disobedience. For example, in Judaism, we have the principle that one must follow the law of the land unless it's requiring you to violate the Torah. Judaism *would* generally tell someone like Thoreau to pay his taxes. It could be a *chillul Hashem* (desecration of the Name of God) and put Jews at risk to engage in tax evasion. However, if the government were to mandate the eating of pork, one would put Jewish law first.

Even though Judaism is in favor of civil disobedience toward a moral means, Judaism is not categorically opposed to violent resistance, self-defense, or morally necessary intervention. For example, when Moshe saw a taskmaster beating an Israelite slave, Moshe killed him, in an action that was not condemned by the Torah. So too, the first Jew, Avraham, in the Book of Genesis enlists others to save his nephew Lot, who has been taken captive by invading kings from Babylonia.

Because Thoreau died of tuberculosis-related bronchitis in 1862, at age 44, we don't know what he thought, definitively, of the Civil War, which achieved his goal of emancipation of slaves through deadly means.

Jews must additionally consider the example Thoreau set by being so strongly and impactfully anti-slavery. It is one thing to hold the Torah value of liberation, and it is another to do the work of liberation in the world. As the rabbis themselves say, "It is not learning which is the essence but rather action."[8]

Thoreau never married and didn't have any children. When he was 23 years old, he proposed to a woman, but she rejected him. He was influenced by Indian spiritual thought via Hindu texts and practices such as flute-playing and yoga, which moved him toward pantheism, a concept we've discussed earlier in this series. Through this belief, Thoreau had a

---

7. Blau, *An Unusual Rabbinic Court Judges Social Problems*.
8. Pirkei Avot 1:17.

desire to connect to nature, which he found also required being free from distractions.

Thoreau wrote in his book *Walking*: "In short, all good things are wild and free."[9]

This unwavering commitment to freedom made Thoreau something of an anarchist. He believed laws were often more likely to oppress humans than to protect them. In the time of slavery and the Fugitive Slave Act, though, that position seemed entirely reasonable.

For Thoreau, actualization of the self meant being free from what, in Judaism, we might call the idol of materialism. He writes in Walden, "Most of the luxuries and many of the so-called comforts of life are not only not indispensable, but positive hindrances to the elevation of mankind"[10] and "Better than love, than money, than fame, give me truth."[11]

As Jews, we should think deeply about how the ways Thoreau believed freedom was achieved. We can embrace his view that the luxuries arounds us are, at best, distractions from what the human can achieve. It is undeniable that materialism is among the most problematic forces in our lives today.

Thoreau shares an essential idea with Judaism in his understanding that, while monetary gains are temporary, we can find the eternal in experiences. Thoreau writes in Walden:

> If you have built castles in the air, your work need not be lost; that is where they should be. Now put the foundations under them.[12]

This bears a striking similarity to what Rabbi Abraham Joshua Heschel writes in his opening chapter of *The Sabbath*:

> The seventh day is a *palace in time* which we build. It is made of soul, of joy and reticence. In its atmosphere, a discipline is a reminder of adjacency to eternity. Indeed, the splendor of the day is expressed in terms of abstentions ... How else to express glory in the presence of eternity, if not by the silence of abstaining from noisy acts? These restrictions utter songs to those who know how to stay at a palace with a queen.[13]

---

9. Thoreau, *Walking*, 68.
10. Thoreau, *Walden*, 15.
11. Thoreau, *Walden*, xl.
12. Thoreau, *Walden*, xli.
13. Heschel, *The Sabbath*.

In Judaism, with Shabbat, we have our own Walden Pond, albeit a less lonesome one, that we can return to for one day a week, rather than, as Thoreau did, for two years straight. Judaism knows, just as Thoreau did, that there is a place both for *Life in the Woods* and for *Civil Disobedience*.

One practical takeaway, for all of us, from Thoreau might be a reminder of the value of taking daily walks.[14] We may not be walking through the forests all day like he was but we can, in our own ways, take walks. We know the significant physical and mental health value but also it can be soul deepening. Thoreau wrote: "I took a walk in the woods and came out taller than the trees." We can gain new perspectives. He wasn't the first philosopher, of course, to promote walking. We know the Greeks often philosophized as they walked together. Kierkegaard wrote: "I know of no thought so burdensome that one cannot walk away from it." For those who were deep thinkers, they needed to escape the book and the pen and paper to regain clarity. Charles Dickens wrote: "If I could not walk far and fast, I think I should just explode and perish." Nietzsche wrote: "All truly great thoughts are conceived while walking."[15] He also wrote: "Do not believe any idea that was not born in the open air and of free movement."[16] So too, the rabbis found great value in deep conversations while walking.[17] Rabbi Menachem Froman wrote:

> ... The Temple also sat on the boundary, on the line between Yehuda and Binyamin. The heart of the Temple, the most important parts, the ark and its cover, were in Binyamin. Why was this so? It was because Binyamin was born on the road. This comes with a great advantage. When you're on the road, you can't be fixed in place, bound by your ideology. You are required to respond, to renew yourself, to flow. People used to say, "On

---

14. See Thoreau's lecture "Walking" first delivered at the Concord Lyceum on April 23rd, 1851. See Rebecca Solnit's "Wanderlust: A History of Walking." Also see "A Philosophy of Walking" by Frédéric Gros.

15. These quotes from philosophers on walking can all be found here: McCarthy, *Whatever the Problem, It's Probably Solved by Walking*.

16. Elkin, 'A Philosophy of Walking,' by Frédéric Gros.

17. See Babylonian Talmud, Taanit 10b: "With regard to two Torah scholars who are walking along the road and there are no Torah matters discussed between them, they are worthy of being burned." Also see Babylonian Talmud 85a for a very rich Talmudic discourse on saving life that occurs while the rabbis are walking. Also see Babylonian Talmud Eruvin 53-54. Also, in Babylonian Talmud Hagigah 15a, famously, Rabbi Meir and his teacher Elisha ben Abuyah learn Torah together as Elisha rides, and Meir walks behind him. So much of the Zohar involves stories of the sages "walking on the way", אחרואב ילוא. It seems to be the main way in which their learning takes place and the Torah they discuss is oftentimes in response to something they are encountering while walking.

the road, don't be right, be smart!" If a car is driving toward you, it doesn't help to yell, "Why are you driving the wrong way in my lane?!" ...[18]

Indeed, let us sit and read, sit and meditate, sit and break bread, but let us also get up and think while we walk together. Sitting is a spiritual practice but so is walking.

---

18. Froman, *Hasidim Tsohakim Mizeh*, 49.

24

Karl Marx (1818–1883)

IS A BETTER WORLD created through the spiritual or the material? What is the nature of the relationship between workers and employers? Is religion really "the opiate of the masses"?

With Karl Marx, we are dealing with without a doubt one of the most influential Jews in history. Norman Lebrecht, in his book *Genius & Anxiety: How Jews Changed the World*, wrote:

> Folk wisdom has it that five Jews wrote the rules of society: Moses said, "The law is everything." Jesus said, "Love is everything." Marx said, "Money is everything." Freud said, "Sex is everything." Einstein said, "Everything is relative."[1]

We could of course spend hours on end ironing out the nuances of that quote, but it remains true that Marx was one of the most important Jewish thinkers ever—in part because Marx intended to be not just a philosopher, but a revolutionary.

Marx was born in Germany in 1818 to assimilated Jewish parents, his mother's father was even a rabbi, however they converted to Christianity before he was born. Marx based his philosophy on a notion of class conflict, laying the foundation for the emergence of communism. With fellow German Friedrich Engels, Marx wrote *The Communist Manifesto*. All of history, they argued there, was *really* about the struggle between the rich and the poor.

As a student of history, Marx believed we could use trends to assess what future societies would look like. So too, in the social sciences, Marx is

---

1. Lebrecht, *Genius & Anxiety: How Jews Changed the World*.

considered the founder of a critical method that rejects speculative ideology in favor of a colder, more clinical approach.

While Marx had little to do with religious Judaism, it would not be wrong to call him a secular messianist. Like Hegel, Marx believed deeply in the betterment of the world through leaps in human progress. However, while, for Hegel, these revolutions were of a dialectical nature[2] through which history achieved its resolution in the modern capitalist liberal nation state. Marx, however, believed that history would further progress through the actions of humans. For this reason, his notion of progress relied on violence and revolution. Progress for Marx is not abstract, but, at its core, about the material economic benefits being delivered equally to all people.

By transferring Hegel's ideas of progress from idealism to materialism, Marx and Engels founded "historical materialism." Historical materialism can be explained as follows:

> The theory postulates that all institutions of human society (e.g., government and religion) are the outgrowth of its economic activity. Consequently, social and political change occurs when those institutions cease to reflect the "mode of production"—that is, how the economy functions.[3]

For Marx, the change needed to overturn capitalist modes of production could not happen on a small scale. Voluntarily joining a *kibbutz* would not be enough to enable liberation. The system of the whole world needed to be overturned.

Marx believed human nature was deeply tied to human labor and its relationship to human actualization. He explored these ideas in his 1867 work *Das Kapital*. For Marx, a person's work is how they transform the world. According to the Israeli scholar Shlomo Avineri:

> Man to Marx is not Homo sapiens, but primarily Homo faber, the creative being who has a unique dialectical relationship to nature and to the objective world, which both sustains him and

---

2. Some would refer to Hegel's approach as mystical. Other scholars suggest that Hegel's writings are marked by a profound commitment to rationalism (albeit rationalism that makes space for contradiction). When he writes about Spirit (or Geist in German) it may be better understood as consciousness than some form of mystical spirit. For Hegel, Geist in the broad sense may be closer to the collective consciousness of human culture but not any transcendent spirit. This approach makes sense since Hegel indicates that he doesn't believe in transcendence (i.e., there may be nothing outside the world/cosmos).

3. Encyclopedia Britannica, *Historical Materialism*.

is also formed by his labor and his activity. Thus human activity constantly changes both nature and man himself.[4]

Capitalism, then, was deeply problematic to Marx, as it forced laborers to give up ownership and control of their work in exchange for money. People worked not for themselves, but for the system and its owners.

What do we—as students of the broader Jewish philosophical, moral, ethical, and religious traditions—think of Marx? First, we must consider whether we, like Marx, view the world as a struggle between classes. On the whole, the Torah does not divide Jewish society between the rich and poor, but it is deeply concerned that the rich and powerful not use their power to pervert justice and oppress those who are vulnerable. Furthermore, the Torah contains a deep concern about kingship and the ways in which a king's wealth and power can lead to taking advantage of the poor[5]. That being said, Judaism, we will see, while it shares certain ideals with Marxism, it is certainly not the case that it aligns fully with it.

At the same time, might Marx's insights on equality line up with the Jewish approach to justice? Marx, in his work *Critique of the Gotha Programme*, popularized the phrase "From each according to his ability, to each according to his needs!"[6]

In the abstract, how different is that, really, from the Torah's teachings? In the Book of Exodus, Moshe says regarding the construction of the *Mishkan* and its accoutrements, "And let all among you who are skilled come and make all that the Lord has commanded."[7]

The Torah goes on to explain:

> And all the skilled women spun with their own hands, and brought what they had spun, in blue, purple, and crimson yarns, and in fine linen. And all the women who excelled in that skill spun the goats' hair.[8]

In essence, the Torah is saying, "From each according to their ability." So too, the Torah almost also tells us, "To each according to their needs." We are taught in Leviticus:

---

4. Avineri, *Karl Marx: Philosophy and Revolution*, 65.
5. For Marx, class conflict hides behind ideology. Many of the early Religious Zionists where essentially socialists/Marxists who saw the Torah as reflecting Marx's concerns and aspirations.
6. Marx, *Critique of the Gotha Programme*, I.
7. Exodus 35:10.
8. Exodus 35:25–26.

You shall not pick your vineyard bare, or gather the fallen fruit of your vineyard; you shall leave them for the poor and the stranger: I the Lord am your God.[9]

Further, in the Book of Deuteronomy, God commands the forgiveness of debts every seven years and immediately adds, "There shall be no needy among you."[10]

In more contemporary terms, Rabbi Dr. Yitz Greenberg derived from the Talmud three ethical values related to the equality of all humans, based on the notion that all people are created b'tzelem Elokim (in the image of God):

1. Every person has infinite value.
2. Every person is equal.
3. Every person is unique.[11]

Jewish thought, in line with Marx, holds the tension between the equal value of all people and the differing abilities and needs of all people. This is illustrated well by an anecdote in the Talmud:

> As a person stamps several coins with one seal, and they are all similar to each other. But the Holy One be Blessed stamps all people with the seal of Adam the first man, and not one of them is similar to another.[12]

And so, both the Torah and Marx espouse equality without uniformity. The difference comes in that, while, to Marx, freedom comes from ownership of one's own labor, in Judaism, the highest form of freedom comes from accepting the obligations and responsibilities of the good.

As such, Judaism doesn't map neatly onto the modern ideas of capitalism and communism. Certainly, the Torah ensures the protection of private property, and there is nothing un-Jewish about the ability of people to go out and make what they want of their own lives. Yet, a contemporary person might scream "Communism!" at the Torah's call for collective responsibility to make sure everyone has their needs met and nobody can be commodified or objectified. One might even call the institution of Shabbat an instance of a class conflict being won by the workers.

We should note the famous quote of Marx that religion is the "opiate of the masses." That makes him incompatible with Judaism, correct? Well,

---

9. Leviticus 19:10.
10. Deuteronomy 15:4.
11. Greenberg, *Personal Service: A Central Jewish Norm for Our Time*.
12. Babylonian Talmud, Sanhedrin 38a.

we first need to look closer at the context of what Marx said. He wrote in his *Critique of Hegel's Philosophy of Right*:

> Religious suffering is at the same time the expression of a real suffering and also the protest against real suffering. Religion is the sigh of the oppressed creature, the heart of a heartless world, just as it is the spirit of a spiritless condition. It is the opium of the people.[13]

While Marx was no follower of religion, he saw it as a response to a deep hole that he entirely believed needed to be filled. His response to religiosity was not pity, but empathy. Religion, he thought, was, in fact, a protest against the very same things he was protesting.

According to the scholar Isaiah Berlin, Marx's affinity for the working class was actually an outgrowth of his Jewish roots. Berlin wrote:

> It is the oppression of centuries of a people of pariahs, not of a recently risen class, that is speaking in him.[14]

Still, we cannot talk about communism and Judaism without addressing how badly it turned out in practice, particularly for Soviet Jews. In the 20th century, we witnessed how, ultimately, communism was a false empowerment that ended up oppressing the poor.

At the time, many under communism did feel their basic needs were being met. When I visited Ukraine in 2003, I met Jews who, after the fall of the Soviet Union, still longed for the return of communism. However, it is undeniable that communism gave way too much power to governments to limit freedoms, including the right to be outwardly Jewish. Communism in its later manifestations wanted uniformity—and preached that your allegiance must be not to God, but to the state.

Judaism is paradoxical in that there is an emphasis on the human need to exist in a collective—we pray in a minyan, study with a partner, and exist as a *people*—while the individual, especially today, retains the freedom to go about fulfilling their obligations in whatever way they see fit.

At the end of the day, it is perhaps best to understand Marx's goals in light of the Torah's vision of messianic redemption. However, where Jews traditionally recognized that such a future would depend at least in part on God, Marx believed humans had the capability to make it possible in the here and now. At the very least, Marx believed in a version of what Jews might call *tikkun olam*. And Marx wouldn't disagree with us in our belief

---

13. Marx, *Critique of Hegel's Philosophy of Right*.
14. Avineri, *Karl Marx: Philosophy and Revolution*.

that the repair of the world is dependent on human action. Where we might disagree is on the method of action necessary. And the entire unfolding of the Jewish tradition has been about determining what specifically our actions in the world need to be.

25

William James (1842–1910)

How do we learn more about the world—by reading concepts in a book, or by experiencing things in real life? How wise is it, really, to be agnostic or undecided in life?

This week we return to America, with the New York–born godson of Ralph Waldo Emerson, William James, one of the founders of the philosophy of pragmatism. "Pragmatism is a philosophical tradition that – very broadly – understands knowing the world as inseparable from agency within it."[1]

For James, we gain knowledge not by observing, but by doing. He cares not about abstract theories as much as which ideas are useful in understanding the world. And one assesses whether an idea is true based on how useful it is for them.

As a child, James spent several years in Europe. He later went to Harvard Medical School, but he became ill and depressed and never practiced medicine—though he did eventually graduate and teach physiology at Harvard.

Most notably, in addition to being a philosopher, James was a pioneering early psychologist. He penned a tome called "The Principals of Psychology," in which he developed an approach that came to be called "functionalist." According to the American Psychological Association Dictionary of Psychology, functionalism is "a general psychological approach that views mental life and behavior in terms of active adaptation to environmental challenges and opportunities."[2]

1. Legg, *Pragmatism*.
2. APA Dictionary of Psychology, *Functionalism*.

According to James, people have a psychological need to hold certain beliefs, particularly religious ones. To James, even though we don't have the tools to prove the existence of God, the notion of God can be seen as true because it is helpful for a person to hold such as belief, as it can enable one to overcome their fear of death and live a more fulfilling life.

Prior to James, it was commonly held that the mind was a largely static structure that could be examined. James, however, argued that one's mind is in an ever-evolving status, constantly influenced by new experiences. This is another move away from theoretical ideological assumptions about humans. The same way, in philosophy, James didn't want external truths but *useful* truths, so too, in psychology, James didn't seek unchanging, objective understandings of the human mind, but useful observations. The mind doesn't just process reality—it also serves one's deeper human needs.

For James, reality is constantly changing, and our observance of anything changes our analysis of it when it enters the realm of experience.

James was a relativist, which to say he understood that different things work for different people. In this sense, he was influenced by Darwin, believing that the strongest ideas, just like the strongest organisms, are the ones to survive. And what makes an idea "fit" for survival is its utility to humans.

James's pragmaticism follows in the tradition of the earlier empiricists, which he used to develop his approach called radical empiricism. In radical empiricism, per the APA Dictionary of Psychology, "reality consists not of subject and object (mind and matter) but of pure experience."[3]

And so, regarding religion, James held that much more important than the objectivity of a religion's truth claims is a person's *experience* with religion.

James believed that experience precedes our emotional labeling of it. He used the example that it's not the case that a person sees a bear, then they feel afraid, and then they run. Rather, a person sees a bear and runs instinctively. The feeling of being afraid sinks in only after. In the thinking of James, a physiological stimulus produces an experience and a response, but our emotions and conscious analyses emerge later.

I think this is also the case with how most people experience religion. We observe and *feel* something deeply before we have a chance to emotionally and thoughtfully react to it.

James's 1897 essay "Will to Believe," is anomalous in that it's a philosophical essay that is also rooted in personal experience, about how he overcame a deep sadness and depression through religious experience.

---

3. APA Dictionary of Psychology, *Radical empiricism*.

For James and his pragmaticism, though, it is not enough to simply follow one's instinctive feelings. One must make up their mind about big ideas. For an idea to be "useful" a person cannot sit on the fence about it. In cases where there are limits to the evidence, a true empiricist, according to James, can transcend the limitations of the evidence and live with the integrity to make a choice that aligns with the integrity of one's life.

We can apply all of this to the claims of traditional Judaism. Do we know, through objective study, that the Torah is true, or that there is a God? No. But we *do* know that Judaism and *mitzvot* have been a meaningful structure that has served the Jewish people for thousands of years. And an additional benefit in Judaism is that one *can* follow commandments and traditions of their people without being sure about the truth claims. And perhaps even a religious experience will even follow.

Similarly, do we have free will? We know we can't in our lifetimes come to an objective answer, but staying undecided, for James, is counterproductive. In the philosophy of James, by committing to believing something, you make it *more true*. Consequently, if I commit to free will being true, I'll act with more freedom and live a better life.

This adds a more practical meaning to how Yiddish writer Isaac Bashevis Singer humorously put it, "We have to believe in free-will. We've got no choice."

Virtually all James's ideas have relevance to how one might live a religious life. But how can we use them to illuminate specific teachings from the Torah?

Personally, I'm struck by James's notion that experience precedes comprehension and how it relates to the Israelites' receiving the Torah at Mount Sinai. In the Book of Exodus, we read:

וַיִּקַּח סֵפֶר הַבְּרִית וַיִּקְרָא בְּאָזְנֵי הָעָם וַיֹּאמְרוּ כֹּל אֲשֶׁר־דִּבֶּר יְהֹוָה נַעֲשֶׂה וְנִשְׁמָע׃

Then he [Moshe] took the record of the covenant and read it aloud to the people. And they said, "All that the Lord has spoken we will faithfully do!"[4]

However, if one takes fewer liberties in translating the Hebrew, "נַעֲשֶׂה וְנִשְׁמָע" means more literally, "We shall do and we shall hear." And, as Jews, we pay careful attention to the word order. First, we do; *then*, we hear? We learn from this that we often don't even understand the significance of the *mitzvot* we do until after we've done them. In accordance with James's

---

4. Exodus 24:7.

advice, one must decide how to live and live that way before coming to any grasp of the truth that might be found in a particular way of life.

It is taught that, when we received the Torah at Mount Sinai, God held the mountain above our heads, in effect forcing us to accept the Torah. The tradition teaches that it was not until the end of the Purim story that the Jews accepted the Torah through their own understanding ("kimu v'kiblu")[5.] We read in Megillat Esther:

> In view, then, of all the instructions in the said letter and of what they had *experienced* in that matter and what had befallen them, the Jews undertook and irrevocably obligated themselves and their descendants, and all who might join them, to observe these two days in the manner prescribed and at the proper time each year.[6]

Here, it was not through coercion but with total freedom that the yoke of Torah was accepted.

The Renaissance-era Italian commentator, Rabbi Obadiah ben Jacob Sforno, argued that the laws of kashrut were given because of the sin of the golden calf. These stipulations weren't part of the original plan, but were revealed later to reconcile the Divine-human relationship after another colossal human failure. He concluded that this was a concession to meet them where they were; the people needed not just the abstract teaching of the Torah but tangible religious experiences that would help them internalize God's teachings in their lives. The people longed for concrete worship (the golden calf) so God gave them concrete ritual (laws for eating).

Even today, though, through things like lighting Hanukkah candles, hosting a Passover Seder, and fasting on Yom Kippur, we're implicitly recognizing that education in the classroom is not enough. We need practices to make Jewish life real. We *do*, and *then* we understand.

So too, the Hasidic tradition teaches that, while Torah learning has its place, we must also put a premium on experience through our own senses. Rabbi Myriam Klotz writes:

> This practice is known as *avodah b'gashmiut* (literally "worship through corporeality"), a term from Hasidic spirituality that refers to the awakening of spiritual life through somatic experience. Avodah traditionally referred to religious actions like prayer or the performance of mitzvot, but the Hasidic masters expanded it to include actions such as eating, dancing or sex.

---

5. Esther 9:27.
6. Esther 9:26–27.

Through prayerful dedication, the practice of avodah b'gashmiut can integrate the spiritual and physical domains into one whole.[7]

And so, at first glance, there might seem to be some flimsiness to James's notion that what *really* matters is a person's experience. Where is the place for objective reality? But I think we all know from our own lives that, while measurable facts are certainly useful, the unquantifiable feelings are what bring us to something higher and deeper.

---

7. Klotz, *Finding God Through the Body*.

26

Friedrich Nietzsche (1844–1900)

Is GOD DEAD? WHAT does such a phrase even mean? Should we live according to the values of our parents, or is it up to us to figure out the best way of life on our own?

Friedrich Wilhelm Nietzsche was one of the most significant philosophers of the late 19th century. At the age of only 24, he became the chair of philology at the University of Basel—though he later had to resign due to poor health. Through his rejection of the prevailing Platonism, Christianity, and egalitarianism, Nietzsche would deeply influence the postmodernist movement to come.

Late in his life, his health severely declined, from dysentery, syphilis, and diphtheria. On January 3rd, 1889, he suffered a nervous breakdown, and he never regained his sanity, spending the last 11 year of his life in a vegetative state, until his death on August 25th, 1900.

What happened at that moment of nervous breakdown? Nietzsche saw a man whipping a horse on the street. Nietzsche ran in between the whip and the horse, yelling for the beating to stop, hugging the horse. He then collapsed crying, never to recover again[1].

Consequently, Nietzsche's mother and his sister needed to take care of him for the rest of his life. A perverted version of Nietzsche's philosophy would come to influence Nazism; this is commonly blamed on Nietzsche sister, who represented him when he was incapacitated and had a deep appreciation for Hitler and fascism.

While some would say Nietzsche sought to destroy the commonly held morality, Nietzsche, in reality, mainly wanted to reevaluate the

---

1. O'Malley, 'The Turin Horse': A tale of animal and human deprivation, and an invitation to feel Nietzsche's pain.

"Judeo-Christian values" that were taken for granted in Germany in his time.

For Nietzsche, Christianity and Judaism promoted a slave morality. Rather than see human beings as free to courageously pursue truth and the strivings of their will, Judaism and Christianity preached a form of submission to a universal moral law that bound all according to the same standard. He believed Christianity and Judaism emerged out of the weakness of being dominated by Rome. Because they could not defeat the Roman armies on the battlefield, they constructed a notion of the good to which all must submit. And so, Nietzsche wanted the people not simply to defer to their belief systems, but to overturn them in pursuit of the highest truths that they set for themselves. Nietzsche saw the slave morality as an illness in Europe that made the people full of resentment against those who had achieved some measure of power and encouraged them to be condemned as evil.

In his view, the Christian leadership of the time was full of hypocrites who preached love but were quick to condemn one another, who put up a façade of weakness, but only in order to take power for themselves. Consequently, he called for those who were strong enough to break the chains of their religion and exercise their own power. (The clerical class was something Nietzsche had personal experience with—his father, uncle, and grandfathers were all Lutheran ministers, though his father died when Nietzsche was a young child, and he was later raised by all women.)

Nietzsche called this "the politics of truth." He saw that, by claiming to hold certain truths, people could grab onto power without necessarily meriting it. It is then only by taking back the claim to truth that the people are able to take back power as well. This was crucial because to Nietzsche, the fundamental human drive is what he called "the will to power." It is a manifestation of the human desire to express one's will upon one oneself and one's surroundings and explains why people are willing to risk their lives in order to acquire and exercise power.

Nietzsche writes in his work *The Will to Power*, "There are no facts, only interpretations," and, "Values and their changes are related to increases in the power of those positing the values."[2]

And so, the only defense against power-hungry people, Nietzsche believed, was a radical insistence on truth. He wrote in *The Gay Science*[3]:

---

2. Nietzsche, *The Will to Power*, 14.

3. These two points may contradict each other. Can one say there are no facts and then insist on truth? When Nietzsche writes about truth, it's not always clear what it means, but it is much more in line with the notion of existential truth than any kind of scientific truth.

> The question whether *truth* is needed must not only have been affirmed in advance, but affirmed to such a degree that the principle, the faith, the relation to it, everything else has only second-rate value.[4]

If Marx thought there was a war of classes, and Hegel thought there was a war within the dialectical tensions of history, Nietzsche believed the battle to be one between wills: the will to power and the slave morality of submission.

In *The Gay Science*, Nietzsche famously uses and reuses the phrase "God is dead."[5] While this is commonly misunderstood as a call for atheism, what he meant to emphasize with it was that the old systems of religion no longer work or fully make sense, yet people refuse to recognize it and remain committed to them.

Nietzsche wasn't anti-religion, but he consistently pushed for what he called "the reevaluation of all values." This was because so many of the things we understand to be good can, if we're not careful, actually limit our affirmation of life and turn us away from it. Or, as the Jewish mystic Rav Kook might have put it, "Let the old be made new. Let the new be made holy."

Nietzsche had a notion of "philosophizing with a hammer." He wanted to smash the accepted dogmatic truisms of western philosophy, almost like Abraham in the midrash of his father's idol shop, or even like Maimonides with his negative theology—we cannot say what God is, only what God is not.

He even saw himself as a quasi-prophetic figure, passionate with what he perceived to be righteous anger. His famous work *Thus Spoke Zarathustra* was even from the perspective of a prophet, Zoroaster, the founder of the once-prominent Persian religion Zoroastrianism.

In *Thus Spoke Zarathustra*, Nietzsche popularized his idea of the *Übermensch*, superman. According to Britannica:

> Übermensch, in philosophy, [is] the superior man, who justifies the existence of the human race. . . . This superior man would not be a product of long evolution; rather, he would emerge when any man with superior potential completely masters himself and strikes off conventional Christian "herd morality" to create his own values, which are completely rooted in life on this

---

4. Nietzsche, *The Gay Science*, 281.
5. Nietzsche, *The Gay Science*, 125.

earth. Nietzsche was not forecasting the brutal superman of the German Nazis, for his goal was a "Caesar with Christ's soul."[6]

As we have seen, the relationship between Nietzsche's thought and the Nazism that would later come in Germany is muddled with later interpretations of his work being ones he almost certainly would have disapproved of. Nietzsche famously broke off his friendship with the composer Richard Wagner over Wagner's antisemitism, and, in *Thus Spoke Zarathustra*, Nietzsche offers a critique of nationalism.[7]

One of his criticisms of Christianity was that it was not life-affirming; it relied heavily on claims about the next life. Thus, it turns us away from what's truly important here on earth and undermines our human potential.

This was part of Nietzsche's rejection of Plato. For Plato, even the most noble things in this world, such as truth and beauty, are only a shadow of the forms in another, higher world. Therefore, to Nietzsche, both Platonism and its influence in Christianity do the damaging work of turning people away from the world that we live in and the things that matter most in it.

Nietzsche had a concept of "the eternal recurrence." Though the idea is rooted in Greek thought, Nietzsche proposed it as more of a thought experiment. If one was condemned to live their life over and over again forever, would they be able to embrace it in its fullness, the good and the bad. For Nietzsche, it was important that we should make each choice as if it were one that we must eternally affirm. The choices we make here and now, he believed, are forever.

Don't we need to be prepared for future challenges, not to mention contemporary ones, toward our cherished ideals? Rabbi Jonathan Sacks wrote in his book *Morality*:

> It was Nietzsche who foresaw what was likely to happen. When people give up their faith in religion, it would not be religion alone that they would lose. They would lose morality, and with it a concern for truth, and then even science would lose its authority.[8]

What should Nietzsche's philosophy mean for us in our time[9]? I think first we should recognize why these ideas might be intoxicatingly attractive

---

6. Encyclopedia Britannica, *Superman*.
7. Moss, *A to Z of Wagner: N is for Nietzsche, Nibelungs and Norns*.
8. Sacks, *Morality: Restoring the Common Good in Divided Times*, 167.
9. Nietzsche had a huge influence on Zionism and Jewish thinking at the turn of the 20th century. His emphasis on overcoming slave morality and existing hierarchies of religious truth was at the heart of the secular Zionist enterprise. His writings had a direct impact on nearly every major Zionist and modern Jewish thinker. For example, Buber,

to teenagers who want to break free from all the rules of their parents, their school, and their religion. The norms that exist often don't make sense, and it is a natural impulse to think one can righteously reevaluate them or even be fully liberated from them all. More than attractive, these ideas might be *helpful*.

However, as you mature, you come to understand the importance of relying on the good things you've inherited, not simply destroy everything. Judaism especially is built on a deep respect for the ideas of our ancestors. While our ancestors' beliefs aren't the end of the story, they *are* the foundation that we choose to build on.

And so, while there is a reverence for the inherited tradition, we also know how important it is to question whether everything we've been taught is actually the highest good. There is a balance to be struck between using the wisdom of those who came before us and affirming our own lives in our time with our own ways of making meaning. We know that it is not good to have either side without the other.

While, for Nietzsche, the vulnerable among us have a drive and a duty to take back their power, in Judaism, we understand that supporting those who need it to be an eternal value. The job of tradition, rather than keeping people in submission as Nietzsche would have it, is to instill us with a morality that is sturdier and goes back farther than a mere play for power. By submitting to the will of God, we in fact *prevent* ourselves from submitting to the will of unjust authorities.

In Judaism, we know that there is a time to say that the misused conceptions of God and the good are dead—but we also know that we then have a responsibility to take the broken pieces of what didn't work and create something newer and truer.

Rosenzweig, Herzl, Ben Gurion etc. Within Nietzsche they could see a call to renewal that Judaism was in desperate need of, and his attack on slave-morality went hand in hand with the Zionist belief that Jews must take power into their own hands to fight antisemitism rather than only rely on God. It is not hard to show how a Nietzschean ethos for overturning tradition can sync nicely with Jewish messianic beliefs. (It's why many have pointed to the similarity between Nietzsche and some of R' Kook's ideas.)

27

Sigmund Freud (1856–1939)

How much do our unconscious thoughts impact our seemingly conscious decisions? How can we access, work with, and when necessary, heal our unconscious selves? Do androids dream of electric sheep, and if so, are they speckled and spotted? And by the way . . . tell me about your mother?

Sigmund Freud, a pioneering neurologist and the founder of psychoanalysis, might seem like a bit of an odd choice for our series on philosophers, but Freud's work had a great influence on many philosophers who came after him, including the entire Frankfurt School, and his ideas can be seen as in conversation with philosophers who came before him.

Born in 1856 to a Jewish family in what is now the Czech Republic, while his paternal grandparents were *hasidic* and his father was known as a bit of a *talmid chacham*, Freud lived a secular life that was nonetheless informed by a love for and command of literature. While he was primarily influenced by the Greeks, hence his naming of the Oedipus complex, the Bible also was of interest to him, and in his later life he would write a book titled Moses and Monotheism.

Rabbi Harold Kushner reflected:

> Sigmund Freud's biographer tells the story of how, when Freud was a child, he was walking with his father in the streets of Vienna when anti-semitic bully knocked the father's fur hat off his head and said, "Jew, walk in the gutter." Freud never forgot that moment of seeing his father powerless and humiliated.[1]

Freud was forced to flee the Nazis at the very end of his life, dying in exile in England in 1939. He is best known for his various and groundbreaking

---

1. Kushner, *How Good Do We Have to Be*, 70.

forays into the human unconscious, gifting us with ideas such as the id, ego, and superego, as well as the Oedipus complex[2], and penning such works as *The Interpretation of Dreams* and *The Psychopathology of Everyday Life*.

His influence is, however, tied at least in philosophy to the work of Arthur Schopenhauer, a proponent of philosophical pessimism, which he elaborates on in *The World as Will and Representation*. Some scholars believe that despite what he might have said, Freud certainly was more than cursorily familiar with Schopenhauer's work throughout the development of his own:

> A close study of Schopenhauer's central work ... reveals that a number of Freud's most characteristic doctrines were first articulated by Schopenhauer ... Schopenhauer's concept of the will contains the foundations of what in Freud became the concepts of the unconscious and the id. Schopenhauer's writings on madness anticipate Freud's theory of repression and his first theory of the aetiology of neurosis. Schopenhauer's work contains aspects of what become the theory of free association. And most importantly, Schopenhauer articulates major parts of the Freudian theory of sexuality.[3]

We won't dwell too long on Schopenhauer–after all, that might feel a little redundant–but perhaps the meaningful question is how each man envisioned working with these similar concepts. Schopenhauer's pessimism about human existence led him to suggest that human happiness is "only like that of a beggar who dreams that he is king."[4] As a result, he was strongly in favor of asceticism as a way to pursue inner peace. Meanwhile, Freud thought that asceticism would likely reinforce a repression of one's drives which he saw as the source of many psychological or behavioral disorders. By failing to take responsibility for one's drives, the individual and the world he interacts with are both left worse off.

One approach Freud discusses ways we can deal with repressed drives is through what he calls sublimation. Instead of being directed towards the physical act, sexual desire can be sublimated into a different activity. This is a very Jewish idea–Yalta famously says in the Talmud, "מכדי כל דאסר לן

---

2. Rabbi Harold Kushner further wrote: "In other words, the story does not have to end with Cane killing Abel in an effort to be the sole recipient of God's, or Eve's, love. (There is an ancient legend, written thousands of years before Freud, that Cain and Abel were quarreling over which one would become Eve's mate after Adam died." (How Good do we have to be, page 133-134).

3. Young, Brook, *Schopenhauer and Freud*.

4. As summarized by Robert Flint in an 1877 lecture, referencing a line in *Will and Representation*.

"רחמנא שרא לן,"[5] for every forbidden thing, there is something similar that is permissible; and the Sages discuss sort of "pathways of fate," suggesting that even if–in some schools of thought–a person's being born at a certain time would destine him to working with blood, he could be a criminal, or he could be a shochet.[6]

So even with the evidence of pain in the world, and the possibility that it might in fact outweigh pleasure, Freud still sought ways for people to actively work–if not on the world, then within themselves–to create something better. He famously said that the goal of psychoanalysis was as follows:

> I do not doubt that it would be easier for fate to take away your suffering than it would for me. But you will see for yourself that much has been gained if we succeed in turning your hysterical misery into common unhappiness. With a mental life that has been restored to health, you will be better armed against that unhappiness.[7]

For Freud, healing began with a journey into oneself, and this is part of what couples him with Nietzsche, and even Socrates: "know thyself!" And Freud would bring this further by establishing it as fundamental to psychoanalysis, that we must enlist the help of others, such as an analyst, in untangling ourselves. This image of untangling reminds me of the famous likely kabbalistic prayer, Ana Bekoach, used by different communities throughout the year: the first line is often translated as a plea for the Divine to "untangle" some aspect of us.[8] While it is unclear that Freud had any formal education in Jewish mysticism, it is often the case that ideas he develops can find similar examples within the Jewish tradition.

While the creation of talk therapy to address and sort through the many forces at play in an individual human mind and life was revolutionary and deeply helpful in the treatment of mental illness and alleviating the distress caused by psychic disorders, it is important to recognize that other interventions are still necessary and helpful for many people. Moreover, I think that all of us here have an understanding that the work we do towards social justice is necessary for full and robust mental and emotional wellness across populations, and that many problems seen as mental health issues in fact are rooted in social inequality and poor material conditions. We have a

---

5. Babylonian Talmud, Chullin 109b.
6. Babylonian Talmud, Shabbat 156a.
7. Studies on Hysteria, 1895, co-written with Joseph Breuer.
8. Ana Bekoach.

responsibility to work towards a world where waking from our most wildly wonderful dreams is not absolutely devastating.

This brings us into some of Freud's more fun, if controversial work, in dream analysis. Freud believed that dreams were a window into the unconscious, and proper interpretation could give us a glimpse of whatever desires are being repressed. He developed an idea of dream symbolism, in which he labeled the *peshat* of the dream "manifest content" and the *remez* as "latent content."

While his method was led by free analysis from the actual dreamer, he did lean heavily into his own quite rigid semiotic key: if you have a dream with manifest content including something like a sword, an umbrella, a skyscraper . . . if it looks phallic, or if it acts phallic, Freud would likely tell you that the latent content is, in fact, phallic.[9] Though the details of this would depend on the individual, he believed that most of our unconscious desires revolved around questions of human sexuality.

Freud concludes, essentially, that a dream is a wish your unconscious fulfills when you're fast asleep, often related to desires and drives that manifested in childhood and which needed to be repressed.[10] In a dream, a sword can represent something sexual, but because Freud has a very broad understanding of human sexuality, it could also mean something we might not typically view as sexual, such as being cared for by someone we love.

Naturally, when we consider dreams as a source of potential information about these unmet needs, they can become a tool for mediating trauma in our lives, especially when we're talking about the earliest events of childhood, which we tend not to remember.

There have been countless critiques of Freud's approach to dreams and psychoanalysis.

> Newly installed in administration, he found himself with a decision: whether to promote a medical researcher named J. Allan Hobson. It shouldn't have been that hard. In a series of famous papers, Hobson had landed body blows on the Freudian idea that dreams arose from unconscious desires, by showing that they actually came from a part of the brain that had nothing to do with desire. He'd proven that the timing and the length of dreams were regular and predictable, which suggested that dreams had less to say about a person's psychological state than about his nervous system. Among other things, Hobson's

---

9. Dr. Frank McAndrew provides some more examples in Psychology Today.
10. The Freud Museum of London elaborates in their education materials.

research suggested that people who paid psychoanalysts to find meaning in their unconscious states were wasting their money.[11]

Like Freud, and unlike most of his contemporaries, the majority of the Jewish tradition wouldn't see a dream as merely the random firing of neurons during the sleep state. But, as with most other things in Judaism, the topic of dreams meets with diverse opinions.

Prophetic dreams are integral to the progression of stories in the Tanakh. It is repeatedly the case that God provides a symbolic message in a dream that ultimately comes to pass. Yosef interprets Pharaoh's dreams about the seven years of plenty followed by seven years of famine[12] which ultimately sets the story of our residency in Egypt into motion, or Gideon gains confidence when overhearing a soldier's bizarre dream[13] in which he is symbolized as barley bread that destroys the Midianite camp. Our cultural narrative takes dreams seriously, so it's no surprise that Chazal do as well, while still acknowledging that there's plenty of room for nonsense, and the power of positive interpretation.

While they famously say that a dream is one-sixtieth of prophecy,[14] that being the rabbinic measurement for "just a smidge" above what is entirely negligible, they nonetheless put forward that we should be willing to wait at least twenty-two years[15] for a good dream to come true; that's about as romantic and hopeful as it gets.

In compiling their own "dream dictionary" in the Talmud, we see a variety of interpretation methods, focused on Torah, and largely conditional. They use the same exegetical and homiletical techniques that they do for other subject matters, bringing proof texts from Tanakh, leaning into puns, and, as always, probing for details. Just a couple of examples: if one sees a pomegranate[16] in a dream, the meaning depends on the state of the fruit—large or small, sliced or whole—as well as the state of the dreamer—are they a Torah scholar or not? A Torah scholar who sees a pomegranate in a dream can expect to engage in the learning and teaching of Torah, however, if one is not a Torah scholar, they can expect to perform plentiful mitzvot. All of these interpretations have positive connotations for the dreamer, with those two in particular finding their evidence in Shir HaShirim. Another

---

11. Lewis, *The Undoing Project*, 291.
12. Starting in Genesis 4:1.
13. Judges 7:13.
14. Babylonian Talmud, Berakhot 57b.
15. Babylonian Talmud, Berakhot 55b.
16. Babylonian Talmud, Berakhot 57a.

example–if a person sees a cat, the interpretation depends on what the local word for "cat" is![17]

In Derech Hashem, the Ramchal speaks at length about the composition of dreams:

> When man sleeps, his faculties rest, his senses are quiet, and his mind is relaxed and hushed. The only thing that continues to function is his imagination, and this conceives and envisions various images. Some of these images arise from the individual's experiences while awake. Others may be the result of substances that rise to the brain, from food or from the body itself. Such are the stimuli for normal dreams, those which are experienced by everyone ... the bond between the body and the Divine Soul should be somewhat loosened while man sleeps ... higher levels of the soul perceive something, they can sometimes transmit it, step by step, until it reaches the animal soul. The imagination is then stimulated and forms images in its normal manner. ... Sometimes this information is greatly confused and intermingled with distorted images arising from the various substances that enter the brain, while at other times, the information is received very clearly ... information that man could not attain with his powers of reason alone, as discussed earlier.

And even in the Gemara, we see an attempt at separating dreams caused by indigestion and those that reflect real prophecy. As the Sages make their way through interpreting a list of dreams that might be uncomfortable for the dreamer, such as having sex[18] with someone forbidden, they clarify that it may not always foretell something bad. If one dreams of a married woman that one has not seen recently or been thinking about then this is a positive sign with regards to one's share in the World to Come.

In summary, Freud's emphasis on the notion of self-awareness is commendable within a Jewish framework, especially in light of a desire to help people and the development of actual tools to dig below the surface.

One of the many Jewish thinkers to engage with Freud was the contemporary Mordechai Rotenberg. He explains quite succinctly:

> On one side of the conflict are our physical urges, while on the other are the demands made by society. Freud describes this conflict as a battle between the principle of pleasure, which is the assumption that all humans seek pleasure, and the principle of reality, which represents the behavior that is expected of an

---

17. Babylonian Talmud, Berakhot 56b.
18. Babylonian Talmud, Berakhot 57a.

individual in any society. According to Freud, the optimal situation is where the reality principle overcomes and replaces the pleasure principle, meaning that our behavior is suited to the reality of our lives.[19]

His ideas may not provide all the answers on how to understand dreams, but this is an area where human knowledge remains limited. Freud was, of course, working with a motive of supporting his own ideas, as were Chazal. As such, the voices of women and people of subcultures or other experiences historically distanced from the academy or the *beit midrash, who might have thought about dreams differently,* aren't represented in much of this material. The Sages did leave the door open for cultural subjectivity, contextual subjectivity, and likely subjectivity on an individual level. While we all have our shared humanity, and the capacity to dream, our personal dreams and what they mean can be as unique as we are.

We are left with many interesting questions for us to think about:

- What role do you think that dreams should have in decision-making? (Consider that Google was invented in a dream, as was the basis for Einstein's theory of relativity.)

- Should contemporary batei din continue to offer dream interpretation as a service? How does that impact your feelings about their legal prowess?

- There's a pretty solid taboo in rabbinic literature around interpreting nightmares as such, with the exception of encouraging repentance. What do you think of dreams as negative diagnostics? (Consider both individual issues, as well as the larger social phenomenon of widespread nightmares in times of crisis.)

- Do you think there's anything we can do with our dreams to help us become better people?

We hold a debt of gratitude to Freud for reawakening our imagination to our lives that exist beyond the surface reality.

---

19. Rotenberg, *The Psychology of Tzimtzum*, 45-46.

28

Edmund Husserl (1859–1938)

How do we know that something exists? Can it be proven by science, or should we rely on human experience?

Edmund Husserl was born in Moravia, which was within the Austro-Hungarian Empire, but is now part of the Czech Republic. He was Jewish, though he wasn't known to be traditionally religious. Husserl became a lecturer at the University of Halle, in Germany, and eventually landed at the University of Freiburg, where Martin Heidegger was one of his students.

Husserl worked within the fields of ontology and phenomenology; phenomenology was his approach to ontology. What does that mean? According to the Stanford Encyclopedia of Philosophy:

> As a first approximation, ontology is the study of what there is ... Many classical philosophical problems are problems in ontology: the question whether or not there is a god, or the problem of the existence of universals, etc. These are all problems in ontology in the sense that they deal with whether or not a certain thing, or more broadly entity, exists. But ontology is usually also taken to encompass problems about the most general features and relations of the entities which do exist.[1]

But it's crucial to note that the great insight of phenomenology is to bracket many of the classic issues of ontology to focus on the structures of consciousness and what they can tell us about human experience of the world.

Husserl is considered the founder of phenomenology.

> Phenomenology is the study of structures of consciousness as experienced from the first-person point of view. The central

---

1. Hofweber, *Logic and Ontology*.

structure of an experience is its intentionality, its being directed toward something, as it is an experience of or about some object. An experience is directed toward an object by virtue of its content or meaning (which represents the object) together with appropriate enabling conditions.[2]

And so, Husserl sought to address the question of what *is* through the lens of what we *experience*. He differentiated himself from previous thinkers in this respect, saying, "Philosophers, as things now stand, are all too fond of offering criticism from on high instead of studying and understanding things from within."

Phenomenology was a groundbreaking idea because it was uninterested in prior ways of understanding an objective reality, which emphasized the speculative use of reason to make conclusions about the world. Precedence was instead given to conscious experience of that reality. This marked a profound shift from the study of abstract truth to the study of human meaning-making.

Husserl was not one to deny that these external things truly exist. Rather, to him, they exist only in relationship to the meaning-making perceiver. "Natural objects," Husserl said, "must be experienced before any theorizing about them can occur."

Husserl was captured by the idea that focusing on pure experience frees us from biases and assumptions. He had hoped that the sciences could be placed on such a firm foundation that they could help us find truth without biases, but he came to conclude that this was not possible. So he wanted to, as an alternative, develop a scientific approach to experience, a way of examining experience that could be held up to scientific scrutiny. Husserl differentiated between a subjective consciousness and an objective "pure consciousness." He said:

> Psychologically experienced consciousness is therefore no longer pure consciousness; [however,] construed Objectively in this way, consciousness itself becomes something transcendent, becomes an event in that spatial world which appears, by virtue of consciousness, to be transcendent.

Husserl was an outspoken critic of Nazism. He said in 1933:

> The future alone will judge which was the true Germany in 1933, and who were the true Germans—those who subscribe to the more or less materialistic-mythical racial prejudices of the day, or those Germans pure in heart and mind, heirs to

---

2. Smith, *Phenomenology*.

the great Germans of the past whose tradition they revere and perpetuate.[3]

The same year, he was suspended from the university due to his Jewish background—and his former student, Heidegger, who was aligned with the Nazis, may have had a role to play in it.

We're not going to give a full section to Heidegger because of his Nazi sympathies, but I think this is a good time to lay down some main ideas about Heidegger's impact. Heidegger had previously wanted to become a Christian priest, but it was in part his encounter with the Jewish Husserl's philosophy that inspired him to change paths. In the 1930s, unfortunately though, he became a member of the Nazi Party.

Though often considered one of the greatest philosophers of the last century, recent research has shown that his Nazi sympathies were not just incidental to his philosophical work but can be seen as an outgrowth of it. Though the Nazis were concerned with being an objective superior race, Husserl and Heidegger were interested in the subjective realm and in human meaning making. Husserl died shortly before the Holocaust.

Like his mentor Husserl, Heidegger, too, was interested in the nature of being and how phenomenology could shed light on it. More specifically, he was concerned with issues of what it means to be human and how a person can live an authentic life. Heidegger's philosophy would influence Jean-Paul Sartre and Hans-Georg Gadamer.

Husserl was also a teacher of Edith Stein, a Jewish philosopher who had converted to Christianity and eventually became a nun, but who was nonetheless murdered in the Holocaust. It was under Husserl's supervision that Stein wrote her dissertation, *The Empathy Problem as it Developed Historically and Considered Phenomenologically*.

Stein articulated a vision of phenomenology that claimed experience to be of a greater essence than other forms of knowledge. "All our own present experiences are primordial," she wrote. "What could be more primordial than experience itself?"

She even gave this phenomenology a theological dimension, saying, "As the possessor of complete knowledge, God is not mistaken about people's experiences as people are mistaken about each other's experiences.

It is notable that Husserl's life almost entirely overlapped with that of another ground-breaking Jew from Moravia, Sigmund Freud, and *both* were students of the German philosopher Franz Brentano. In fact, one of the critiques of Husserl in his time was that he was too concerned with the psychological. However, where Husserl focused on the structures of consciousness,

---

3. Evans, *The Coming of the Third Reich*, 421.

it was Freud who argued for the unconscious, those aspects of ourselves that escape our phenomenal awareness.

In the Jewish world, Husserl's influence found its way to Rabbi Abraham Joshua Heschel, who also drew upon phenomenology in his examinations of prophecy and religious experience. While Heschel believed Jewish law to be fully binding, he was concerned that too often an exclusive focus on Jewish law served to obscure the importance of religious experience in religious life.

The importance of conscious experience is deeply rooted in the Jewish tradition. A teaching from the Baal Shem Tov tells us[4] במקום שחושב האדם שם הוא כולו, which is often simplified as, "You are where your thoughts are."

Phenomenology, especially as explained by Edith Stein, deals with "intersubjectivity," which we can call the space between your subjective experience and mine. This is the space in which we encounter the Other, and is what serves as the basis for empathy. In Judaism, we recognize that empathy requires stepping beyond one's subjective experience and into someone else's through an encounter with them and their reality. It is unfortunate the work of Husserl, and especially his student Edith Stein, did not spawn a significant field in Germany in the 1930s for the specific study of empathy.

Buber's I-Thou is basically a phenomenology of empathy and dialogue. It was perhaps the most popular philosophical book in Germany in the early 20th century. Even so, Buber was more of a popular thinker than an academic one who affected intellectual trends in the university. It is also worth noting that Levinas studied with Husserl. He is probably the most famous proponent of the phenomenological method in the 2nd half of the 20th century. He also turns phenomenology towards ethics but not through the idea of empathy (the notion that we can know the other or get in their head). Rather, he uses phenomenology to stage how the encounter with the Other fundamentally shapes our subjectivity by placing demands on us. What makes Heidegger so problematic is that his use of phenomenology is almost exclusively focused on the individual's experience of the world rather than their encounter with their fellow human beings. Stein and Levinas stand in direct contradiction to this by centering the encounter with the Other.

We know from our Jewish experience that it is one thing to do a physical act of kindness, but another to be empathetic, to have a true person-to-person connection. We don't want to just help people coldly. We want to do compassionate things and *be* compassionate people.

Further, just as there are aspects of philosophy that focus on our empirical experience of the external world and others that focus on a study of

---

4. Toldot Yaakov Yosef, Chayei Sara 21, 69.

the inner experience, we know that Judaism contains both dimensions as well. We certainly care about the objective realm such as about Jewish tradition and the concrete ways in which it can be lived by means of ritual objects, mitzvot, the Land of Israel, the study of tangible texts and languages, and the healing of sick bodies.

But, especially since the time of the Baal Shem Tov, we've made the modern move of caring deeply about the interior world of each person. The inner life is not only meaningful—it's where we actually live.

Even outside the Hasidic tradition, though, Judaism has a concept of avoiding *hirhurei aveirah*, avoiding detrimental thoughts. Yes, it is important that we avoid immoral behaviors, but we also care about ethical intentionality and developing a moral consciousness.

From Husserl and phenomenology, we can learn to try to listen more closely to our own unfiltered experiences, and we can, through our best efforts at empathy, attempt to understand one another. Modern philosophy and the Jewish tradition both teach us that, while some things can be empirically observed, there is no replacement for the realm of the soul and in the inner self—in ourselves and in others.

29

John Dewey (1859–1952)

WHAT SHOULD THE SCHOOL day consist of? Is it better to learn by listening to a lecture? By doing practice exercises? By talking to others? By going on a field trip?

Here we return to America with John Dewey, the thinker who helped set the stage for contemporary education in this country by encouraging critical-thinking skills rather than simple indoctrination. By introducing the world to a notion of education that relied heavily on learning by *doing*, Dewey, who born in Vermont, changed our system of schooling in a way that persists to this day.

Like William James, Dewey was in the school of pragmatism;[1] under pragmatism, we cannot know what is fully true, so we need only to find truth that helps us navigate the world. (This idea would be critiqued by Bertrand Russell, who believed pragmatism had forfeited the philosophical search for truth.)

But, for John Dewey pragmatism played a key role in education because the purpose of education was to impart knowledge that will meet human needs and fulfill human purposes. Dewey referred to his pragmatism as "instrumentalism," which holds that "the value of any idea is determined by its usefulness in helping people to adapt to the world around them."[2]

In Judaism, we are having instrumentalist thoughts all the time. For example, can we make the truth claim that God hears and answers our prayers? Probably not. But we know how the words of prayer can change

---

1. Alongside James, the American Charles Sanders Peirce was a founder of pragmatism.
2. Encyclopedia Britannica, *Instrumentalism*.

our lives. Prayer, then, for many of us, is a good thing, and perhaps even true, on the grounds that it is useful. This reminds me of a Hasidic teaching:

> Perhaps the most important single line for me is the statement attributed to Rabbi Pinhas of Koretz, a contemporary of the Ba"al Shem Tov: 'People think that you pray to God,' he said, 'but that is not the case. Rather prayer itself is of the essence of Divinity.'[3]

Part of what Dewey advocated for in his instrumentalist education philosophy was that learning should not be abstract but hands-on. A person must learn not only from books but from interaction with real people and environments. A teacher talking at the front of the room, for Dewey, was not sufficient.

In a way, this was subversive, making education less about an authority figure handing knowledge to a passive student. Instead, the student would participate experientially. As Jews, we can of course understand what he's talking about. In Jewish education, one is supposed to mainly learn hands-on with a *chavruta*, and the teacher is there to assist you as someone who is more experienced.

Dewey believed that education was of practical importance for more than just the students; it was needed for a healthy democracy. Dewey was born right before the Civil War and lived through Reconstruction, the Gilded Age, World War I, and World War II, so he saw in his lived experience how crucial it was to have a well-educated citizenry that could think on its feet to solve real-world problems.

Dewey himself helped found the NAACP and the ACLU,[4] and he saw a deep need to support democracy and academic freedom in opposition to the rising fascism he was witnessing in the world.

His impact on the American culture was so deep that, to some degree, we can today look at America's status as a world superpower and see that it is because of our pragmatic concerns and actions that Dewey's country came to be a global leader. This has its complications as well. More than being a nation of theologians and philosophers, America became a nation characterized by economic strength, military power, and technological innovation.

Yes, America made great gains because our ways of thinking have enabled us to solve problems and make practical advances. But perhaps we've lost something as well, an exalted place for ethics, relationships, and matters of the eternal. And maybe, in our time, the same critique is worthy of the

---

3. Green, *God, Prayer, and Religious Language*, 13-28.
4. Stack Jr., *John Dewey and the Question of Race: The Fight for Odell Waller.*

State of Israel. Both countries, at one point or another, have celebrated being a "startup nation" that was building something great out of nothing. Might it be more remarkable for America and for Israel to deepen their sense of the sacred? Is there not space to inspire a renaissance toward spiritual journeying?

We should not need to choose between one side or the other. Instead, we can consciously make space for both. We know the educational project should indeed be heavily pragmatic and humble on matters of the unknown. At the same time, we know the life of the mind and soul are of deep value, and they are what make pragmatic success worth achieving in the first place.

If we recall from our examination of Thomas Hobbes, there is a stream of thought that says people by nature are not pro-social and need a "social contract" to reign in their behavioral excesses. Dewey, however, fundamentally disagreed, believing people may be inherently good to one another from the start[5]. This upbeat outlook on human nature makes it much easier for one to say education should be student-driven and experience-based, rather than about a teacher taming their uncivilized pupils.

Morality, for Dewey, was more like creating art than memorizing principles. He wrote, in his book *Art As Experience*:

> Imagination is the chief instrument of the good ... art is more moral than moralities. For the latter are, or tend to become, consecrations of the status quo, reflections of custom, reinforcements of the established order. The moral prophets of humanity have always been poets even though they spoke in free verse or by parable ... Art has been the means of keeping alive the sense of purpose that has out run evidence and of meanings that transcend indurated habit.[6]

It is art that keeps our moral selves alive and moving. And, for Dewey, ethical principles exist only in the real world. He wrote:

> Fraternity, liberty equality isolated from communal life are hopeless abstractions. Their separate assertions lead to mushy

---

5. Although scholars suggest this, this may not be entirely clear for Dewey though. He does critique social contract theory, but that is because he recognizes that individuals never gave up anything to form a collective. Rather, one can only be an individual if one is first part of a collective. Dewey may not think the child is inherently evil and therefore needs some sort of extreme discipline to become good, but that may not be the same as saying a child is inherently good.

6. Jasper, *The Art of Moral Protest*, 1.

sentimentalism or else too extravagant and fanatical violence which in the end defeats its own aims.[7]

We can absolutely see the parallels here with the Jewish tradition. When we read the Prophets of the Tanakh, we are indeed also reading a form of moral poetry. And, when we learn *Pirkei Avot*, we're learning not just rules but ethics in the context of the lives of the ancient sages, which encourages us to think hard about the function of morality in our own lives. We can even see the parallel in the Zohar, a work in which the sages don't learn in a study hall—they learn while walking around the Galilee.

Rav Kook also writes explicitly on aesthetics and morality.

> The wondrous tzaddikim, for whom this world does not exist with its boundaries, limitations, and lowliness; it is they who make the physical world precious and give honor to it because they see within it a supernal world, its pure illumination from the source of life, its beauty and its goodness elevated with great exhilaration. A sensitivity to the pleasantness and beauty of the physical world increases with these tzaddikim to a level of supernal holiness and refinement until they live a full life that contains all the vitality of aesthetic pleasure, which brings delight to life at a very high level. Their spiritual senses, even with regards to aesthetic matters such as the beauty that exists in appearances, song, the nation, and morality, expand exponentially until they are viewed as the sources of beauty and order in life.[8]

Rav Kook also encouraged the establishment of Bezalel Art School in the letter below, which also touches on similar themes from the text above:

> By the Grace of God, To the leaders of the honored society for the study of Hebrew art, the Bezalel Association, Shalom. One ray of light has shined on us from amidst the thick fox of our presently dark world . . . One of the clear signs of revival is the honorable pursuit that is to emerge from your honored association- "The revival of Hebrew art and aesthetics in Israel." The sigh of our very talented brothers, masters of aesthetics and the arts, who are finding a rightful place in the highways and byways of society is heartwarming and beautiful; for a heavenly spirit has carried them to Jerusalem, set as a seal upon our hearts, to crown our holy city with their pleasant designs . . . No one can be but joyous at this sign . . . This important field of aesthetic arts can truly bring a blessing and open the livelihoods

---

7. Jasper, *The Art of Moral Protest*, 363.
8. Kook, *Shemoneh Kevatzim* 1:804.

and provisions to many of our brothers' families that live in the holy land ... It will also nurture the sensitivity for beauty and purity with which the precious children of Zion are so blessed, and it will uplift many depressed souls, giving them a clear and illuminating view of the beauty of life, nature, and work, of the honor of labor and diligence. All those are exalted principles that fill the souls of all Jews with feelings of delight and glory.[9]

Further, one of Dewey's ideas, that certainly jibes with Judaism, is that we are not just to memorize hard and fast rules, but rather learn values that are applied in the world. Dewey moves education from an authority to an experience. He writes:

In morals a hankering for certainty, born of timidity and nourished by love of authoritative prestige, has led to the idea that absence of immutably fixed and universally applicable ready-made principles is equivalent to moral chaos ... [There is] another manifestation of the desire to escape the strain of the actual moral situation, its genuine uncertainty of possibilities and consequences. We are confronted with another case of the all too human love of certainty, a case of the wish for an intellectual patent issued by authority.[10]

While it may appear that Jewish law also attempts to reduce ethics to rules, the Torah also makes clear that one must "Do what is right and good in the eyes of God."[11] According to the rabbis, this means one must be willing to go beyond the letter of law, as certain situations may demand. Halachic rules can provide a basis for our ethical actions, but they are never meant to serve as their final limit.

Dewey was influenced by Charles Darwin in that he believed humans were interacting with the natural world but not separate from it. Consequently, we are affected by our social environments. We are not fixed selves. We are constantly adapting in response to the world around us. Dewey took from Darwin—who himself was in the tradition of the Ancient Greek thinker Pericles—the idea that nature is in a constant state of change.

Dewey made a critique of ancient religion, saying that humans, especially historically, would deal with uncertainty in the world by turning to the gods. Instead, he believed we should seek to master the world ourselves.

We can even understand this to be a criticism of the Torah, which encourages the people to follow the commandments so that they receive the

9. Letters of Rav Kook, Vol 1, Letter 158.
10. Dewey, *Human Nature and Conduct*.
11. Deuteronomy 6:18.

right weather for their crops. To someone like Dewey, it is better to instead learn to predict weather patterns and build irrigation systems. We should do things to respond to crises rather than praying for help and making religious meaning out of them.

This too, is reflected in the Jewish tradition, such as in our notion of *tikkun olam*, that redemption will not happen without human participation.

Rabbi Joseph B. Soloveitchik, argues that we must navigate between the need for just human or Divine control. In his essay "Majesty and Humility," the Rav teaches that the religious charge is partially to be majestic—to be God-like and to master our environments. On the other hand, he recognized a side of the human experience that is deeply humbling as we are faced with the fact of how little power and control we truly have. Every attempt we make to master our environment inevitably also shows us the limits of what we can do.

I believe, as Jews, we can't reject Dewey. But we can find a place to reconcile the instrumental with the eternal. I like the illustration of Shabbat. We define the activities that are prohibited on Shabbat, our taste of the World to Come, by our practical work in the world. The Mishnah identifies what pragmatic, useful work looks like, and then we take a brief break from it at least one day out of the week. For sure, we place a high premium on the useful and the real—*but* we also make space for what is greater. And these two realms can inform and strengthen one another as we strive to live our best lives. As Jews, we ought to be both instrumentalists (operating within the messiness of democracy and societal norms) and idealists (dreaming of a new world and a next world).

30

Martin Buber (1878–1965)

Is RELIGION ABOUT OUR relationship with God, or with other people? How can we know God in a world that feels so far removed from the stories of the Bible? How can we know other people in a world that seems to demand that we be productive and make a profit at all times?

Normally, in this series, we look at a world-famous philosopher and how their ideas relate to Judaism's. With Martin Buber, however, we have a fascinating case of someone who lived steeped in the Jewish tradition and allowed that to shape his philosophical work, which in turn came to be respected all over the world.

Distantly related to Karl Marx, Buber grew up an Orthodox Jew in Austria (his grandfather was the orthodox scholar Solomon Buber).[1] He spoke German, Yiddish, and Hebrew and was a scholar of philology (the study of language and texts). However, he broke from the confines of his tradition and became deeply engaged with the non-Jewish philosophers that we've been exploring here. He married a woman raised Catholic who converted to Judaism. He was a very early Zionist, though he stayed in Germany as a professor at the University of Frankfurt Am Main until he resigned in protest when Hitler came to power in 1933. Fortuitously, he would leave Germany for Jerusalem just in time in 1938. He became a professor of philosophical anthropology in Jerusalem at Hebrew University.

Before the State of Israel was founded, Buber was a strong supporter of a "binational solution" in Palestine (a one-state solution). Afterward, he supported a regional federation of Israel and Arab states. Buber's view of Zionism was called "Hebrew humanism," which, rather than emphasizing

1. Shenker, *Now, Jewish Roots*.

nationalism, was concerned with the revival of Jewish culture and ethical life.[2] The Jewish state was a means toward renewing and actualizing a Jewish culture. Buber may have respected Herzl greatly but, as a cultural Zionist, he certainly disagreed with much of his vision. He also criticized Ben Gurion on the plans with Arab refugees.

Buber rejected the idea that he was a philosopher or theologian—he viewed his work as being in the realm not of ideas but of personal experience. He knew nothing of the study of God, only a person's relationship to God. After making *aliyah*, Buber became the preeminent Jewish philosopher, best known for his "philosophy of dialogue."

In Buber's view, people can have two kinds of encounters: I-It (*Ich-Es*), and I-Thou (*Ich-Du*). I-It encounters are transactional. For example, when you order food at a restaurant, you'll likely be nice to the person at the counter, but the interaction is happening only for the purpose of you getting food and the worker getting money. This is not wholly bad; you *want* to be able to have professional relationships with the doctor handling your health, the customer at your business, or the person changing your tires.

However, Buber insisted that these I-It relationships are not enough to sustain a human being. Crucially, he believed, we need I-Thou relationships, the kind in which we seek to gain nothing from the other person, and the other person seeks to gain nothing from us. These are relationships in which we are engaged simply for the sake of the other. In fact, according to Buber, I-Thou encounters are the way we can know the Divine. He writes in his book *I And Thou*:

> Extended, the lines of relationships intersect in the eternal You. Every single You is a glimpse of that. Through every single You the basic word addresses the eternal You . . . In every sphere, in every relational act, through everything that becomes present to us, we gaze toward the train of the eternal You; in each we perceive a breath of it; in every You we address the eternal You, in every sphere according to its manner. All spheres are included in it, while it is included in none. Through all of them shines the one presence.[3]

Buber argues for dialogical existence, famously saying, "All actual life is encounter."[4] For Buber, there's a level of infinity and universality, indeed a transcendence, that emerges in an I-Thou encounter.

---

2. Schaeder, *The Hebrew Humanism of Martin Buber*, 11.
3. Buber, *I And Thou*, 123, 150.
4. Chow, *All Actual Life is Encounter: Martin Buber's Politics of De-politicization*.

This is entirely compatible with the Jewish worldview, especially as articulated by the Hasidic tradition. In fact, translating and interpreting Hasidic teachings for a modern audience was a passion of Buber's. And reading his work on this topic can show one why Buber was so inspired by the idea that, by recognizing one another, we can come to recognize God. Buber wrote in his work *Hasidism and Modern Man*:

> This is not the place to present the teachings of Hasidism. They can be summed up in a single sentence: God can be held in each thing and reached through each pure deed. But this insight is by no means to be equated with a pantheistic world view, as some have thought. In the Hasidic teaching, the whole world is only a word out of the mouth of God. Nonetheless, the least thing in the world is worthy that through it God should reveal himself to the man who truly seeks Him; for no thing can exist without a divine spark, and each person can uncover and redeem that spark at each time and through each action, even the most ordinary, if only he performs it in purity, wholly directed to God and concentrated in Him."[5]

God can be revealed through all things, Buber understood, and what clearer way is there to find God than through sincere human-to-human encounters? This is especially appealing in our contemporary world, in which the notion of God feels out of reach, unknowable, and maybe even doubtful. Buber eases our discomfort and loneliness by saying:

> Man cannot approach the divine by reaching beyond the human; he can approach Him through becoming human. To become human is what he, this individual man, has been created for. This, so it seems to me, is the eternal core of Hasidic life and of Hasidic teaching.[6]

Today, the need for dialogue has never been more apparent. We need genuine dialogue between Israelis and Palestinians. We need genuine dialogue to deal with our partisan conflicts in America. And we need genuine dialogue within all of our communities and families. But, as we learn from Buber, this does not mean simply getting people into a room to negotiate potential gains for each side. That will limit it to an I-It encounter. What it means is attempting to grasp the other person as a Thou, a human being created in the image of God, and apprehending the greatness of what that means. Talking to the other, Buber teaches us, is a truly religious enterprise.

---

5. Buber, *Hasidism and Modern Man*, 41.
6. Buber, *Hasidism and Modern Man*, 34-35.

Religion, we must know, is not as simple as keeping *kashrut* and Shabbat, or signing onto the principles of one's faith. To be religious is to be in dialogue, to have real relationships with people and be changed by the Divinity that those relationships reveal to us.

And yet, I think as Jews we can take it a step further. Rabbi Jonathan Sacks, in his book *Judaism's Life-Changing Ideas*, penned a critique of Buber. He wrote:

> To be a Jew ... is not just a matter of believing or behaving, but also of belonging. Martin Buber wrote a famous book about spirituality called *I and Thou*. It had a huge impact on Christian theologians, much less so on Jewish ones. The reason is self-evident. Judaism is less about the I-and-thou than about the we-and-thou. It is constructed in the first-person plural of togetherness ... All-of-us is greater than any-of-us.[7]

Where Rabbi Sacks' critique may have been misplaced was in considering Buber to be a radical individualist when he wrote books and books about Zionism. Though I recognize that his book I-Thou can be read that way, it was only intended to be the first book in a longer series that would explore questions of collectivity. Buber understood and wrote extensively about the necessity of Jewish peoplehood for the Jewish individual.

Perhaps to find the fullest form to dialogical existence, it is not enough to relate as a self to others. We must also break down the barriers of the self so that we encounter others without the fences that divide us standing in the first place. Judaism, we know, is about more than personal experience. It is about collective consciousness, the kind we experienced at Mount Sinai. Buber's own argument is that there is no individual without the collective. The collective includes not just the small number of Thous I may encounter but the larger collective/community from which the individual emerges.

The difference here is the difference between individual instances of loving-kindness and lasting societal change for justice. This does not mean we should throw out Buber and his *I And Thou*—it means the Jewish tradition is equipped to build on it.

There have been many other disagreements with Buber's I-Thou. Rabbi Zachary Truboff writes:

> Buber imagines I-Thou in a way that is similar to most liberal conceptions of morality, which argue we should have no problem encountering the other, knowing the other, and loving the other. All it takes is a bit of education, a willingness to work

---

7. Sacks, *Judaism's Life-Changing Ideas*, 116.

on oneself, and empathy. Rosenzweig and Levinas, however, understand the ethical relationship in a far more challenging manner. For them, what is revealed in the I-Thou encounter is just how strange and foreign the other really is. We grasp this only rarely and have to be willing to let it disrupt our lives rather than assume it will reinforce a pre-existing worldview.[8]

This is something Rabbi Avi Katz Orlow already began to do, when he explored the relationship between Buber's *I and Thou* and the popular Israeli singer Arik Einstein's 1971 song where he sings: "You and I—We will change the world."

By bringing this text together with Buber's *I And Thou*, Rabbi Katz Orlow saw Buber's philosophy of dialogue as a call not just for human dignity, but potentially even for society-wide justice.[9] He wrote:

> What did Einstein mean when he wrote אני ואתה - You and I? Perhaps it is just the Hebrew translation of the Jewish Philosopher Martin Buber's idea of Ich und Du- I and Thou. Buber wrote, "Feelings dwell in man; but man dwells in his love. That is no metaphor, but the actual truth. Love does not cling to the I in such a way as to have the Thou only for its "content," its object; but love is between I and Thou. The man who does not know this, with his very being know this, does not know love; even though he ascribes to it the feelings he lives through, experiences, enjoys, and expresses."[10] Life is not just about experience and sensation, rather life finds its meaningfulness in relationships. The attitude of the "I" towards "Thou" is a relationship in which the other is not separated by discrete bounds. Bad things happen in society when we objectify each other. It is only through the אני ואתה I-Thou relationship that we can hope to see positive social change.[11]

With his philosophy of dialogue, Buber took us part of the way there, by showing us that, to see God, we must learn to see beyond ourselves. What's next is what we do with those I-Thou encounters. Each one of them, we will learn, is an opportunity to change the world for the better.

8. Sent to me in an email on April 27th, 2023 and shared with his approval.

9. In Buber's Paths of Utopia, he makes clear that he sees the I-Thou relationship as the foundation of utopian community. For example, the kibbutzim were a model of this for him. He felt that social change occurred not by trying to change the state but by creating utopian communities that could serve as ideal models and that over time they could supplant the oppressive conditions of capitalism and the state.

10. Buber, *I And Thou*.

11. Orlow, *From Optimism to Activism*.

31

Ludwig Wittgenstein (1889–1951)

ARE WE ABLE TO say what we truly mean? Do even well-intentioned words have the power to lead us astray? How can we understand one another better?

Born in Austria toward the end of the 19th century, Ludwig Wittgenstein had three Jewish grandparents, though his family had largely assimilated into the Christian culture and religion. It's unclear how engaged in Judaism he actually was, and his works contain an ambivalent attitude toward his Jewish roots.

Wittgenstein's major philosophical contributions had to do with language—and "language games." Wittgenstein's most famous work, and his only one published within his lifetime, was his *Tractatus Logico-Philosophicus*, or *Logical Philosophical Treatise*.

For Wittgenstein, philosophical problems are primarily problems of language. We propose ideas and raise questions, but much of what we think to be perplexing about life is a result from failing to use language clearly and precisely. Only through a careful examination of our words and the ideas we think they communicate can we come to a greater understanding about ourselves and the world. Here he found fierce disagreement from his peer Karl Popper[1], who believed that philosophical problems were real problems to solve. We can begin to understand how significant this disagreement can be when we consider theodicy, the question of why bad things happen to good people. Is the problem our perceived lack of Divine justice to be resolved through language or to be solved with logic?

---

1. It should be noted though that its not clear that this encounter ever really happened.

LUDWIG WITTGENSTEIN (1889-1951)

According to Wittgenstein, even once we fully clarify language such that many of the philosophical problems we struggle with go away, we will always be stuck on and bewildered by the fact that there is existence itself. He wrote:

> Not how the world is the mystical, but that it is . . . We feel that even if all possible scientific questions be answered, the problems of life have still not been touched at all. Of course, there is then no question left, and just this is the answer. The solution of the problem of life is seen in the vanishing of the problem.[2]

For Wittgenstein, language rarely reveals our intentions clearly. Just as clothes conceal the true body, language has a tendency to conceal the true reality of thought.

Think back to the time of the Covid-19 emergency, when are all wearing masks. Were those masks forms of protection—or actually disguises? Likely, we used them as both! Either way, thinking about the relationship between masks and language brings us to a fascinating debate about the adequacy of language to portray our true thoughts, our true reality. In modernity, we stake a lot in language. Consider Freud's notion of talk therapy to reveal the hidden truths from childhood, which depended upon speaking to the psychoanalyst. Yet, in postmodernity, from the influence of Wittgenstein, the idea has emerged that language can offer an utterly inadequate symbolism of truths understood much deeper, that cannot be conveyed in language.

Perhaps said more simply, Wittgenstein's point is that we don't really understand how language works (i.e., how it conveys meaning) in part because we use it without thinking. He is just noting that language is rarely as transparent as we want it to be.

According to Wittgenstein's understanding of language, people often miscommunicate despite their best intentions to speak clearly. Language is meant to be referential, the words we speak refer to specific ideas and things. However, it almost is never the case that our words convey meaning as precisely as images, which we understand as referring to something concrete. Unlike pictures,

> Language disguises the thought; so that from the external form of the clothes one cannot infer the form of the thought they clothe, because the external form of the clothes is constructed

---

2. Horgan, *Was Wittgenstein a Mystic?*

with quite another object than to let the form of the body be recognized.³

For this reason, Wittgenstein believed we must be exceptionally careful with our words, how we use them and when we speak them. In general, human beings tend to take language for granted. However, Wittgenstein makes clear just how central it is to human existence. Language is not only the way we communicate with others but functions to structure the very contours of our existence, as he famously writes, "The limits of my language mean the limits of my world."⁴ In a sense, Wittgenstein felt it was better to err on the side of silence rather than use words in a confusing manner. He concludes the Tractatus with a statement that Maimonides himself would have agreed with: " What we cannot speak about we must pass over in silence."⁵

Judaism, of course, has a long history of understanding the power of speech to do good and bad. The Torah makes clear that God uses language to create the world, "God said, "Let there be light"; and there was light,"⁶ and this idea becomes particularly important to kabbalah and Hasidut. According to the mystical tradition, it is God's words that serve as the building blocks of all creation. However, language can be used not only to create but also to destroy. We learn from the Talmud:

> Anyone who humiliates another in public, it is as though he were spilling blood.⁷

From here we come to understand the severity of speaking negatively about others. In the Jewish tradition, one can perhaps find echoes of Wittgenstein caution about using words inappropriately in the following teaching from *Pirkei Avot*:

> Shammai used to say ... speak little, but do much; and receive all people with a pleasant countenance.⁸

With his second major work, *Philosophical Investigations*, published after his death, Wittgenstein posited that language is about more than just pictures, but rather "games."⁹ What exactly did he mean by this? It was

---

3. Wittgenstein, *Tractatus Logico Philosophicus*, 45.
4. Wittgenstein, *Tractatus Logico-Philosophicus*, 4:7.
5. Wittgenstein, *Tractatus Logico-Philosophicu*, 7.
6. Genesis 1:3.
7. Babylonian Talmud, Bava Metzia 58b, translated by The William Davidson Talmud (Koren - Steinsaltz).
8. Pirkei Avot 1:15, translated by Dr. Joshua Kulp.
9. See YouTube: The School of Life, *Philosophy - Ludwig Wittgenstein*.

not to claim, as did Humpty Dumpty in Alice in Wonderland, that "When I use a word, it means just what I choose it to mean—neither more nor less." Rather, by calling language a game Wittgenstein meant the language functions by its own set of rules that are independent from any objective reality. Different contexts require us to say and act in certain ways if we want to accomplish our goals. In this approach, language is not merely a method of relaying information, rather it is a tool that we use to achieve certain outcomes depending on the situation. Miscommunication happens when people misunderstand the "language game" being played. For example, when one runs into an acquaintance at the supermarket, our language games dictate one should greet them with the phrase, "How are you?" However, it is rarely the case that we expect an answer of more than a few words. If in that moment, they were to launch into a speech about their life story, we would think to ourselves they misunderstood the language game that was to be played.

Naturally, as Jews, we *love* language and language games. For many of us, our week centers around the reading of the Torah, but that's not enough—the rabbi must explain it to us in a sermon. Also, the Torah often lacks clarity and specificity, so we have the Mishnah, which began as an oral tradition set up to easily be memorized. But how do we know what we're supposed to take away from the Mishnah? From here we get the Gemarah, with all its debates and legends from the rabbis who painstakingly sought to wring more and more meaning out of the existing tradition. However, the Jewish obsession with trying to understanding the texts of our tradition does not end here. The Jewish canon is full of commentators, who were often grammarians, who still believed that we had not been able to get the full meaning out of the existing words, so they added more words to the mix. They asked more questions and proposed even more answers.

While, for Wittgenstein, language can be understood either through precise analysis or by determining what language game is being played, in the Jewish tradition, we seek to resolve the problem of unclear language by adding layers and layers of more language.

By the time we get to the Hasidic tradition, around the end of the 18th century, wordplay itself becomes the way of adding entirely new, simultaneous meanings to the existing meanings of the texts[10]. The neo-Hasidic contemporary rabbi has expressed why he loves this method of using existing words to draw out new meanings and new Torah. He said on his podcast:

---

10. To be sure, this was not a new practice but is the very essence of midrash itself. What is new is the new and radical ways this was done.

> I'm obsessed with wordplay ... When I encountered *Chasidut* (when I encountered Hasidic texts) I found ... the words are *substance* ... The way that Hasidic approaches to texts manifest is that each word, each letter, each phrase is itself *substance*—it has character. And so, if there's an *alef* showing up here, (*alef* being the first letter of the Hebrew alphabet) then you have in play all the meanings of *alef*... And then, next level up, you get certain words that, every time those words come up, you can tie them to every other instance of that word in other texts. You start to be in this mind-frame and this heart-frame of basically punning. I know it sounds maybe trivializing, but ... it unlocked a lot for me.[11]

For all of us immersed in Torah learning, we can unlock the mysteries behind the surface of the words and letters. What the letters and words literally mean to us is only a tiny fraction of what the words can fully convey to us. For Wittgenstein, we get meaning from clarifying the meaning of language and by understanding the different "language games" we play. In the Jewish system, we have an ever-evolving process of exploring the meaning of language through the process of midrash.

In the Talmud, we find the famous story that even Moshe—the receiver of the Torah, who passed it on to us—wasn't able to understand all the depths of the text. We read in Tractate Menachot:

> Rav Yehuda says that Rav says: When Moses ascended on High, he found the Holy One, Blessed be He, sitting and tying crowns on the letters of the Torah. Moses said before God: Master of the Universe, who is preventing You from giving the Torah without these additions? God said to him: There is a man who is destined to be born after several generations, and Akiva ben Yosef is his name; he is destined to derive from each and every thorn of these crowns mounds upon mounds of *halakhot*. It is for his sake that the crowns must be added to the letters of the Torah.[12]

Whereas Wittgenstein was focused on the way language was used, the Talmud points to an additional dimension of language, the shape of the very letters themselves. The crowns placed on them by God are understood as conveying a meaning of their own over and above what one might discern in the word alone.

11. *Judaism Unbound Podcast*: "Episode 369: Jewish Mysticism".
12. Babylonian Talmud, Menachot 29b, The William Davidson Talmud (Koren - Steinsaltz).

Language, we learn from the work of Wittgenstein, is an imperfect tool, however, it is the primary tool we have as human beings—the one we've relied on for millennia and will continue to rely on for the foreseeable future, despite our current image-saturated culture.

However, by cultivating a moral consciousness that shows us that words are imperfect in our hands and are potentially dangerous, we can learn to be more cautious, more empathetic, and more equipped to find new meaning in ancient wisdom.

32

Jean-Paul Sartre (1905–1980)

WHAT IS THE PROPER way to live a human life? Is there a set path in front of us, or is the world a totally open frontier for freedom?

Jean-Paul Sartre was one of the leading French existentialists. One of Sartre's most famous phrases is "Existence precedes essence." That is to say: there is no predetermined essence that shapes how one is to live their life— it is the concrete fact of one's existence and the freedom that goes along with it that allows one to choose how they live their life. According to existentialism:

1. Existence is always particular and individual—always *my* existence, *your* existence, *his* existence, *her* existence.
2. Existence is primarily the problem of existence . . . it is, therefore, also the investigation of the meaning of Being.
3. That investigation is continually faced with diverse possibilities, from among which the existent (i.e., the human individual) must make a selection, to which he must then commit himself.
4. Because those possibilities are constituted by the individual's relationships with things and with other humans, existence is always a being-in-the-world—i.e., in a concrete and historically determinate situation that limits or conditions choice.[1]

Sartre deals extensively with what it means to act "in good faith," to be authentic based on your freedom. Living in bad faith, on the other hand, to

---

1. Encyclopedia Britannica, *Existentialism*.

Sartre, would mean believing a role determined by other people who want to tell you what you are is what ultimately defines you.

He did much of his writing in cafés; we typically imagine Sartre with a cigarette in one hand, a coffee in the other, and an enthralled audience around him. But the café scenery influenced his thought as well. It was while watching a waiter *play the role*, so to speak, of a waiter that Sartre came to understand such a person as not affirming their freedom.

Much like an ambitious and dreaming teenager, Sartre did not like the idea that most people are willing to put limits on their own selves and lives. George Kateb wrote:

> The Human disposition, according to Sartre, is to deny our possibilities for the sake of the comfort of a bounded and well-defined identity, as if we could be nothing but what we are, and as if we were destined to be only one thing forever. One plays a role as if it were co-extensive with one's entire capacity for being. [This stance], by denying possibility, produces a welcome prison of self-induced limitation.[2]

Sartre's ideas emerged firmly in the context of World War II. In the war, he was drafted by the French army and held as a German prisoner.

Sartre's thought separated what he called "being-in-itself" from what he called "being-for-itself." An example of something that is "being-in-itself" would be a rock. It has no mind of its own, no will or agency, and doesn't really change until it is destroyed. However, humans exist *for* themselves. We're not determined or fixed or definite, the way objects are. We're constantly in motion and in a state of variability—until we're dead and unable to change ourselves anymore. Sartre explained:

> Consciousness is a being, the nature of which is to be conscious of the nothingness of its being.[3]

While it may not sound comforting to think of our being as nothingness, Sartre did not see it that way, The fact that humans have no fixed essence allows them to change who they are. It grants them the freedom not to be defined by the way of religion, science, or culture may seek to do so. In 1943, he published his famous work *Being and Nothingness*. In it, he argues that a human life is a type of loan, and each of us has the responsibility of creating our own life. We have a responsibility to create ourselves. We are terrifyingly free.

---

2. Kateb, *The idea of individual infinitude*, 7, 42–54.
3. Kaufmann, *Existentialism from Dostoevsky to Sartre*.

While freedom can be empowering, it can also create tremendous anxiety for us. To be free means to be totally responsible for oneself, believing there is no purpose to life that can simply be handed to us. Rather, one must construct it on their own. In America and in Judaism, we love to think of freedom as an entirely positive term. But to Sartre, freedom is oppressive because the burden of responsibility is so high. We are, in Sartre's words "condemned to be free."

Sartre is often remembered by the coldly pessimistic quote, "Everything that exists is born for no reason, carries on living through weakness, and dies by accident."

He is also famous for the line, "Hell is other people," though this is not an actual quotation but a takeaway from his 1944 play *Huis Clos*, or *No Exit*. The play depicts three characters who have no freedom because they're in Hell. Trapped together in a small room, they are forced to confront the ways in which they cannot escape perceiving themselves through the eyes of others. In doing so, they have no freedom to create themselves, and each one inevitably finds themselves tortured by the others. Sartre shows us that "Hell is other people" because, when we're not free to create ourselves, all we can do is pick at one another.

Living in a time of turmoil, Sartre felt an obligation to participate in political issues—and he ended up taking positions that advocated for violent revolution against colonialism around the world. Involved in the New Left, he was an apologist for Soviet communism, and he called the Cuban Revolutionary Che Guevara the "era's most perfect man."[4] Sartre supported movements that seemed to be grounded in virtue, but came to be dominated by power-hungry, and often violent, individuals.

In 1945, Sartre wrote an essay "Anti-Semite and Jew." Here among many other ideas offered, he defines a Jew as one who is perceived by another to be a Jew. This was written after Paris was liberated from Nazi occupation in 1944 when the world was only beginning to make sense of the Holocaust, antisemitism, and the role of Jews in secular societies.

What do we, as Jews, make of Sartre? We know from our annual experience of the communal journey from Egypt to Mount Sinai and the individual journey from Elul to Yom Kippur that the spiritual life does require the hard work of struggling with self-accounting and self-reflection. While it can be easy and comfortable to simply embrace an identity thrust upon you and not question how you are to live, Judaism asks that we do more. In this respect, Sartre is in line with our worldview, as both place an emphasis on our duty to determine our own unique mission and purpose.

---

4. Guevara, *The Bolivian Diary: Authorized Edition*.

One modification might be that perhaps we *do* have an essence that precedes our existence. Being a person with a soul, made in the image of God, puts upon us needs and responsibilities we didn't necessarily ask for. Stated more modestly, perhaps it is not the essence of our souls that makes us responsible but rather our relationship to God that makes us never completely free (just like one in a robustly committed relationship with a spouse and child is never completely free to do as they wish). And yet, *wherever* our life's purpose comes from, it's on our hands to carry it out. While, for Sartre, liberation comes from creating one's own self, in Judaism we seek to reconnect to the essence that precedes us. To return to God and to return to one's essence, we find, is the highest form of freedom.

And, counterintuitively, we often find this liberation through practices that might at first seem self-limiting. More than doing what one wants, we value the importance of being of service to God and to our fellow human beings. A parent who spends all their time trying to be radically free and reinvent themselves is not in fact finding the highest form of freedom, not if their ignoring their obligations to their children. However, one who commits their time to working a hard job and taking care of their children is in fact finding greater liberation by living out their purpose. (Of course, such a parent should have the societal support that makes this more possible and less personally taxing.) The journey from Egypt to Sinai shows us that true freedom comes in the form of responsibilities and opportunities for service.

Freedom, we see, is not the same thing as self-actualization. For Sartre, we would be in "bad faith" to by default commit ourselves to an inherited traditional morality. Whereas, for many Jewish thinkers, to live in accordance with the Torah is itself the highest actualization, because it enables us to transcend our self-interests in favor of a higher calling.

Sartre doesn't simply think one must reinvent themselves. He knows we can't be "free" in every decision we make. And there are parts of ourselves that we cannot choose (like our height). In Being and Nothingness, he places a great emphasis on what he calls "the project," what we might think of as an existential life project. For Sartre what's most important is that we choose the endeavors that bring meaning to our life rather than just simply accepting them because they have been imposed on us. Another way to think about it with a Jewish application is that for Sartre, it's not enough just to do mitzvot because the rabbi says God commands it. It has to be something that one chooses freely for oneself and commits to as a source of meaning that orients one's life.

We can imagine, though, that Sartre might want to push back on the notion that we can live our fullest lives without pursuing all of our personal desires. Professor Yehuda Gellman analyzed the gulf between Sartre's approach to actualization and Rebbe Nachman's, saying:

> In his *Existentialism is a Humanism*, Sartre gives the example of the person who thinks of himself as a poet, though he has hardly written a poetic line in his life. He *is* a non-poet, no matter what he says about himself to himself. Just so, the son of the king might *think* of himself as a *hindik (turkey)*, but he is not, and by the end he does not act like it. However, unlike Rabbi Nachman, Sartre was all in favor of bringing out "transcendent" self-image into alignment with our actual reality. Anything short of that would be what Sartre called "bad faith." Here, though, Rabbi Nachman would be allowing a rupture between our self-image and our reality as lived.[5]

The Jewish answer to this criticism, though, should be simple: In a world in which we can't do everything, we must have some values that are higher than others. If one must choose between following their wildest dreams and living in accordance with eternal truths, the choice should not be all that difficult.

And so, Sartre is both right and wrong. It *is* generative to break free from so many of the assumptions about what we need to be. Maybe we *don't* need to be the richest, the best-looking, the most productive, or the person who gets the best Instagram vacation photos. However, Jewish wisdom teaches us that we *will* ultimately submit to the will of something, and that something *should* be rooted in the ethic of responsibility that gives our lives meaning.

---

5. Lopes Cardozo, The Tent of Avraham. Gellman, *Rabbi Nachman x 2: The Unreflective Self*.

33

Emmanuel Levinas (1906–1995)

WHY ARE HUMANS OFTEN so tragically cruel to one another? What spurs us to take action in the world? What teaches us, on a soul level, that acts of loving-kindness are necessary?

Emmanuel Levinas was born in pre–World War I Lithuania, but he moved to France for his studies. During World War II, he worked as a translator for the French military, and he was taken as a German prisoner of war, which ironically benefitted him, because unlike so many of his fellow Jews, he wasn't taken to a concentration camp.[1]

Levinas had a deep interest in the Talmud, but as a philosopher he is best known for his work on the ethics of alterity (otherness). This came about because the Holocaust pushed Levinas to rethink the great problems of philosophy. He wondered: How could a society as famously enlightened as Germany's, the one that gave birth to the greatest modern philosophers, have committed the atrocities of the Holocaust?

His answer was that the dominant philosophy of the time had become too far removed from basic ethical concerns and emphasized abstractions that could cause us to forget our ethical responsibilities to others. Consequently, a paradigm shift in philosophical thinking was in order. The question of what it means to be human could not be answered through logic and the imagination but was to be found first and foremost in the face of each person we encounter.

When we encounter the face of another human being, Levinas believed, it should be as if we're standing at Mount Sinai hearing God commanding us. "The dimension of the divine opens forth from the human

---

1. Ivry, *A Loving Levinas on War*.

face.[2]" The human face demands so much of us that we are pulled into a Divinely commanded level of commitment. "The proximity to God, devotion itself, is devotion to the other man.[3]" One need not even hear the other speak for this to take place, for in encountering the other, we hear them communicating with us through the presence of their face.

This isn't exactly the same as Levinas's fellow Jewish thinker Martin Buber's philosophy of dialogue. This is because, for Buber, the encountering of the Other is not so much about the political and moral implications that spring from it. From Buber's perspective, it is about understanding and recognizing the other as a person different from myself, yet nevertheless in relationship with me all the same.

For Levinas, however, the encounter with the face of the other places obligations and responsibilities on us. It compels us in a way that will inevitably have both ethical and political ramifications.

This should not be seen as empty, feel-good rhetoric. The implication is that, when somebody needs me, even if I turn away from them, I cannot escape the demands that their face puts on me. Instead, I am forced to confront the consequences of my actions.

Levinas's idea here comes from the synthesis of two camps: the dialogical philosophy of Martin Buber and Franz Rosenzweig and the phenomenology of Edmund Husserl and Martin Heidegger—the key modification being that we must go beyond the abstractions of phenomenology and ontology. To see why, one must look no further than Heidegger's own participation in the Nazi Party. The danger of such an approach is that one loses sight of the presence of the Other, and that it is they, more than any philosophical concept, which structure my existence.

Naturally, it is not hard to see the parallels between the demands of the human face identified by Levinas and the demands of the image of God in each person as expressed in Judaism. While, for Levinas, the image of God is in the human face, in Jewish thought, it's in the person's entire being, but can be represented by the face. The face is significant for Levinas because it reflects the location of human subjectivity. In Totality and Infinity, he specifically focuses on the eyes. In seeing the eyes of the Other, we must confront their absolute freedom and unknowability. We know there is "someone there" but we will never know them fully. He was also probably influenced by Rosenzweig (and the Torah) which describes revelation in terms of an encounter with God's face.

---

2. Levinas, *Totality & Infinity: An Essay on Exteriority*, 78.
3. Levinas, *In the Time of the Nations*, 171.

In Judaism we have the idea of *achzariyut*, or cruelty. What specifically does cruelty entail? The medieval commentator Abraham ibn Ezra says that cruelty is to make someone like a stranger (*ach zar*). In making someone like a stranger to you, someone whose face and presence you don't know, we negate our responsibilities to them, thereby allowing us to be cruel.

At the same time, we must resist the urge to fear otherness. For some, it makes sense to love other people because we can see ourselves in them. But for Levinas this is not the case. Rather, our obligation to the other comes from the confrontation with their face through which we experience their otherness. There is no great achievement in treating others well because they are just like us. As human beings, we do that naturally. Instead, it is precisely the fact that the other is not like us that puts us in relationship with and obligation to them. Levinas takes the Torah's imperative that we must see ourselves as having been slaves in Egypt and develops it in the following fashion:

> The trauma I experienced as a slave in the land of Egypt constitutes my humanity itself. This immediately brings me closer to all the problems of the damned on the earth, of all those who are persecuted, as if in my suffering as a slave I prayed in a prayer that was not yet oration, and as if this love of the stranger were already the reply given to me through my heart of flesh. My very uniqueness lies in the responsibility for the other man; I could never pass it off to another person, just as I could never have anyone take my place in death: obedience to the Most-High means precisely this impossibility of shying away; through it, my 'self' is unique. To be free is to do only what no one else can do in my place. To obey the Most-High is to be free.[4]

For Levinas, and in our justice work, we must recognize that those we work beside and those we seek to help are always radically other. In order to love the stranger, we must first recognize how much of a stranger they are. Levinas is forcing us to confront the fact that the stranger isn't some holy angel that has descended from heaven who must be treated with love and care. They are instead different from me. Their wants, desires, and values, may in fact upset me deeply. Justice work in a Levinasian sense means being open about this (something we are loathe to do in the politically correct world we live in).

In the Psalms, David understands God as commanding him "Seek My face!"[5] David says:

---

4. Levinas, *Beyond the Verse: Talmudic Readings and Lectures*, 142.
5. Psalms 27:8.

> In Your behalf my heart says:
> "Seek My face!"
> O Lord, I seek Your face.
>
> Do not hide Your face from me;
> do not thrust aside Your servant in anger;
> You have ever been my help.
> Do not forsake me, do not abandon me,
> O God, my deliverer.
>
> Though my father and mother abandon me,
> the Lord will take me in.[6]

How much is this just like a human-to-human interaction? David, in need, seeks the face of God—and he is frustrated that God seems to be hiding God's face from him. Why? Because in a face-to-face interaction, God would see the need to be of assistance to David, to help him in ways even his father and mother won't. For all of us, made in the image of God, the duty is no different. This point is emphasized by Rosenzweig, a significant influence on Levinas, who explains: "A man who asks, cannot be disregarded; one must turn away one's eyes to reject his entreaties. As long as one meets him face-to-face, his request must be granted."[7]

Rabbi Shneur Zalman of Liadi read the face in these verses as intimately connected to the heart. In the Tanya, he did some wordplay in Hebrew, recognizing that David says, "My *heart* said for You, 'Seek *panay* (My face).'" The Alter Rebbe said this means we must seek the *pnimiyut* [innermost level, though the word sounds like "my face"] of the heart.[8] Seeking the face of God is deeply connected with our own inward spiritual journey.

Today, many of the great evils of the world are not perpetrated face-to-face. On the large scale, poverty does not occur because I, in my car, pass by an individual person who needs help. We have systems that force millions of Americans to live without their needs met and allow billions of people to live in deep poverty in the Global South. Even in our communities, we ship our unhoused neighbors to encampments, thinking we can put the needs of the other out of sight and out of mind.

Factory farming is not different. We don't see the animals we eat until they're wrapped and refrigerated in the grocery store. To be sure, Levinas did not apply his ethics to animals. Similarly, but more aligned with his

---

6. Psalms 27:8–10.
7. Rosenzweig, *Understanding the Sick and the Healthy*, 98.
8. Tanya, Part IV; Iggeret HaKodesh 4:1.

thinking, we put imprisoned people and the problems they face far away, so that almost none of us need to see them. Even warfare is something we can try to do through cyber strategies, drone attacks, and distant missiles. We can degrade the other far more easily when it takes less work to turn away from their face.

But what about the Holocaust, which consisted of a great deal of face-to-face killing. There, ideology—enforced by the hierarchy of the society—was the curtain between one person and another. The ideology of progress had even low-ranking Nazis believing that it was worthwhile to wipe the Jews and others out. He describes his own experience of this during World War 2. He served in the French army only to be captured and sent to a German prisoner of war camp. He describes his time there as follows:

> The French uniform still protected us from Hitlerian violence. But the other men, called free, who had dealings with us or gave us work or orders or even a smile - and the children and women who passed by and sometimes raised their eyes - stripped us of our human skin. We were subhuman, a gang of apes"[9]

In the aftermath of the war, Levinas made it his life's project to remove these metaphysical barriers to seeing the other.

With modern technology, we love to have the *illusion* of seeing the other. We look at pictures on *Face*book and interact distantly, though with image-saturation, on Zoom. We like to think these ways of seeing each other are no worse than doing so in person, but in fact, much of the time, we can totally miss the other. It's easy to feign the projection of presence when we're sitting in front of a camera but in reality, we might be perusing email or social media when it looks like we are making eye contact. There is no replacement for face-to-face presence. And we would be doing ourselves a favor as a culture by trying to make face-to-face presence preferable, perhaps even required, as often as possible, especially when there are ethical consequences at stake.

By spending time with one another, we realize that each of us is profoundly different, yet paradoxically bearing the same image of God. The call to seek the face helps us realize the potential of others, and it helps us realize the importance of ourselves. Rabbi Menachem Mendel of Kotzk, known as the Kotzker Rebbe, memorably offered a teaching, which is a bit confusing at first.

> If I am I because I am I, and you are you because you are you, then I am I and you are you. But if I am I because you are you,

---

9. Levinas, *Difficult Freedom*, 152-153.

and you are you because I am I, then I am not I and you are not you.[10]

Rabbi Mark Asher Goodman wrote, "In other words, if I am only acting this way because I am trying to be like you, then I'm not really being myself. And maybe you're not either."[11]

The lesson of Levinas is that we have to see others in order to help others become who they're destined to be. And through this relationality, we will live out the purposes of our own lives as well.

---

10. Goodman, *Life Lessons from Recently Dead Rabbis: Hassidut for the People*, 130.
11. Goodman, *Life Lessons from Recently Dead Rabbis: Hassidut for the People*, 130.

34

Hannah Arendt (1906-1975)

WHAT CAUSES PEOPLE TO do evil? Do they set out to harm others, or do they lack free choice by finding themselves in evil systems? What can be done about the problem of authoritarianism?

Born in Germany into a secular, Jewish, middle-class, progressive family, Hannah Arendt would become one of the most influential political philosophers of the 20th century.

In her higher education, Arendt received just about the best German philosophical mentorship possible; she studied with Martin Heidegger and Edmund Husserl, and her doctoral supervisor was the existentialist philosopher Karl Jaspers.

In 1933, the year after Hitler came to power, Arendt was arrested for doing research into antisemitism, which was illegal. She was eventually released from prison, and she fled Germany, ultimately landing in the United States.

Having been a Jew imprisoned in Germany, Arendt's awareness toward restoring the social wellbeing of Jews was acute, and she helped many young Jews emigrate to Israel. She would go on to write many influential books, become Princeton's first female full professor, and even have an asteroid named after her.

Arendt engaged different philosophical questions, but she most notably addressed issues of power and evil by looking at the dynamics of authority and democracy. She famously covered the trial of Holocaust mastermind Adolf Eichmann as a journalist, and in doing so she popularized the concept and phrase of "the banality of evil."

But before that, in her 1951 work *The Origins of Totalitarianism*, Arendt examined the emergence of communism and Nazism. Controversially, she saw them as having a number of similarities. Even though many have a tendency to distinguish between these ideologies, Arendt was interested in totalitarianism in all its manifestations.

The major point she made was that World War I and the Great Depression created an atmosphere of uncertainty and political instability in many European nation states. People wanted a clear path forward amid the chaos and were welcoming to demagogues and authoritarians who claimed to offer a clear path to prosperity. Their pursuit of raw power ultimately led to undermining the basics of democracy and transforming existing social structures to maximize social control.

In 1958, Arendt published *The Human Condition*, in which she critiqued Western philosophy and modern capitalist middle-class life by suggesting that we've lost our connection to labor and worldly experiences, trapping ourselves in the abstractions of the mind.[1] She questions if we may have lost the sense of a public sphere where an individual can act politically and distinguish themselves and instead, all we have is a private sphere where individuals pursue their self-interest in a consumerist fashion. And so, Arendt wanted Western philosophy to return to placing a premium on the concrete.

In *On Revolution* (1963), Arendt opposed the idea of Marx and Hegel that revolutions are the products of historical forces. Rather, she believed, they come from direct action. Furthermore, she saw a major distinction between the French and American revolutions. The American revolution was to be admired because it never gave up on pursuing the fundamental principle of freedom and eventually enshrined it in the Constitution. However, the French revolution eventually turned against its own principles and drifted into terror and Napoleon's dictatorship. For Arendt, human initiation and brilliance can bring about great change in the world, but, without a grounding in morality and remaining committed to it, they can also cause harm.

We can see this as a point of tension with her later claim that Eichmann was part of an evil machine. Are problems caused by people, or systems? What is freedom in the thought of Arendt? Are we just cogs in a system, or are we free to change things?

Her work that might hit closest to home for us as Jews, though, is *Eichmann in Jerusalem: A Report on the Banality of Evil*. As a reporter for *The New Yorker*, Arendt covered the trial that marked the first and only time the State of Israel has put someone to death. What made her perspective unusual

---

1. This might sound a little bit like the thought of Levinas, who saw the Holocaust as emerging from a culture in which abstract thought removed Germany from a focus on human dignity.

was that she believed Eichmann, a key perpetrator of the Holocaust, to be a cog in an evil system, rather than an evil person himself. She wrote:

> The trouble with Eichmann was precisely that so many were like him, and that the many were neither perverted nor sadistic, that they were, and still are, terribly and terrifyingly normal. From the viewpoint of our legal institutions and of our moral standards of judgment, this normality was much more terrifying than all the atrocities put together.[2]

By Arendt's account, Eichmann was a totally normal person one might run into on the street or in a restaurant. Seeing this ordinary-looking man held in a glass witness box during the trial made it seem to her that anyone, if put in the wrong situation, could be made into a monster, that they could end up just following orders from above.

According to Thomas White:

> Arendt found Eichmann an ordinary, rather bland, bureaucrat, who in her words, was 'neither perverted nor sadistic', but 'terrifyingly normal.' He acted without any motive other than to diligently advance his career in the Nazi bureaucracy. Eichmann was not an amoral monster, she concluded in her study of the case, Eichmann in Jerusalem: A Report on the Banality of Evil (1963). Instead, he performed evil deeds without evil intentions, a fact connected to his 'thoughtlessness', a disengagement from the reality of his evil acts. Eichmann 'never realised what he was doing' due to an 'inability . . . to think from the standpoint of somebody else.' Lacking this particular cognitive ability, he 'commit[ted] crimes under circumstances that made it well-nigh impossible for him to know or to feel that he [was] doing wrong.'[3]

This idea would be challenged in 2011 by the German philosopher Bettina Stangneth in her book *Eichmann Before Jerusalem*. Stangneth strongly refuted Arendt's idea that Eichmann was a powerless part of a system, arguing instead that he was a vicious antisemite who took immense pride in the fact that he murdered so many Jews.

Another critique came from the Jewish scholar of mysticism Gershom Scholem, who held that Arendt in her reporting on Eichmann was overly harsh in her judgement of Jews during the Holocaust. Elements of her analysis gave the impression that those forced to serve on Jewish councils set

---

2. Arendt, *Eichmann in Jerusalem: A Report on the Banality of Evil*.
3. White, *What did Hannah Arendt really mean by the banality of evil?*

up by the Nazis were no better than collaborators and that Jews could have done more to resist Nazi oppression. Scholem claimed that such assertions could only be made by one not sufficiently grounded in the suffering of the Jewish people, and it did not reflect a love of the Jewish people. Scholem wrote to Arendt in a letter:

> I don't picture Eichmann, as he marched around in his SS uniform and relished how everyone shivered in fear before him, as the banal gentleman you now want to persuade us he was, ironically or not.[4]

In the thought of Arendt, people generally don't do wrong because they find joy in it or want to do evil. Rather, they lose the ability to think critically and become victim of oppressive political systems that capitalize on those weaknesses, to make them do unthinkable things. Arendt was so deeply interested in politics and she believed we have to repair these systems that have such a profound impact on skewing people's moral decision making.

Arendt ultimately concluded that, while Eichmann did not set out to do evil, he had become a person unfit to live among the rest of us. She wrote:

> And just as you supported and carried out a policy of not wanting to share the earth with the Jewish people and the people of a number of other nations—as though you and your superiors had any right to determine who should and who should not inhabit the world—we find that no one, that is, no member of the human race, can be expected to want to share the earth with you. This is the reason, and the only reason, you must hang.[5]

It is important to note that whatever specifically brought Eichmann to do what he did, his case remains the only time that Israel has used the death penalty. To this day it is debated whether even this one exception should have been made. However, most Jews would agree that, even if one is against the death penalty generally, the scope and irrefutable documentation of Eichmann's brutality made the death penalty warranted.

This approach is not far off from what is expressed in the Talmudic tradition, that humans are capable of justly carrying out the death penalty only in exceptionally rare cases, if ever. We learn from the Mishnah:

> A Sanhedrin that executes a transgressor once in seven years is characterized as a destructive tribunal. Since the Sanhedrin

---

4. Prochnik, *What Gershom Scholem and Hannah Arendt Can Teach Us About Evil Today*.

5. Arendt, *Eichmann in Jerusalem: A Report on the Banality of Evil*.

would subject the testimony to exacting scrutiny, it was extremely rare for a defendant to be executed. Rabbi Elazar ben Azarya says: This categorization applies to a Sanhedrin that executes a transgressor once in seventy years. Rabbi Tarfon and Rabbi Akiva say: If we had been members of the Sanhedrin, we would have conducted trials in a manner whereby no person would have ever been executed. Rabban Shimon ben Gamliel says: In adopting that approach, they too would increase the number of murderers among the Jewish people. The death penalty would lose its deterrent value, as all potential murderers would know that no one is ever executed.[6]

This debate is important to think closely about today, as it remains contentious in Israel whether terrorists should be executed. How much should immersion in a destructive culture be a mitigating factor for the punishment of an individual? Would even a senior soldier in a totalitarian or terrorist regime have little choice in their actions? If someone is no longer a danger to others, what is there to gain by killing them? Should we do it for justice? Revenge? To make them as an example to deter future killers?

A wise reading of the religious, philosophical, and sociological wisdom would tell us that the death penalty should almost always be avoided.

In my interpretation of Arendt, I believe one of her goals was communicating that, to prevent evil from reoccurring, we cannot place all the blame on individuals. We must see the role of the systems that produce evil and ensure that those systems don't continue to emerge. It may look as though Arendt was weak, giving a partial moral pass to Eichmann. But she wanted to go after totalitarianism at large.

Many decades later, with authoritarianism and fascism reemerging in the world to a not-insignificant extent, we can see how the worst in people can be brought out by what is around them. This is true not only with Putin, Trump, and Bolsonaro, but with the whole populist mindset that they exploit. To be sure, Arendt's critique of totalitarianism was certainly tied to her views on combatting antisemitism. Fascist government control never ends up well for the Jews.

Perhaps the lesson we can take from Hannah Arendt is less about the banality of evil and more about the fragility of justice and how diligently it must be protected and cultivated.

---

6. Babylonian Talmud, Mishnah Makkot 1:10, translated by The William Davidson Talmud (Koren – Steinsaltz).

35

Simone de Beauvoir (1908–1986)

WHAT DOES IT MEAN to be a woman? What are we to make of the thousands of years of intellectual history that have disregarded the experience of women? How are we to move forward in a society built on male-dominance?

By making us reconsider everything that we've inherited, Simone de Beauvoir was a revolutionary figure for the way philosophers think about human existence.

Beauvoir was a French existentialist, with a background in phenomenology. Existentialist philosophy rests on "an interpretation of human existence in the world that stresses its concreteness and its problematic character."[1] It's a philosophy that struggles to understand what it means to be a person in the world. Her work was wildly controversial, and it was even forbidden by the Vatican. Beauvoir had a long romantic relationship with Sartre, but she never married or had kids.

Beauvoir was a pioneering second-wave–feminist philosopher, her famous book being *The Second Sex*, published in 1949. Beauvoir saw that philosophy, for almost all of its history, was done from a male perspective. Philosophers, who were men, used the word "man" as a substitute for "humanity" (much like the way the Hebrew word *adam*, which can refer to a person of any gender), but in doing so, they had a tendency to see men and not woman as representative of what it means to be human.

This, she saw, was obviously a flawed way of thinking—it leaves out most of the human population. By seeing men as the standard, she argued, women are viewed as equal only in areas in which they are deemed to be the same as men. Beauvoir noticed that even men who have served as allies in

---

1. Encyclopedia Britannica, *Existentialism*.

feminism relied on the argument that women are equally valuable because they're equally capable. Even for them, the source of female dignity came from women being able to do the same things as men.

And so, Beauvoir pointed out that men and women *are* different biologically. This makes much of the prior philosophical canon flawed, because it ignores the fact that women exist in the universe differently—whether we're talking about the relationship to the body, to others, or to the world. Women have phenomenologically different experiences and spheres of consciousness that are dependent on the social structures that define femininity. To be sure, she wants to transcend gender in the sense that women are existentially free in the same way as men and society must change to accommodate women rather than limit them.

Beauvoir merged the existing feminism into a feminist existentialism. Women did not necessarily choose to be women, but they could choose how they were to interact with the social construct of femininity. Beauvoir saw the immense societal pressure than was put on women to act and be certain ways. Similar to the way Sartre saw a waiter in a café as playing the role of waiter, Beauvoir saw that women were made to occupy the role of woman in a way that was not necessary.

Beauvoir most famously wrote, in *The Second Sex*, "One is not born, but rather becomes, a woman." She wanted women to choose: What kind of woman do you want to be? For Beauvoir, women should not feel compelled to be like men in order to be accepted and at the same time, they should not be compelled to be a typical woman in the way it was socially constructed. With this she was talking not only about the quest for authenticity, but about the strategy for how women can achieve freedom.

Seeing the way Beauvoir challenged the fundamental male-centered assumptions of philosophy, we can be inspired to take the same approach to Judaism, which for almost its entire history was in many ways centered on men and the male experience. We can recognize that the Torah was given in a time of deep patriarchy, and it consequently was understood as directed to a male audience. This resulted in men being more literate and educated throughout Jewish history. We can think hard about what it means that certain commandments have long been interpreted as being geared toward men.

It also must be recognized that even when a woman goes against the long-enforced stereotypes and decides to learn the Talmud, she must peer into an ancient history of alienation. The tradition is primarily a collection of male voices and when women are discussed in the Talmud, it's almost always from a male perspective. Women are generally taught *about*, rather than being the teachers themselves.

We can ask: How do women deal with this problem, of their intellectual inheritance being dominated by male influence and male-normativity?

One option that women can take is to reject all Jewish thought prior to feminist innovation—and perhaps even to reject Judaism altogether, as it inevitably relies on millennia of patriarchal history.

However, if you're looking for Jewish wisdom, presumably because the tradition has brought meaning to your life from childhood up through the present, this probably doesn't sound like a desirable option.

Alternatively, one might want to reject the explicitly patriarchal texts and traditions, but not reject Judaism itself. Women could rewrite the tradition, inventing an entirely new Judaism. This was an approach similar, but more radical, to one taken by Jewish feminist thinkers like Professor Judith Plaskow in *Standing at Sinai*. If the old way is irredeemably patriarchal, women need to create a new way that is fundamentally different. To be sure, Professor Plaskow did not want to invent a new Judaism which she is skeptical of, but she did want to reinterpret the tradition. We cannot just say that women are now equal rather we must do the harder intellectual work of reinterpretation.

If the tradition writ large was shaped through a male lens than it must be re-examined as well. And so another related path to take—one we can call "egalitarian"—might be to reinterpret and re-translate all that has been given to us. We can understand God to be gender-neutral, and we can understand the commandments to apply to all people equally. That way, women can be brought into the male-created system as equals.

A more traditional option is to uphold all that had developed under the old system—in which men studied Torah, were the arbiters of Jewish law, and performed the majority of mitzvot in synagogue and elsewhere while women received little in the way of religious education and had their religious life limited primarily to the home. We can maintain the authenticity of the tradition and build a new feminist path on top of what has already existed. This would be the approach advocated for by Professor Tamar Ross in *Expanding the Palace of Torah*. Here she also writes about how important it is for Orthodox feminists to retain some sense of gender difference:

> For the Orthodox feminist, the Jewish element in her feminism is not merely a description of the nature of the burden of tradition that she must contend with in order to achieve equality. Due to the more complex nature of her commitments and loyalties, she will not be inclined to view the traditional conception of gender as a totally negative affair. Many aspects of her womanhood are cherished elements of her self-identity and communal attachments, or serve as signifiers of other values that she has

internalized. For her, the sanctification of differences between men and women in Jewish tradition is corroborated by her sense that such differences bear true benefits despite the risks.²

The Orthodox feminist might make halakhic arguments for expanding women's leadership and women's participation in rituals but not necessarily by making egalitarian claims. The claims might be about pathways to serve God or about the search for meaning.

Of course, different Jewish feminists will choose differently. But regardless of how we go about moving forward in a more equal world, we learn from Beauvoir that it is not enough for a Jewish feminist to be only an intellectual critic. We cannot merely critique what exists. The task upon Jewish women is to choose what kind of women they want to be. And the burden on male allies is to provide non-judgmental space for women on the journey of repairing the Jewish tradition to one that honors the dignity and spiritual-growth needs of all people. To be sure, Jewish feminism and feminist critique is, in its most robust form, not just about helping women. Feminist critique can help reveal modes of domination and oppression that affect all Jews, and by becoming active contributors to the tradition, women can help shape it in transformative ways, perhaps even redemptive in that they can solve problems long thought unsolvable from a more limited perspective.)

Naturally, this rethinking is also a gift to Jewish men, who will learn they need not be compelled to conform to a narrow or common perception of masculinity, rather creative options are always open to them. Men will have the opportunity to discover what it means to be a Jewish man in a way that is meaningful to them.

As the rabbis explain, "there is no person that has not their hour."³ Each person, we know, is created for their own purpose in the world, and not simply to conform to the expectations of others including notions of femininity and masculinity that were passed down to us by others. We are each here to pursue a life that is authentically meaningful to us.

Beauvoir teaches us that gender is not a small issue in philosophy and religion. Each of us has the task of truly journeying into the best way to live our role in the world, for the sake of equality and liberation, and for the sake of our souls and spiritual journeys.

As Beauvoir wrote in her book *The Coming of Age*:

---

2. Ross, *The View from Here: Gender Theory and Gendered Realities*, 221.
3. Pirkei Avot 4:3.

I am incapable of conceiving infinity, and yet I do not accept finity. I want this adventure that is the context of my life to go on without end.

We see here what it means to be a person who does not accept a predetermined life, but who sees life as something that must be taken on and discovered by each individual.

36

Isaiah Berlin (1909–1997)

WHAT DOES IT MEAN to be truly free? Is it enough to be free from the impositions of tyrants and masters, or do we need something more?

Isaiah Berlin was born an Eastern European Jew and, escaping persecution from the Russian Empire, he immigrated to Britain when he was 11. Ultimately, he ended up at Oxford and became a world-famous intellectual. Berlin was a descendant of leaders of Chabad, and he would refer to the Lubavitcher Rebbe as "my cousin."[1] We can see how breaking free of the Russian Empire as a child made Berlin's philosophical work particularly interested in freedom.

Berlin's biggest idea, which he introduced in 1958 in his short work "Two Concepts of Liberty," was his distinction between negative and positive liberty. Negative liberty is freedom from external constraints or impositions, while positive liberty is the freedom to pursue what we believe to be the good. We can trace the idea of negative liberty back to John Stuart Mill, but the contribution of Berlin is that it is not only freedom *from* oppression that matters, but also freedom *to* affirm what we want to affirm and pursue it.

For me, Berlin's distinction between negative and positive liberty is clearly demonstrated in the Jewish story through the connection between the Exodus from Egypt and the receiving of the commandments at Mount Sinai. The Jewish people are achieving negative liberty when they are freed from enslavement in Egypt. No longer must their days be determined by what Pharaoh wants of them. But freedom *from* enslavement is not sufficient

---

1. Boteach, *The Great (and Imperfect) Hope That Is Chabad*.

on its own. We are not fulfilled until we have the freedom *to* live according to God's will and guidance for a just and holy life.

So too, one can see this distinction in the current State of Israel. On the one hand, a Jewish State enables Jews to be free from the marginalization of living as second-class citizens as was the case in many parts of the world, but more importantly, it enables something even greater which is the freedom for the Jewish people to actualize our own destiny.

Meanwhile, in America, the Bill of Rights is the defining political document that establishes negative liberty for all of America's citizens. The First Amendment, though it precedes Berlin's work, includes the Establishment Clause and the Free Exercise Clause. Together, these ensure the government cannot force a religion on the people, *and* individuals are free to practice the religion they want.

And so, Berlin's dual notion of freedom positioned him as a major advocate for the pluralism we support today. We know we cannot force our views on others, and we know others must be free to have their own beliefs, just as we are free to have ours. While in our time we often take this for granted, we should recognize that it's a departure from the kind of political thought that was often dominant in the first half of the twentieth century. Philosophers who came before Berlin, tended to have grand unified theories, such as communism and fascism, which attempted to understand humanity's role in the history of the universe.

This idea of positive and negative liberty sounds great, but there is a point at which the two can clash. It is often the case that a strong definition of positive liberty will often come into conflict with negative liberty. For example, when there is communism that tells people what the good life is to pursue, that articulation of positive liberty now tramples on the negative liberty. It is not sufficient for it simply to be proposed theoretically but to be made real, people must conform to its dictates. This is where Berlin's pluralism comes in. He argues that modern politics must refrain from claiming the authority to define the good and impose it on others. Instead, every person must be free to figure out what is good themselves within reason, so that the liberty of all can be upheld. This will be far from easy. Berlins writes:

> True pluralism is much more tough-minded and intellectually bold, it rejects the view that all conflicts of values can be finally resolved by synthesis and that all desirable goals may be reconciled. It recognizes that human nature generates values which, though equally sacred, equally ultimate, exclude one another, without their being any possibility of establishing an objective hierarchical relation among them. Moral conduct may therefore

involve making agonizing choices, without the help of universal criteria, between incompatible but equally desirable values.[2]

Each of us will have to make really hard choices and feel the loss even when we make the best decision we can.

> The notion of the perfect whole, the ultimate solution in which all good things co-exist, seems to me not merely unobtainable – that is a truism – but conceptually incoherent . . . Some among the great goods cannot live together. That is a conceptual truth. We are doomed to choose, and every choice may entail an irreparable loss.[3]

This, of course, gets far more complicated when we move beyond individual choices into the realm of societal norms and laws. In 1969, Berlin published his most important work, in *Four Essays on Liberty*, which explored the tension between freedom and equality. While Hegel and Marx believed in a single spirit or force moving history, suggesting there was a kind of determinism behind human progression, Berlin's view was not so simple, as he believed many complicated factors influenced societal change historically.

And, just as he wanted to complicate our understanding of history, Berlin sought to complicate our understanding of moral life. Here he rejects singular principles such as utilitarianism and Kant's categorical imperative—and suggests, rather, that there are many human values to juggle and hold together. Often, those values are conflicting and what becomes essential is learning how to navigate this tension without allowing things to descend into violence.

The capacity of Berlin's thought to uphold the value of all people made him a crucial thinker during the challenges of the 20th century. In 1992, Berlin told a humorous story on British radio about the time when, during World War II, Winston Churchill believed he'd invited Isaiah Berlin to lunch, but had mistakenly invited Irving Berlin, the Jewish-American songwriter.

Thinking he was speaking to the philosopher, Churchill said, "Mr. Berlin, what is the most important piece of work you have done for us lately, in your opinion?" Irving Berlin's answer: "I don't know, it should be 'A White Christmas,' I guess."[4] Churchill continued to ask him questions, not realizing who he was talking to and eventually asked him when he thought the

2. Berlin, *Russian Thinkers*.
3. Berlin, *The Proper Study of Mankind*.
4. Excerpt from edited transcript of "Desert Island Discs."

war might end. In response, Irving Berlin told Churchill, "Sir, I shall never forget this moment. When I go back to my own country, I shall tell my children and my children's children that in the spring of 1944 the Prime Minister of Great Britain asked me when the European War was going to end."[5] This comical story illustrates the extent to which Isaiah Berlin was viewed as an influential thinker by one of the most significant world leaders at that time.

For our lives as Jews, perhaps Berlin's biggest contribution is his insistence on pluralism. Though pluralism is relatively new to philosophy, we can find its roots far back in the history of the Jewish tradition. We read of a debate in the Talmud, in Tractate Eruvin:

> Rabbi Abba said that Shmuel said: For three years Beit Shammai and Beit Hillel disagreed. These said: The *halakha* is in accordance with our opinion, and these said: The *halakha* is in accordance with our opinion. Ultimately, a Divine Voice emerged and proclaimed: Both these and those are the words of the living God. However, the *halakha* is in accordance with the opinion of Beit Hillel.[6]

Even if God declares that the Jewish law is in accordance with the rulings of Beit Hillel, God also makes clear that the rulings of Beit Shammai are also to be considered as part of the word of God. Even if Beit Hillel is correct, there is a spark of truth in the position of Beit Shammai. The notion here is that there can be moral pluralism given the complexity of human intentions and human understandings. We know there are many noble pursuits that are good and conflicting in all of our lives. We are often weighing not the good versus the bad, but the good versus the good.

Another example of pluralism comes in Pirkei Avot, in which we read the saying from Hillel:

> Do not separate yourself from the community, Do not trust in yourself until the day of your death, Do not judge your fellow . . . until you have reached [their] place.[7]

Perhaps there is a reason why these seemingly discontinuous statements are joined together. We cannot separate ourselves from the community *because* we need to rely on others. And even if we think others are not

---

5. Excerpt from edited transcript of "Desert Island Discs."

6. Babylonian Talmud, Eruvin 13b, translated by The William Davidson Talmud (Koren - Steinsaltz).

7. Pirkei Avot 2:4, translated by Dr. Joshua Kulp, modified for gender neutrality.

sufficiently upstanding, we are rarely in a position to judge them and act as if we have a right to impose our will upon them. Pirkei Avot further teaches:

> Ben Zoma said: Who is wise? He who learns from every man, as it is said: "From all who taught me have I gained understanding" (Psalms 119:99).[8]

The very fact that one can and must learn from all people means that their opinions and values have validity even if they differ from our own. Furthermore, the Talmud says[9] that the Torah one should learn is the Torah that one's heart is most pulled to. Each of us must follow our own religious passions even as they differ from one another. This too is a pedagogical pluralism that each of us need to engage in spiritual practices and learning that uniquely fill us up. We should not just pour the same content into our students and children but rather empower them to think creatively and follow their unique interests as well.

In the Jewish tradition, we see the value of pluralism, and recognize that none of us have a monopoly on the truth. Not only this but we can even find pluralism within ourselves, which often contain multiplicity and paradox. Yes, a key purpose of spiritual work is to create unity within the self, but that requires raising the sparks of the multitudes we contain. And it is no different with the multiplicity within our families, in our communities, and in the world.

---

8. Pirkei Avot 4:1, translated by Dr. Joshua Kulp, modified for gender neutrality.
9. Babylonian Talmud, Avodah Zara 19a.

37

Albert Camus (1913–1960)

How are we supposed to accept the existence of an unjust world? How are we supposed to say that life is good in a world full of war, poverty, and disease? What is the purpose of life if we're all going to die one day anyway?

Albert Camus was born in French Algeria. His father was killed in World War I, and he was consequently raised by his mother in extreme poverty. Camus suffered from tuberculosis, a disease that recurred throughout his life and significantly impacted his thought. Camus's most famous work is a novel called *The Plague*, which is about living in the face of a cruel and absurd world.

Camus would move to France and become involved with the French communist party. During World War II, he joined the French resistance to the Nazi occupation. During this war, in his 1942 work, *The Stranger*, Camus wrote about a fictional settler in Algeria who kills an Arab man.

Camus was an existentialist. Much of his writing focuses on the struggle that, in our personal consciousness, we feel that life is meaningful—yet, when we zoom out, we get the sense that the universe is vast and we are but an infinitesimally small part. How, then, can life have meaning?

How can we handle this contradiction? Camus believed that rather than turn away from it, we must truly lean into and embrace the meaninglessness of human existence. While that might sound depressing to some, for Camus it is what enables us to live well.

Camus powerfully illustrates this idea through the Greek myth of Sisyphus, a character condemned by the gods to eternally roll a boulder up a hill only for it to keep falling back down. Camus saw this as paradigmatic of human existence with all the seemingly meaningless things we feel obligated to do. Even the parts of life that are most meaningful to us, such as following a dream or raising a family, are ultimately meaningless from the perspective of the universe. Why, then, should we live? What reason do we have to keep on persevering?

According to Camus, one cannot escape the absurdity of human existence. Like Sisyphus, we try to impose meaning on the world, but it is often like pushing a boulder up a hill. Though we may be able to move it some distance, eventually, our efforts will fail, and the boulder will roll back down again. In the face of such absurdity, Camus argues that human beings are unique in that we can make meaning out of what is objectively meaningless. We can choose to embrace the absurdity of life and in doing so, discover our freedom to rebel against it. In the end, we may fail, but we will do so as free beings.

Camus's notion of the absurd might not resonate for all of us at all times, but at times of personal crisis, we may feel it is necessary to question everything. It is undeniably valuable to affirm our own meaning-making amidst the absurdity of life. Some might dismiss an internally driven sense of meaning, failing to see its cosmic relevance. But, in fact, meaning that comes from within us can, at times, be *more* meaningful, as it's imposed not from an outside source, but from our own deepest intuitions. To be sure, Camus doesn't argue that we can just impose our own meaning on the world because there is no objective meaning. The world constantly resists those efforts (hence the boulder always rolls back down again). However, Camus is saying that even though we know the boulder will roll back down (that life is meaningless), we can choose freely to keep pushing it up. We can act heroically in the face of the absurd, and when we do, we are perhaps most human.

How does this compare with how Judaism addresses the feeling that life is ultimately meaningless? For example, how do we deal with the despair of being unable to fully repair a world whose injustice seems absurd?

First, we can look to our father Abraham. When God said that Sodom and Gomorrah would be destroyed, Abraham famously protested, saying:

> "Far be it from You to do such a thing, to bring death upon the innocent as well as the guilty, so that innocent and guilty fare alike. Far be it from You! Shall not the Judge of all the earth deal justly?"[10]

Even though Abraham's protest ultimately did not save those people, his example shows us that there is nothing wrong with identifying absurdity when we see it. More importantly, he is willing to do so to God directly.

---

10. Genesis 18:23.

When we recognize the contradictions of our existence, such as our mortality, the shortness of life, and just how minuscule the amount we can achieve seems to be, it is easy to want to give up. Yet Judaism fights against this by instilling an awareness of time and a sense of urgency. What we do matters even if we can't always see the long-term consequences of our actions. We read a slightly anxious statement to this effect in *Pirkei Avot*:

> Rabbi Tarfon said: the day is short, and the work is plentiful, and the laborers are indolent, and the reward is great, and the master of the house is insistent.[11]

Despite the fact that we're limited in our ability to bring about justice—and even in our ability to know what justice is—we learn from the tradition, in the continuation of Rabbi Tarfon's statement:

> It is not your duty to finish the work, but neither are you at liberty to neglect it.[12]

In a sense, R' Tarfon acknowledges the absurdities of human existence. Despite our best efforts, it is rarely the case that a human life ends with the world's problems being fixed. Yet, that does not diminish our responsibility in trying to address them. In the temporal, we have the chance to connect to things that are eternal, even if they do not yet achieve perfection. This is put most poetically in the conclusion to the Book of Ecclesiastes. First, the teacher reiterates the near-despairing thesis of the book:

> Before the silver cord snaps
> And the golden bowl crashes,
> The jar is shattered at the spring,
> And the jug is smashed at the cistern
>
> And the dust returns to the ground
> As it was,
> And the lifebreath returns to God
> Who bestowed it.
>
> Utter futility—said Koheleth—
> All is futile![13]

But then, the book concludes with an answer to all of this futility:

---

11. Pirkei Avot 2:15.
12. Pirkei Avot 2:16.
13. Ecclesiastes 12:6–8.

The sum of the matter, when all is said and done: Revere God and observe His commandments! For this applies to all mankind.[14]

Yuval Noah Harari, a popular secular Israeli historian and the author of Sapiens, reflects on how he rejects Judaism because making meaning of the world, in the face of inevitable destruction from climate change and other major threats, doesn't make sense. He, following a Buddhist approach, prefers to orient himself, when faced with the absurdity of life, around the problem of suffering rather than the problem of meaning. Perhaps we cannot address the absurdity of our existence in any coherent way but perhaps we can address our suffering around it.

A different, Jewish, way of looking at it is that we can view God as having created the world specifically in order to have someone to express lovingkindness to. Our existence is inherently meaningful because we are born out of that need of God's to connect to us. If this was just to fulfill God's need, so to speak, something would seem wrong with creating a broken world. But we can learn to see creation as an ultimate act of kindness, as a necessary extension of love.

We can also grapple with the absurdity of life in the strain of religious thought that tells us we're nothing—and also everything. The story is retold by Martin Buber:

> It was said of Reb Simcha Bunem, an 18th century Hasidic rebbe, that he carried two slips of paper, one in each pocket. One was inscribed with the saying from the Talmud: Bishvili nivra ha-olam, "for my sake the world was created." On the other he wrote a phrase from our father Avraham in the Torah: V'anokhi afar v'efer," "I am but dust and ashes." He would take out and read each slip of paper as necessary for the moment.[15]

In his own way, Reb Simcha is acknowledging the same contradiction noted by Camus. On the one hand, we are nothing but "dust and ashes." Nothing we do is permanent, and when compared to God, our efforts will always fall short. But at the same time, we can see that, despite our infinite smallness next to God, we also have the power to be more impactful than we can even imagine. The Hasidic Masters tells us that our mitzvot are effective not only in this realm, but also in healing the heavenly sphere. Even if we try to think less mystically, we can imagine the ripple effect of our good deeds and see that, just by making one good decision, we can set a chain reaction of healing into motion that we never could have anticipated.

---

14. Ecclesiastes 12:14.
15. Buber, *Tales of the Hasidim: Later Masters*, 249-250.

Perhaps Leonard Cohen explained it best, when he said.:

> You look around, and you see a world that cannot be made sense of. You [can] either raise your fists, or you [can] say hallelujah.

Yes, the world is absurd. But that is not the end of the story. There is still work to be done.

38

John Rawls (1921–2002)

WHOM DO YOU FEEL most obligated to help? Yourself? Your family? Members of your religious community? Your own country? Everyone in the world?

After the nuclear bombing of Hiroshima, John Rawls resigned from the U.S. Army and entered the world of philosophy, in which he'd focus on politics and ethics. Rawls met Isaiah Berlin while studying at Oxford and went on to become a Harvard professor and teach Thomas Nagel and Martha Nussbaum.

One of Rawls's most important books is called *A Theory of Justice*, published in 1971. The work answers questions of "distributive justice," of how we might distribute resources in the world in an equitable manner.

As we saw in the thought of Berlin, Rawls recognized the competing values of equality and freedom. Though we can try to distribute resources to everyone equally, it will always be done at the expense of people having the freedom to choose what to do with their own resources. So too, in a society that gives everyone the freedom to work for and buy what they want, there are inevitably poor people who suffer. Classically, the conflict between freedom and equality is a complex one. If we want to ensure everyone has an equal share of material resources, the only way to do this is through central planning and distribution. As a result, one doesn't get to do whatever one wants. Rather, you have to do what the system requires in order to ensure that everyone can be equal. The more freedom granted to the individual, the more they get to choose how they want to be in the world. Freedom inevitably leads to inequality because it allows for there to be an unequal distribution of power and resources. For example, freedom means we don't put a limit on how much money billionaires can make.

Rawls's conclusion was that, in reality, it is not a binary choice between freedom and equality. We shouldn't try to weaken one in service of the other. Rather, we should work for both to be robust. He referred to the integration of these values as "justice as fairness."

Fascinatingly, Rawls imagined starting a society all over again, on a desert island. By imagining a perfect society, we might be able to move the real one closer to the ideal. To better imagine a world that maximizes both freedom and equality, he offered a thought experiment that he called "the original position." In it, he believed we should imagine a "veil of ignorance." We should picture ourselves being completely blind to the race, gender, ability, and social class we'll be born into and create a world that we'd be happy to live in, one that we think will be most fair for the average individual without overly compromising their freedom. We want a society that we'd say is fair without knowing anything about where we might end up in it.

Rawls used this experiment to theorize the "difference principle." He believed that, given this veil of ignorance, not knowing where we ourselves would land, we would be motivated to limit inequality and improve the status of every person, especially those who are worst-off.

Rawls believed that the way to best achieve equality is to ignore social status. He followed in the tradition of Hobbes's social-contract theory, insisting that we create a contract as a society and accept the rules together because it is beneficial for all, and not just the elite. However, Rawls believed the social contract now needed an upgrade to address the factors that lead to social inequality.

Rawls also advocates for civil disobedience as a response to society's inequality and injustice. In *A Theory of Justice*, he defines it as:

> A public, nonviolent, conscientious yet political act contrary to law, usually done with the aim of bringing about a change in the law or policies of the government.[16]

Rawls's ideas are especially interesting to observe from a Jewish perspective, as Jewish law has traditionally distinguished between one's obligation to their fellow Jews and other human beings. It makes me ask the question: Do we as Jews feel too obligated to our own people and not enough to the world?

I think the wisdom of the Jewish tradition shows us that Jews' obligations operate on two different levels for good reasons. As Jews, we have the right, maybe even the obligation, to value the wellbeing of members of our own community, for we are not only a nation but a family. According to the

---

16. Rawls, *A Theory of Justice*, 364.

Jewish tradition, it is unfeasible for every person to feel obligated to the entire world. Instead, we are part of concentric circles of people, starting with ourselves and our family, then a slightly looser connection with our friends and community, then to perhaps our state and country.

Only at the broadest reaches of our ethical imagination are most of us able to consider the needs of the whole world—and perhaps this is good, because, all else being equal, we are best able to help those whom we know best. Of course, this is not at all to mitigate the importance of helping those with fewer resources globally. Though our primary obligation may be to those closest to us, living in globalized world somewhat changes that equation. We may prioritize our fellow Jew, but it would be unethically atrocious if we refused to extend our ethical efforts beyond this.

And so, we see that there's nothing inherently wrong with choosing to be charitable to Jewish causes, or volunteering more with Jewish agencies. Just as there would be something intuitively wrong with helping a stranger before your parent, it is the same within our communities.

That said, we cannot stand for a world that doesn't strive for a certain amount of equality among all people. I think the dynamic here is well illustrated by the organization HIAS. HIAS was originally called the Hebrew Immigrant Aid Society and did the work of resettling Jews. Once Jewish refugees became a comparatively much smaller problem, HIAS reoriented itself toward helping refugees all over the world. We learn that, just as we advocated for Jewish refugees in World War II, we should advocate for others as well. We see that communal obligations can give us a pathway toward a universalistic cause. We can use the particular to realize the universalistic.

One of the most prominent tensions within the Jewish community right now is that between the parochialists—those who want a tightly knit Jewish community that looks out for itself—and those who only want to look outward, who believe that advocating for any Jewish interest at all is backwards at best or wrong at worst.

Perhaps the more authentic Jewish view is to have a comfort with both, as is stressed throughout the tradition. The Talmud, in Tractate Gittin, explains that, even though Jews are commanded to set food aside for poor members of the Jewish community, it must be available to gentiles as well. We read:

> The Mishna teaches: One does not protest against poor gentiles who come to take gleanings, forgotten sheaves, and the produce in the corner of the field, which is given to the poor [pe'a],

although they are meant exclusively for the Jewish poor, on account of the ways of peace.[17]

The *Talmud* goes on to explain that, just as we must feed gentiles alongside Jews, we do for them other acts of charity and justice as well. It is recorded:

> Similarly, the Sages taught in a *baraita* (*Tosefta* 5:4): One sustains poor gentiles along with poor Jews, and one visits sick gentiles along with sick Jews, and one buries dead gentiles along with dead Jews. All this is done on account of the ways of peace, to foster peaceful relations between Jews and gentiles.[18]

Naturally, we are most aware of those in close proximity to us, who are usually more like ourselves. But, as we interact with the broader world, we see that we're obligated to others precisely because even those who are different from us have needs that mirror our own. There shouldn't be a tension between tribalism and universalism because, when understood correctly, the differences between ourselves and others are both artificial and useful. They're useful because they assign us a closer group of people to be connected to, but they are artificial in that we are ultimately not different from those outside of our own communities.

It is recognition of our oneness that should enable us to work to actualize Rawls's vision. Might we find that we care less about the struggles of an Iranian village because of the Ayatollahs that declare their desire to destroy Israel. If we're opposed to the death penalty, are we just as opposed to it when it's given to someone who's harmed Jews? Would we feel the same about economic justice if we didn't know what kind of a household we would be born into?

At the same time, while there needs to be some blindness as it relates to policy and belief, here we can't fully embrace naivete. For example, Jewish law prohibits selling weapons to someone who is known to be violent. Similarly, we can give *tzedakah* indiscriminately while taking measures to prevent fraud.

The Torah demands that we interrogate our biases by aspiring to procedural justice that treats others fairly and equally, regardless of what we may think of them. We read in the Book of Deuteronomy:

> You shall not be partial in judgment: hear out low and high alike. Fear neither party, for judgment is God's.[19]

17. Babylonian Talmud, Gittin 61a.
18. Babylonian Talmud, Gittin 61a.
19. Deuteronomy 1:17.

Achieving justice can often mean recognizing that we have biases and considering what we can do to combat them, so as to ensure that the law is impartial and fair. A leading Harvard psychologist, Professor Steven Pinker, who rejects the notion that humans are born as blank slates, argues for how his biological views align with Rawls' notions of justice:

> Can one really reconcile biological differences with a concept of social justice? Absolutely. In his famous theory of justice, the philosopher John Rawls asks us to imagine a social contract drawn up by self-interested agents negotiating under a veil of ignorance, unaware of the talents or status they will inherit at birth—ghosts ignorant of the machines they will haunt. He argues that a just society is one that these disembodied souls would agree to be born into, knowing that they might be dealt a lousy social or genetic hand. If you agree that this is a reasonable conception of justice, and that the agents would insist on a broad social safety net and redistributive taxation (short of eliminating incentives that make everyone better off), then you can justify compensatory social policies even if you think differences in social status are 100 percent genetic. The policies would be, quite literally, a matter of justice, not a consequence of the indistinguishability of individuals.
>
> Indeed, the existence of innate differences in ability makes Rawls's conception of social justice especially acute and eternally relevant. If we were blank slates, and if a society ever did eliminate discrimination, the poorest could be said to deserve their station because they must have chosen to do less with their standard-issue talents. But if people differ in talents, people might find themselves in poverty in a non-prejudiced society even if they applied themselves to the fullest. That is an injustice that, a Rawlsian would argue, ought to be rectified, and it would be overlooked if we didn't recognize that people differ in their abilities.[20]

One of the Jewish thinkers to grapple with Rawls was Rabbi Dr. Walter Wurzburger. He liked that Rawls combined the utilitarian and Kantian approaches. That is to say, every person is an end onto themself yet we must care about the consequences for the masses as well. Without Rawls, Wurzberger implies, every tribe just lives in its own ghetto.

It is a wonderful thing for Jews to embrace Rawls's universalism, but we shouldn't ignore the fact that we often need particularistic communities to achieve it. Ideally, we can learn to be a tribe without ghetto walls.

20. Pinker, *The Blank Slate*.

39

Michel Foucault (1926-1984)

WHAT IS POWER, IN the context of human societies? How is it concentrated or dispersed, and how does it move through and between different systems?

Born into an economically and socially stable family in 1926 in France, Michel Foucault received a solid education and originally studied psychology—despite his father's wish that he, too, become a surgeon. In his youth, he had significant mental health struggles, which doctors attributed to his being a gay man in a society that did not embrace such an identity.

He went on to earn his doctorate in philosophy, studying at the Ecole Normale Superieure, where he was influenced by Jean-Paul Sartre and Louis Althusser. Focusing on relationships between power, knowledge, and society, his great works continue to influence philosophy and social science discourse today. Some of his significant works include *Madness and Civilization* (1961), *Discipline and Punish* (1975), and the multi-volume *The History of Sexuality*, published after his death in 1984 from complications related to HIV/AIDS. In his work on madness, he explores our societies' fear of the irrational and the outlier ("the mad") and we learn how about how society can come to scapegoat those that awaken what we're collectively afraid of.

Often cited as a post-modernist and post-structuralist, one of his major ideas, following Nietzsche, is that ideas are not eternal, but rather emerge over time through the structures and discourses that make up human society. To properly understand them, we must participate in what he refers to as "genealogy," a term borrowed from Nietzsche, in which the development of ideas are analyzed over time. This process often reveals the contingent nature of ideas we assume to be unchanging while also digging up evidence from the past that may point to counter narratives about how concepts and beliefs came to be and what their meanings might actually be.

One of the major insights of Foucault is the way in which discourses shape our understanding of the world. While the term is normally understood as communication through speech, Foucault has something much bigger in mind with it. For him, discourses are the language, knowledge and institutions that determine how we make sense of the world. They are what make something knowable to us, thereby granting it a sense of ontological truth. Perhaps the most famous analysis of discourse in his writings is found in The History of Sexuality, part 1, where he examines the development of modern notions of sexuality. The common understanding is that before the developments of the last century, sexuality was a repressed feature of human life, particularly in the Victorian era. It existed but wasn't meant to be talked about publicly, and it is only with the sexual revolution of modernity that we can now acknowledge the proper place of human sexuality in human life.

Foucault, however, disagrees with this narrative and sees sexuality not as something that has been revealed by removing repression and prohibition, but as having been produced by discourses such as science and politics. In the nineteenth century, science began to view sexuality as a matter of human health, and therefore it was understood to be something that could be done and experienced in ways that were both healthy and unhealthy. As a result, sexuality needed to be monitored and policed, for a society has a responsibility to ensure the welfare of its citizens. It became an object of the law and therefore something to be defined and legislated. Additionally, because sexuality is an amorphous concept, the only way to get at it was through speech. People would have to describe their experiences of sexuality to others who would then analyze them to determine what they mean. It was only by talking about sex could the truth of sexuality emerge, an idea that would come to the fore with psychoanalysis.

From this example, Foucault was able to see that power rarely functions as we think it does. Rather than being situated in positions of authority which then issue dictates that we must submit to, power is found in the language and structures that enable us to understand the world around us. The language and institutions of science, health, education, and therapy can cause us to view ourselves and others in very specific ways, thereby imposing powerful constraints on our existence.

In Foucault's way of thinking, "Power is not something that is acquired, seized or shared, something that one holds on to or allows to slip away; power is exercised from innumerable points,"[21] and the consequences of this, he explains, is that "points of resistance exist everywhere in the power network. Hence there is no single locus of great Refusal, no soul of revolt,

---

21. Foucault, *The History of Sexuality*, 94.

source of all rebellions, or pure law of the revolutionary."[22] In a sense, power is a multidirectional affair, akin to what we see in physics. The force of gravity exerted by the earth is strong and holds all of us down. But that doesn't preclude us from also exerting force upon ourselves and each other. In fact, if it wasn't for gravity, we wouldn't be able to move at all. We would take one step into space and keep on floating forever. We often experience power as a force that restricts us, but it is also what makes agency possible.

In order to best illustrate the complexities of power, Foucault dedicated significant energy to examine the development of modern prisons. He contends that it wasn't that long ago when criminal punishment was often conceived of primarily as a public spectacle, such as hanging, which demonstrated the power of the king and was intended to send a message to his subjects. However, it eventually shifted to primarily a form of imprisonment which secludes criminals from the rest of society.

According to Foucault, prisons functioned differently from the rest of society, but in doing so, also served as the forerunner for many aspects of modern life. In prison, criminals were subjected to a comprehensive disciplinary regimen that regulated what they wore, how they talked, what they eat, and how they acted. Failure to comply with them would lead to punishment. Foucault went so far as to argue that the ideal form of a prison would be one in which convicts were not policed by guards but rather policed themselves. To explain this, he turned to Jeremy Bentham's idea of the Panopticon, a prison designed so that all inmates could be monitored by one person. While each inmate could not be certain they were being watched at any given time, they knew the possibility existed and therefore had to monitor their behavior to ensure they did not transgress the rules and be punished. For Foucault, the model of the Panopticon became a metaphor for the way in which modern society does not demand subservience to a king but inculcates within us an awareness that we are being watched by others and must make sure to adhere to a set of standards and values. Those who fail to live up to them are then pathologized and criminalized.

While at first glance there is little in common between Foucault and Judaism, because so much of the Jewish tradition has been shaped around the experience of being a minority, it often shows a sensitivity to the nuances of power articulated by Foucault. In Egypt, Pharaoh subjugates the Jews through a form of state slavery, and eventually declares all Jewish baby boys to be killed as soon as they are born. However, enacting this decision requires the participation of the Egyptian midwives who tend to the Jews. While women are not typically considered for a position of power in

---

22. Foucault, *The History of Sexuality*, 95-96.

Egyptian society, the midwives' role in delivering infants makes them an important part of the social structure. As Foucault noted, the point of power is the point of resistance, and the midwives are able to resist Pharaoh and save the Jewish babies by telling him that the Jewish women give birth too quickly for them to carry out his genocidal plan. Their resistance to Pharaoh does not seek to bring about a revolution but it saves lives nonetheless.

Similarly, in the Megillah, Esther is an orphan who is essentially abducted and made the bride of Achashverosh, the most powerful man in the known world. Though she may be the queen, she is incredibly vulnerable, for Achashverosh can dispose of her easily at any time. Meanwhile, Haman uses his political powers as the king's favored minister to carry out his genocidal agenda against the Jews, completely unaware that the greatest threat to his plan will come from a woman who appears to be without any real power. Mordechai urges Esther to act, despite her apparent lack of power, and she goes and speaks to the King in a way that turns the entire story upside down.

While much of Judaism seems to be on the same page as Foucault when it comes to his descriptions and critiques of power, it gets more complicated when we factor in how his ideas about language and knowledge relate to all of this. The rabbinic project assumes a continuity of tradition and religious truth that Foucault's critical approach seeks to undermine. Nevertheless, the rabbis would probably agree with Foucault that language, more than anything shapes our understanding of the world. As the book of Genesis makes clear, God created the world through speech, an idea that is developed by Sefer Yetzirah, an early mystical work, and then later taken up in Kabbalah in fascinating ways. However, it is not only God who shapes the world through language but human beings as well. God's first task for Adam after being created and placed in the Garden of Eden is to give names for each of the animals God presents to him. The discourse of halacha is all about ascribing the proper halachic category to the objects and actions we encounter in life, a discourse that is produced through the study of texts and the social interactions of rabbis and laypeople.

Foucault's ideas have had a powerful influence on academia in the humanities and on the study of Talmud in particular. Scholars have attempted to apply Foucault's insights about the way discourse shapes sexuality to rabbinic texts which frequently make gender and sexuality an object of study. In addition, Foucault's genealogical method has been used critically to undermine commonplace notions of Jewish history to show the existence of alternative understandings and counter narratives.

What do the ideas that Foucault presents mean for us? How can we better examine what our actions do? How can we gain perspective on how our language and what we think we know about the world inhibits our ability to contribute to meaningful change? What kind of power do you have that you feel you could make better use of? What kind of power do you have that you feel might be too dangerous? How can you disperse that power? How can we work with the institutions we interface with—particularly those where we have some amount of power—to not function as tools of oppression?

Foucault is a challenging thinker who can inspire us to think more deeply about power dynamics in all their forms, and who can help us think about the way we relate to ourselves in new and important ways.

40

Noam Chomsky (1928–Present)

ARE HUMAN VALUES, AT the core, fundamentally universal and only divided by specific language and expression? Should behavior only be determined as ethical if one acts according to universal principles and not selectively out of self-interest?

Noam Chomsky was born in 1928 to Jewish immigrants, both of whom were active in their local religious community in Philadelphia and believed strongly in the importance of education. Chomsky recalls that they were both "heavily involved in the revival of Hebrew," and insistent upon strong educational foundations so that the Jews in their community would be capable of robust free thought. As such, even though he now identifies as non-religious, he still finds some of his ethics rooted in Judaism, such as an assertion found in his Haftarah portion, from Zechariah[1], not by might, not by power, but by the spirit of the Divine.[2] This, perhaps, serves as good support for Chomsky's commitment to pacifism.

Having first made a name for himself in the field of linguistics—some call him the "father" of the modern field, Chomsky is now one of the best-known public intellectuals in the English-speaking world, having branched out into political activism, social criticism, analytic philosophy, and even cognitive science. To date, he has written over a hundred books and been engaged in debates with many other significant thinkers.

Just to take a moment to name what some of you likely already know—Chomsky has strong opinions perceived by many to be anti-Israel.

---

1. Which he cited, in Hebrew, during an interview we had together a few years ago. See YouTube: Valley Beit Midrash, *Activism, Human Nature, & American Repentance: Noam Chomsky Interviewed by Shmuly Yanklowitz*.

2. Zechariah 4:6.

To borrow the words of one of his more famous intellectual nemeses, Alan Dershowitz says that Chomsky "hates America, hates Israel [and], hates western democracy."[3] That's a pretty concise summary of most of the controversies. As always, we're going to do our best to thoughtfully engage with ideas that Noam Chomsky puts forward even if some of us don't agree with any or all of them.

Chomsky actually insists that his activism, his political philosophy, and linguistics are inextricably connected. One of his major ideas in the field of linguistics sure does sound like a broadly applicable philosophy: linguistic universals, chiefly universal grammar. Chomsky believes that there is innate, or a priori knowledge, built into the human brain that is not dependent on one's native language, and that it manifests as a universal grammar one can identify in all human languages. This universal grammar enables human beings to have a shared understanding of things even as we may express things quite differently in French, Fijian, or Finnish Sign Language.

Some of us who know or are learning other languages may question if that's true to our experience, but to give an illustrative example, most would agree that hunger is a natural sensation universal to all human beings. Our body tells us that we need to eat, and because that's so basic, all languages must have a way to relay that information. In English, we say "I am hungry," which sounds ridiculous to speakers of other languages—hunger is hopefully temporary, so why would we express hungriness as if it's an integral or immutable part of our identity? Other languages would say "I have hunger," or even "hunger is upon me," while in American Sign Language, one visually signals an empty upper digestive tract. All of these manners of expression are certainly different and might contribute to different relationships with hunger, but in this case most of us would likely agree with Chomsky that the meaning of hunger is universal even if its expression is not. Even if we don't know anywhere near the majority of the world's languages, we would probably still feel safe betting that hunger is more or less the same around the world.

But where are the limits? We know that many cultures have conceptual words that are generally agreed to be "untranslatable," though we of course try. This is actually one of the great challenges in Jewish learning—working with ancient texts, ancient knowledge, ancient language . . . and trying to find a way to express it in modern terms, navigating modern sensibilities.

---

3. As quoted by Ahmed N. Mabruk, reporting for *The Harvard Crimson* on a debate between the two.

But what about those difficult-to-define things that do at least seem universal... like peace, fairness, friendship, love?

Chomsky famously debated our old friend—perhaps frenemy, Foucault on topics of power, justice, and human nature. Foucault questioned whether there was such a thing as an unchanging notion of "justice" or "injustice", arguing instead that our understanding of these concepts is a product of the kinds of societies we live in.

Chomsky disagreed with this so fervently that he interrupted Foucault during their debate to say:

> "I think that there is ... some sort of an absolute basis, ultimately residing in fundamental human qualities, in terms of which a real notion of justice is grounded."[4]

He further argued that while existing justice systems embody all manner of injustices, they are "groping towards" an ideal of universal, true human justice.

This theme of universality also shows up in his critiques and prescriptions with regards to political power. Chomsky holds that the ethical standards that an actor applies to himself should be the same as he is willing to see all other actors in a system act out, and that he should in practice allow them to act out. He argues that we engage in elaborate rhetorical choreography to justify a lopsided view of justice, whether in our favor or to the disadvantage of others.

He says that the American political system, for example, is chiefly concerned with preserving the financial interests of corporations, and as such the options that voters are given at the ballot box are largely superficial. Instead of being presented substantive options, political discourse tends to obsess about language and small details—which serve only as a distraction—rather than focus on the matters that deeply address our national pursuits. Globally and historically, Chomsky claims, the ruling class limits the political options of democracy by concocting language to define their financial interests as a moral baseline that is unquestionably legitimate.

He gives the example of what is referred to as "the Responsibility to Protect" doctrine. In 2005, the United Nations adopted it as a political principle, defined as an ethical mandate for the international community to take action to prevent genocide, war crimes, ethnic cleansing, and crimes against humanity wherever they may be happening. Sounds reasonable, doesn't it?

Surely, Chomsky isn't in favor of crimes against humanity? And that's precisely the point: the language adopted by the UN is too vague and

---

4. An excerpt from their 1971 debate, viewable on YouTube.

inscrutable to be clearly actionable, but whatever actions are taken in pursuit of it are given the appearance of being morally cleansed in public imagination. NATO's bombing of Serbia in 1999 was billed as a way of mediating the crisis in Kosovo, but this contrasts significantly with what the average person typically imagines humanitarian intervention to be, like feeding starving children. Furthermore, why would the Responsibility to Protect be invoked to legitimate intervention in Serbia but not in similar or worse crises in Africa? Where and when the international community chooses to act in the name of humanitarianism, it is often the case, Chomsky argues, that it does so only to protect its financial interests.

> "Nothing serious is contemplated about the worst catastrophe in Africa, if not the world: Eastern Congo, where ... multinationals are once again being accused of violating a UN resolution against illicit trade of valuable minerals and thus funding the murderous conflict ... there is no thought of invoking even the most innocuous prescriptions of [the Responsibility to Protect] to respond to massive starvation in the poor countries. The UN recently estimated that the number of those facing hunger has passed a billion, while the World Food Program of the UN has just announced major cutbacks of aid because the rich countries are reducing their meager contributions, giving priority to bailing out banks ... years ago UNICEF reported that 16,000 children die every day from lack of food, many more from easily preventable disease. The figures are higher now. In southern Africa alone it is Rwanda-level killing, not for 100 days, but every day."[5]

At first glance, it might seem that Chomsky's basic idea about ethical universalism is perfectly Jewish. After all, didn't Hillel the Elder famously summarize the Torah as "that which is hateful to you, do not do to another?"[6] Yes, and the end of that quote that often gets left out is a command to go study Torah. And that is where we find some complexity, if not complication.

For example, Chomsky's pacifism[7] might be noble to a significant extent, Judaism is different from some other religions in that while we are forbidden from taking the life of another person under most circumstances, if we know that another is setting out to kill us, we have a duty to kill him

---

5. Excerpted from lecture given at UN General Assembly in 2009, readable on his website.
6. Babylonian Talmud, Shabbat 31a.
7. Al Jazeera English, *Noam Chomsky on the War Against ISIL | UpFront*.

in order to prevent our own demise. While the language most of us know this by is in the Gemara[8], it comes from a passage in the Torah[9] that says, essentially, that one isn't liable for killing a home invader, with the presumption that anyone entering your home with the purpose to steal must also be willing to maim or murder you to get his way.

It's difficult to comprehend an ethic that says we must do nearly anything to save a life—including, in situations of self-defense, potentially taking the life of another. But the Torah is fine-tuned to shades of grey Chomsky is not a fan of. However, it's not a language game for the Torah. There are real exceptions, or sites of nuance, that are necessary for an ethical system to be truly ethical.

In many places in the Rabbinic literature, as well as in other scholarship, we have tried for thousands of years to accept what might seem like contradiction. With one midrash in Exodus Rabbah[10], the Sages take up the task of reconciling the contradictions of Torah—and of human life—by citing the giving of the Torah, "all at once." Birth and death happen all at once, sickness and healing in the same moment, and so too do we find situations where the right thing in one context inevitably contradicts appropriate behavior in another. One example they give is that of yibbum—in that very long section in Leviticus listing out all of the people you're not supposed to have sexual relations with, one of those people is your brother's wife. But if he happens to be your older brother, and he unfortunately leaves behind a childless widow, we know that Levirate marriage is viewed as a real act of justice in that it is seen as enabling the deceased husband to have a child through his brother.

There are even more direct examples of hierarchies, if not actual contradiction, within ethics that seem like contradictions in practice. Jews aren't supposed to eat pork. Jews aren't supposed to eat on Yom Kippur. Those are the sort of basic laws that are so obvious that gentiles will sometimes castigate Jews who don't hold by them. Yet Jewish law spells out in fine detail how exactly to go about eating pork on Yom Kippur—if you're pregnant and feel an overwhelming, unyielding need to eat some.[11] This isn't hypocrisy. This is a reflection of our valuing of life over any number of other values, even strong values that relate to communal cohesion.

We don't always hold everyone in our community to the same standards because people have different abilities, different needs, and unique

---

8. Babylonian Talmud, Mishnah Sanhedrin 72a.
9. Exodus 22:1.
10. Exodus Rabbah 28:4.
11. Babylonian Talmud, Yoma 82a.

relationships with the Divine, even as we share a larger Covenant with generalized norms.

One of the interesting features of Torah law is that even though it is designed for a particular people, it also provides a simplified legal system for other peoples in the Noahide Laws. The seven commandments, and all the details that would be incorporated within them, can be seen as a universal morality of sorts. While Jews in traditional communities may need to take time out of their day to make sure a new sweater wasn't made with a forbidden mixture of fibers and to diligently search out and destroy all chametz ahead of Passover, the non-Jewish nations are told: no murder, no stealing, no eating the flesh of an animal while it is still alive, no blasphemy, no sexual immorality, no idol worship . . . and everyone must establish courts. The definitions of some of these prohibitions are debated within the Jewish tradition and it is obvious that there are cultures in the world that do not see some of these prohibitions as problematic. But they can still serve as a baseline for how we might conceive of justice and morality for all human beings.

Jewish law seems far more comfortable with expressing universality with respect to "*lo taaseh*" (prohibitions), as can even be seen in the statement of Hillel the Elder "that which is hateful to you, do not do to another." But even within that, we know there are exceptions. Perhaps underneath the complexities of law, there is some sort of universal truth that we, as humans, can only grope our way towards, though it remains to be seen whether it is what Chomsky thinks of as justice.

41

Jacques Derrida (1930–2004)

JACQUES DERRIDA IS ANOTHER philosopher who was born Jewish, in French Algeria in 1930. Derrida was definitely within the post-structuralist and post-modern camps, but he distanced himself from those worlds. The main critique of Derrida is that he is deliberately difficult to understand.

His famous idea is the philosophy of deconstruction, "a way of criticizing not only both literary and philosophical texts but also political institutions," and in doing so, it "attempts to render justice. Indeed, deconstruction is relentless in this pursuit since justice is impossible to achieve."[1]

In the words of philosopher Mark C. Taylor:

> The guiding insight of deconstruction is that every structure—be it literary, psychological, social, economic, political or religious—that organizes our experience is constituted and maintained through acts of exclusion. In the process of creating something, something else inevitably gets left out.[2]

What Derrida was doing was attacking reason's pretensions to provide systematic and absolute explanations of the world. Whereas many thought language accurately depicted reality, Derrida saw this as something of an illusion, a fact which could be discerned when one carefully examined the meaning of texts. By looking at them closely, deconstruction showed how texts cannot offer any clear and unambiguous meaning and any attempt to claim that they do always requires repressing other possibilities or making claims to authority that cannot be justified. Derrida's famous quote here is "There's nothing outside the text." Texts, for Derrida, cannot tell us some

1. Lawlor, *Jacques Derrida*.
2. Taylor, *What Derrida Really Meant*.

outside world truth. They just tell us about the texts themselves, and even then, their meaning is far more open than it is closed.

To Derrida, there is no stable way to talk about truth as it emerges from language; language is inadequate to express truth in any absolute sense. However, the illusion that language can express unambiguous truths is at the heart of what Derrida calls the metaphysics of presence. Since its very beginning, philosophy has aspired to make unambiguous claims about human beings, the world, and the nature of existence. For Derrida, such claims always fall far short of what they promise, particularly when one examines the texts that purport to demonstrate them. As Derrida saw it, every text has contradictions in it, no text is fully coherent, and deconstruction offered a way of trying to read texts while aware of gaps. As a result, it enables one to be skeptical of the kinds of metaphysical claims so often used to perpetuate systems of hierarchy.

Many have noted the similarity between deconstruction and rabbinic hermeneutics such as midrash, which is also deeply sensitive to the way in which texts can offer multiple meanings. However, where deconstruction is often used to undermine claims of authority and power, midrash, on the other hand, uses the inconsistencies and contradictions of texts as a license to fill in the gaps and expand the meaning of the text. For us, contradictions are generative. We don't say a story is nonsensical because aspects of it contradict each other and simply dismiss it out of hand. Instead, we see contradictions as being there to teach us something. With regards to the Torah and its apparent contradictions, Rav Kook said it best[3]:

> We as yet do not know the specific nature of prophecy and divine inspiration, nor do we even know if it can be that there are no contradictions in prophetic and divinely inspired sayings, as is the case in well-reasoned lectures, for perhaps the phenomenon which is beyond our comprehension is also beyond our conditions for perfection, and all its contradictions are in harmony on some level, in no need of reasoned solutions. Nature does not fear contradictions, as does science, since it is incalculably greater than science. This is faith's majesty ...[4]

As "people of the book," we accept that language certainly can't convey everything, but we know that language *can* be the clothing of truth, and perhaps the only way we can approach it. While language can't fully describe God, we cannot turn to God in prayer if we cannot address God by name.

---

3. *The Letters of Rabbi Abraham Isaac HaCohen Kook*, letter 478, 108.
4. Goodman, *The Last Words of Moses*, xxxvii.

There is a saying from Rav Tzadok of Lublin: "I heard in my youth that HaKadosh Baruch Hu created a book, and that book is the world. And the Torah is a commentary on that book."[5]

When we find contradictions in a text, we have many choices or interpretive moves. We could say the two contradictory verses are actually saying the same thing. We can suggest that the two verses are each teaching something new and here too not contradicting each other at all. Or we can say a new meaning emerges from a real contradiction. In any case, for a student of Torah, contradictions expand our engagement rather than limit us.

In the Jewish tradition, we allow texts to relate to each other across locations and generations. We understand Maimonides in relationship to Nachmanides, and Nachmanides in relationship to the Talmud. No text gives us the perfect truth, but each one potentially points us to another text. That's the greatness of Jewish learning it's always pointing us to other texts and the meaning of one can only be discerned in relation to all of them.

In deconstructing a text, you are not invalidating it as much as going deeper into its discovery and seeing how incomplete it is without complementary works. To be sure, Derrida certainly doesn't think the text itself can give us access to some absolute truth, in part because the text is inherently incomplete and in part due to the limitations of language. Jews, on the other hand, are more committed to truth as can be found in language.

This is especially relevant in the realm of prayer. Rabbi Dr. Alan Brill recounted Rav Shagar's use of Derrida in this respect:

> Rav Shagar acknowledges that for many their prayers are without benefit or hope. To offer a path of continuing to pray despite this lack of hope, he finds a parallel to Derrida's prayer as without hope in which Derrida nevertheless says despite the despair and lack of hope, there is always a possibility of that one may be answered.
> ... Shagar equates Derrida's prayer without hope to Rebbe Nachman's Void, the Halal Ha-Panui, which is seemingly empty without hope. However, according to Shagar, prayer has the possibility to cut through the void. In addition, God must be in His seeming absence. Not because of a holism in which everything is God, rather because there is always the possibility of breaking through the void. In the meantime, prayer is an impossibility, yet we still pray.[6]

Yes, language has its limits. But, whether in text or in speech, we have no better tool.

---

5. See YouTube: Joey Rosenfeld, *Book of Redemption 13: Zohar Introduction*.
6. Brill, *Prayer without Hoping- Rav Shagar*.

42

Daniel Dennett (1942–current)

THE 21ST CENTURY SAW the rise of what some call the "New Atheism," a movement characterized by a markedly lower tolerance for religion, especially religion that attempted to impose its values or beliefs through politics.[1] The phrase "New Atheism" was coined by journalist Gary Wolf in a 2006 article for *Wired*, where he profiled the thinkers "mounting a crusade against God."[2] Although it may seem like a counterintuitive topic for Jewish exploration, here we will be exploring one of the "four horsemen of the new atheism," Daniel Dennett. The other three horsemen might be slightly more familiar to us: Richard Dawkins, Sam Harris, and the late Christopher Hitchens.[3] But we'll be focusing on Dennett.

Born in 1942, Daniel Dennett is an American natural philosopher with an interdisciplinary approach—using evolutionary biology and cognitive psychology to understand the philosophy of the mind.[4] He is an extremely vocal atheist and secularist.

By way of definitions, *atheism* is generally defined as a lack of belief in God. However, many atheists do not go so far as to deny God exists, simply that they lack belief.[5] Nevertheless, the *new atheism*, as championed by Dennett and company, tends to be less tentative and assertively argues that

---

1. Hooper, *The Rise of the New Atheists*.
2. Wolf, *The Church of Nonbelievers*.
3. Poole, *The Four Horseman review – whatever happened to the 'New Atheism.'*
4. Encyclopedia Britannica, *Daniel C. Dennett*.
5. American Atheists, *What is Atheism?*

all religions are false.[6] *Secularism* is the principle of separating the state from religious institutions and beliefs.

Dennett's atheism and secularism are far more than merely personal beliefs. As of 2017 he was a member of the Secular Coalition for America advisory board and a member of the Committee for Skeptical Inquiry, as well as an outspoken supporter of the Brights movement,[7] which asserts that all public policy should be based on science alone.[8] One of Dennett's most famously held positions is that religion is simply the result of *evolutionary biology*, meaning it is the product of our evolutionary needs and not evidence of God. Evolutionary biology largely refers to the study of the evolutionary processes, for example natural selection, that resulted in diversity of life on earth. It attempts to evaluate human physiology and behavior by exploring how they might have assisted human beings to survive over the course of millennia.

Of particular interest for us will be his views on the mind and free will. In philosophy, the question of *free will* refers to a millennia-long discourse over whether humans have the ability to act freely and what the moral implications of that freedom (or lack of it) might be.[9] Free will is generally seen as opposed to *determinism,* which asserts that all events including human decisions are inevitable.[10] (In religious terms, we might call this fate.)

As you might expect, Dennett believes that morality, like religion, is just another product of humanity's evolutionary needs. However, he is not a relativist and is critical of post-modernism and their overall skepticism toward truth. A quote from Dennett:

> Postmodernism, the school of "thought" that proclaimed "There are no truths, only interpretations" has largely played itself out in absurdity, but it has left behind a generation of academics in the humanities disabled by their distrust of the very idea of truth and their disrespect for evidence, settling for "conversations" in which nobody is wrong and nothing can be confirmed.[11]

Indeed, Dennett has nothing if not respect for facts, at least scientific ones. Viewing human nature through an evolutionary lens, he identifies as an *adaptationist* and believes that many but not all of our human traits

6. Encyclopedia Britannica, *Daniel C. Dennett.*
7. Institute of Art and Ideas, *Daniel Dennett.*
8. The Brights, *Who Are the Brights?*
9. O'Connor and Franklin, *Free Will.*
10. Encyclopedia Britannica, *Determinism.*
11. Dennett, *Dennett on Wieseltier V. Pinker in The New Republic Let's Start with a Respect for Truth.*

are the result of evolutionary adaptions. However, this is distinct from the now outmoded *pan-adaptationism*, which argues that all (not just many) of our human traits are the result of evolutionary adaptations. In evolutionary biology, *adaptation* refers to the adjustments of organisms to their environment in order to improve their chances of survival; adaptations are passed down to the next generation; this is part of *natural selection*.[12] For example, the fact that today's human immune genes reflect an evolution based on which genetic variations were able to survive the Bubonic Plague in the mid-1300s.[13]

Now we may return to the concept of free will versus determinism, a question that for Dennett is decided by the extent to which our behaviors are influenced by our genetics and their long evolutionary history or whether we have the freedom to choose for ourselves. In this debate, Dennett embraces free will. Get ready for another -ism: Dennett is a proponent of *Compatibilism*, which means he believes that free will and determinism aren't at odds, but rather are compatible with one another. There is a pathway, he believes, in which we can be coherent and not inconsistent while embracing both. While our genetics may produce certain constraints for how we can act, within those constraints, human beings can use reason to choose different outcomes. He has argued that humans alone among the animals have evolved minds that give us free will and therefore moral responsibility.[14] For a Jewish source that articulates a similar idea to compatibilism, although in a decidedly non-atheistic fashion, we might turn to Pirkei Avot:

"Everything is foreseen yet freedom of choice is granted."[15] Meaning, God foresees all that we will do, nonetheless, we are still free to do it. How responsible are we if we don't embrace our free will? The Torah's radical insight is that all humans are deeply responsible for themselves, their family, the community, and the world at large. We aren't let off the hook.

To be fair, even though Dennett embraces a naturalism and determinism that suggests we are not at all as free as we think we are, that doesn't mean responsibility goes out the window. He argues that people want to be held responsible because being deemed responsible gives them social status and privilege. When you don't act responsibly you lose your job, lose

---

12. National Geographic, *Adaptation*.

13. Klunk, Vilgalys, Demeure, et al., *Evolution of Immune Genes is Associated with the Black Death*.

14. Dennett and Caruso, *Just Deserts*.

15. Pirkei Avot 3:15.

your license, or go to jail but when you do act responsibly you get a raise or receive social praise.

Dennett seeks to develop a philosophy of the mind that is rooted in *empirical evidence*, meaning, evidence gathered through scientific observation. In a way, Dennett advocates for bridging philosophy with the sciences—that empirical research shouldn't be left solely to the sciences, but rather that it has a place in the philosophical realm where we talk about the nature of life, the mind, and human experience. Much of his work concerns consciousness. As an atheist, he believes there is nothing beyond the brain. There is no external God; nor is there an internal soul. And if it turns out there is a soul, Dennett has said, he believes it will be explained by science and evolution: "There ain't no magic there," he said to the *New Yorker* in an interview on the topic. "Just stage magic."[16]

One of his most controversial moves is to deny the existence of *qualia*, a term that philosophers use to refer to our subjective experiences of personal consciousness, such as the smell of perfume, the pain of a headache, the colors of a sunset. Qualia are at the heart of many theories of consciousness, because they often describe a relationship between the outer world and inner experience. Dennett doesn't deny people experience pain or see colors, but he rejects the idea that qualia exist as some sort of purely subjective experience apart from reality.[17] He believes we have all the scientific tools to measure and assess all aspects of human consciousness that may exist. However, countless neuroscientists push back on his claim. And for good reason! Just because I can't see your subjective experiences, it is absurd for me to assume that you don't have them.[18] In fact, one could argue that Dennett fundamentally misunderstands the basis of science and proof—that as you can't reject qualia[19] without evidence to reject it. One needs evidence to prove something exists but also one needs evidence to prove something definitively does not exist. That said, Dennett may overstate his claims, but he does have a lot to offer us in terms of bridging disciplines, and in particular, making a bridge for empirical research to enter the philosophical realm.

---

16. Rothman, *Daniel Dennett's Science of the Soul*.
17. Dennett, *Consciousness in Contemporary Science*.
18. See for example Ramachandran, V.S. and Hirstein, W., "Three laws of qualia: what neurology tells us about the biological functions of consciousness", *Journal of Consciousness Studies*, Volume 4, Numbers 5-6, 429-457.
19. One might say differently that Dennett isn't denying that experiences defined by others as qualia exist but that he is saying those experiences are objective ones and based on reality.

There's a real parallel here with the Talmud, where some halachic positions are rooted purely in abstract legal thought, while other positions are rooted in social reality. Interestingly, there are famous instances in the Talmud where a dispute is resolved by the rabbis saying, *Puk hazei mai ama davar*, essentially, "Go out and see what the people are doing."[20] In such a case, abstract theory means little, and the halacha is to be decided by the empirical behavior of the people. In one such case, the rabbis were unsure as to what blessing should be made after one drinks water. So, they instructed that one must check and see how people currently act in regard to this question. We need halakha that takes into account both the theoretical and the sociological. Something would be empty about Talmudic discourse if the primary lens were sociological; yet, something would also be missing if the law were completely detached from human experience.

In a similar vein, we need both science and religion/philosophy in order to fully describe the world. Most of us probably feel in our hearts that the question of the soul, for example, can never be resolved through empirical data. Rabbi Adin Even-Israel Steinsaltz says on this matter:

> After many generations of observation, it is generally accepted that the soul is located in the brain. However, scientists and philosophers, as well as other thinking people, know that this sort of definition is merely convenient shorthand and not really a description. Even those who locate the soul in the heart or brain know that these organs are pieces of flesh. They are, at best, points of contact with the soul, but do not constitute the soul itself.[21]

From what I have read, it seems to me that as Rabbi Steinsaltz is asserting that there is some immaterial part of the self which seems to be beyond the physical. The best academics—the stars of the scientific community—include a lot of people who would seem to agree with Rabbi Steinsaltz. Take for example the scientist Francis Collins, former director of the Human Genome Project, who is quite outspoken about his belief in God, and recognizes there can exist things beyond human understanding.[22]

Rabbi Jonathan Sacks, of blessed memory, noted some of the limitations of science in his book on morality:

> ... there is something intrinsically dehumanizing in the scientific mindset that operates in detachment, driven by analysis, the

---

20. See for example Babylonian Talmud Berachot 45a and Eruvin 14.
21. Steinsaltz, *The Soul*, 4.
22. Horgan, *One of the World's Most Powerful Scientists Believes in Miracles*.

breaking down of wholes to their component parts. The focus is not on the particular—this man, that woman, this child—but on the universal. Science per se has no space for empathy or fellow feeling. That is not a critique of science, but it is an insistence that science is not the sum total of our understanding of humanity.[23]

That Dennett completely rejects the value of subjective experience is a little confounding. It's interesting that he himself is not an academically trained scientist, and yet many working scientists actually embrace the mystery and humility of what is beyond our comprehension. You might say they keep science in its own lane about what it can prove and disprove.

Conversely, we can really understand Dennett's frustration with religious individuals who completely reject science, and instead insist that religious belief should shape public policy. Many religious fundamentalists insist that God will protect us even as scientists are telling us that it is humans who need to take direct action. Just look at climate change: No one can, in good faith, brush off the conclusive science regarding how human actions are making the planet uninhabitable. Climate change is real. Science is real. Our discussion on implications of Dennett's claims should not suggest otherwise.

What I am asserting, rather, is that religion can respect science and vice versa. Rather than viewing them as in battle or in tension, we can view science and religion as in collaboration. I personally embrace both the science of evolution and the creation story of Genesis. You can read Genesis as a creation story offering spiritual and moral lessons, as opposed to a scientific history of the universe. It's possible to fully embrace both as true, and many thinkers do. Francis Collins, the geneticist I mentioned before, has said, "The God of the Bible is also the God of the genome."[24] He's a Christian. From the world of Jewish thought, Daniel C. Matt, the brilliant translator of the Zohar, wrote a book called *God and the Big Bang*, which finds points of overlap between science and spirituality—examining how physics and Jewish mysticism can mutually illuminate one another.[25]

One of the most powerful examples of a Jew who embraced religion and science is the Rambam, who as well as being one of the great minds of Jewish thought was also a working physician who treated patients. Much of his writing bridges the gap between disciplines. In his *Guide for the Perplexed*, the Rambam outlines a "negative theology," which essentially states

---

23. Sacks, *Morality: Restoring the Common Good in Divided Times*, 231.
24. Horgan, *One of the World's Most Powerful Scientists Believes in Miracles*.
25. Matt, *God and the Big Bang: Discovering Harmony Between Science & Spirituality*.

that it is impossible to assert anything positive about God because of the limits of our human comprehension; rather we can only understand by ruling out what God is not.[26] This is an almost-empirical approach to theology. It also feels possible that the Rambam's pursuits as a doctor may have informed his approach to Jewish wisdom. For him, treating patients and tending to the soul was not a contradiction, and the fact that he saw them as complimentary in and of itself is a kind of refutation of Dennett.

That said, I don't think Jews—or anyone—should outright reject atheists who land in places like Dennett. Even if such thinkers overstate their claims as Dennett does, they are not threats to society, presuming they have a moral framework that enables them to know right from wrong. Rather, we must remember that all philosophy throughout time has had blind spots, and that Dennett's emphasis on studying the mind and consciousness is worth learning from.

One of the great frontiers of consciousness is of course AI, Artificial Intelligence. You might imagine that Dennett would embrace AI, since he seems to view people as machines to some degree—with nothing beyond the physical. However, it turns out that Dennett is actually deeply concerned by AI. He fears we may come to misunderstand the systems of artificial intelligence, and start to think that AI possesses their own intellectual power as if they were human. He warns that companies using AI to create "counterfeit people" are eroding the trust that makes civilization possible: "These counterfeit people are the most dangerous artifacts in human history, capable of destroying not just economies but human freedom itself."[27]

Asking what makes humans different from AI is a very Jewish question. One of the great interests of Torah scholars is what makes humans different from animals? From angels? From God? And now we can add to that, what makes humans different from the most advanced machines? For those of us that embrace the uniqueness of each person's internal experience and their soul, we may view technology and machine learning as useful, but understand that it is in no way a replacement for or superior to human capability.

As we continue to explore new realms of consciousness in the expanding field of AI, it's clear now more than ever that science cannot dismiss the soul. We must all think carefully about how to safely and responsibly integrate AI into the society we want to live in—one that acknowledges the sanctity of each human.

---

26. Navon, *Intro to the Guide of the Perplexed: Negative Attributes.*
27. Dennett, *The Problem with Counterfeit People.*

Dennett's ideas may not directly intersect with Jewish traditional thought but he offers a smart springboard for further conversation to deepen our sophistication on significant theological and philosophical issues.

43

Peter Singer (1946–Present)

ARE HUMAN LIVES WORTH more than animal lives? Is someone who spends $5,000 on a vacation morally guilty for not using that money to save someone's life? Should we rethink our entire system of living in order to maximize the wellbeing of all living creatures?

Born to a Jewish family in Australia, Peter Singer is one of the great living philosophers. He recently retired as a professor of bioethics at Princeton, and in addition to being distinguished within the world of academia, he is also well-known as a public intellectual. One reason for this is that he has devoted significant energy towards writing for a popular audience, not just an academic one. But also, his work deals with issues of great concern to all of our lives.

Singer is a fervent utilitarian, though he's evolved in the nuances of the utilitarianism he espouses. Early in his career, Singer was a "preference utilitarian" which held that "actions are right if they maximize the satisfaction of preferences or desires, no matter what the preferences may be for." [1]

However, this philosophy is controversial because people can have preferences of many different kinds, including things many would consider immoral. If harming another would give one greater pleasure than the pain caused, under preference utilitarianism this would be allowed. Singer later changed his view to "hedonistic utilitarianism," which argues that "the right action is the one that produces (or is most likely to produce) the greatest net happiness for all concerned." [2]

---

1. Encyclopedia Britannica, *Preference Utilitarianism*.
2. Internet Encyclopedia of Philosophy, *Hedonism*.

This approach helped make Singer a leading philosophical proponent of animal rights. In his 1975 book *Animal Liberation*, he made the first strong philosophical case for animal rights. He argued that in maximizing the greatest net happiness, we must also take into consideration the suffering of animals. Animal rights[3], we see, are a natural consequence of utilitarianism. If we truly want to minimize suffering on a mass level, and not just for human beings, the cruelty that so many animals endure must absolutely be taken into account.

It should be to no one's surprise that Jewish texts can be found to support this view. However, the Jewish tradition has tended to focus on defending animal welfare rather than promoting a narrower understanding of "animal rights." This is to say that, while the Torah doesn't have a clear notion of "animal liberation," it provides clear injunctions to reduce the suffering of animals that are put to human use.

For example, we read in the Book of Deuteronomy: "You shall not muzzle an ox while it is threshing."[4] The reason for this is that, if an animal is being made to work for you, it must also be able to eat.

While human beings may have a right to use animals, there is still a moral concern for them that must be respected. While there is a distinction between animal welfare and human welfare, they exist on the same level as possessing the value of being living creatures that God intentionally created with compassion, even if they differ in that only humans are created in the image of God.

We see that, even though, animals don't have the right to not be eaten, there is still a dignity to them that must be respected. The Torah immediately goes on to explain that, just as animal blood demands our decency, one cannot shed human blood. To be sure, one cannot kill a human because of their dignity as being created in the image of God, not because of any relationship to animal blood, but the blood connection is nonetheless still there. While there is a distinction between animal welfare and human welfare, they exist on the same continuum as possessing the dignity and sanctity of being living creatures, albeit on different levels.

And so, there is a Torah concern for animals, but Singer takes it further. In an email exchange, Singer once told me that not only does he not believe in human dignity being higher than the dignity of animals, he doesn't believe in "human dignity" at all. To state what's probably obvious, Singer doesn't believe in God, so why should he think human beings are

---

3. Singer is clear that he philosophically rejects the notion of "rights" (human rights or animal rights) but that he is okay with the language because he is aligned with the movements in their goals.

4. Deuteronomy 25:4.

created in the image of God? For atheists, the burden is on them to argue why human life is worth more than animal life. His concern is not with the isolated moral concern of dignity but about pain and pleasure at large. To Singer, human suffering is not more important than animal suffering. Or, as he put it decades ago in *Animal Liberation*:

> All the arguments to prove man's superiority cannot shatter this hard fact: in suffering the animals are our equals.[5]

In Judaism, this is not upheld, as it is humanity, specifically, that bears the image of God and the higher levels of the soul. Human life, we see from the Torah, must take precedence over animal life. Although we should be compassionate to animals and treat their suffering as having enormous ethical weight and implications for how we live, in the Jewish tradition, we cannot conflate the dignity of humans with our need to reduce suffering for animals.

These conflicting views between the Torah and Singer's philosophy can make us ask the question: Does one human matter more than two animals? What about 10 million animals? How many animals might we be willing to kill to save one human?

In my engagement with Singer's thought, I not only see animal rights in a different light but also find that his views on how we treat the elderly to be divergent from Jewish values. Because of his rigid insistence on a rational utilitarianism, Singer believes we as a society are spending too much money on keeping people alive at the end of life, when it is clear that the quality-of-life declines so precipitously. Rather than prolong the life of the elderly, Singer claims the ethical thing to do would be to allocate more resources towards saving many more young people.

Famously, when Singer's mother was near the end of her life, his family spent a large amount of money to keep her alive. To his credit, Singer acknowledged that, when it was the case of his family, his ethics demanded a cold utilitarianism that had been too difficult to uphold.

In another area in Singer's thought, I find to be similarly problematic, he makes clear that he does not seem to value the moral concerns of those who have special needs. He believes that society should not devote large amounts of resources to accommodate a small group of people. This is another instance of a clash between Singer's view that we must maximize pleasure and reduce suffering and the Jewish belief that all people are infinitely precious.

---

5. Peter Singer, *Animal Liberation*.

For Singer, "rights" are unimportant; what matters is the wellbeing of the most people. Judaism has to disagree. The Jewish tradition values the dignity of every individual, not the sum total of pleasure experienced by the masses. As the rabbis say:

"Why was Adam, the first human being, created alone? To teach you that one who destroys a soul, the Torah treats it as if one has destroyed an entire world. And conversely, one who saves a soul, the Torah treats it as if one has saved an entire world."[6]

It is also important to know that Singer has long been a driving force in the movement for "effective altruism." In 2022, Gideon Lewis-Kraus explained in *The New Yorker* that effective altruism "takes as its premise that people ought to do good in the most clear-sighted, ambitious, and unsentimental way possible. Among other back-of-the-envelope estimates, E.A.s [effective altruists] believe that a life in the developing world can be saved for about four thousand dollars."[7]

William MacAskill, a young Scottish utilitarian philosopher, explores "long-termism," the notion that future lives may matter more than those currently alive given how many more people will exist in the future. One not only can, but perhaps must, prioritize climate change for future generations to come over current moral needs given how many people are to come! Is it true that future people matter as much as those alive today? If it is so hard to figure out how to do good by those alive today isn't it that much harder to support those not even existing? On the other hand, we certainly can't discount future lives as morally irrelevant. If we drop a glass and don't clean it up, does it matter if it'll hurt someone in 2 minutes, 2 years, or 20 years? Totalitarian regimes often offer short-term benefits but here we are looking at humanity from a longer perspective. Should we be more concerned with helping one million people today or 2 billion in some decades to come? Taking utilitarianism to this next level is not simple.

It is notable the way Singer challenges us to think about philanthropy differently. Singer makes the argument that it is not possible to ethically justify living with luxuries. If you choose to spend your money on unnecessary expenses, you are in effect saying, "I know I can save a life with this money, but instead I choose this luxury." Singer's utilitarianism leads him to believe that, without even intending to harm another, one can be complicit in suffering and death.

In his book *The Life You Can Save: Acting Now to End World Poverty*, Singer even invokes the Jewish tradition to demonstrate that giving one's

---

6. Babylonian Talmud, Mishnah Sanhedrin 4:5.
7. Lewis-Kraus, *The Reluctant Prophet of Effective Altruism*.

money to reduce poverty is not just a good deed—it's a moral obligation. He writes:

> The Hebrew word for "charity" tzedakah, simply means "justice" and as this suggests, for Jews, giving to the poor is no optional extra but an essential part of living a just life. In the Talmud (a record of discussions of Jewish law and ethics by ancient rabbis) it is said that charity is equal in importance to all the other commandments combined, and that Jews should give at least 10% of their income as *tzedakah*.[8]

In general, as Jews, we should grapple with the ideas found in today's "effective altruism" movement. We *do* need to be more careful about directing our *tzedakah* to save lives, rather than just pouring large sums of money into passion projects and luxuries. We *should* be seriously challenged by the levels of luxury we live with. To be sure, we understand as Jews that life is a gift to be celebrated and enjoyed. But that comes with the responsibility of also thinking critically of how we allocate our time and resources toward a higher moral calling.

The life we are given is such a precious thing, and Singer understands that it is incumbent upon us to not waste it, to think carefully about how we can best use the opportunities we have, and to act in a way that is morally reputable. Even if the paths he thinks we should take are often different from the ones I'd endorse, I find Singer asks the questions we must engage with in order to live ethical lives.

---

8. Peter Singer, *The Life You Can Save: Acting Now to End World Poverty*.

44

Martha Nussbaum (1947–Present)

SHOULD THE LAW CARE about our feelings? How do emotions impact individual behaviors, and how does that translate into the function of systems?

Hailed by some as one of the most important philosophers in modernity, and certainly one of the most important woman thinkers of our time, Dr. Martha Nussbaum's work in philosophy has engaged significantly with the Ancient Greeks, Political Philosophy, Feminism, Classics, Existentialism, and ideas about justice. Unsurprisingly, she is the Ernst Freund Distinguished Service Professor of Law and Ethics at the University of Chicago's School of Law, while also holding a joint appointment in the Department of Philosophy, as well as associate faculty roles in Classics, Political Science, and the Divinity School.

Originally, Nussbaum studied theatre before pursuing graduate work in philosophy, receiving her master's and PhD from Harvard. She has since written two dozen books and received the Kyoto Prize, Berggruen Prize, Balzan Prize, and more than sixty honorary doctorates from universities around the world.

Also of note, while Dr. Nussbaum was born in 1947 to a Protestant family in New York City, she converted to Judaism and is now an active member of KAM Israel's congregation and choir in Chicago, and I am grateful for her influence on and participation in my own life, notably: a talk she gave in 2004 is what prompted me to give up meat, and I was privileged to conduct a video interview with her a couple of years ago.

Dr. Nussbaum, while continuing to contribute throughout the breadth of the world of philosophy with an emphasis on ethics, is perhaps best known for her work with what is called a neo-Aristotelian capabilities approach. Rather than emphasize abstract rights, it instead focuses on the capabilities that are unique to being human by asking the question, ""What are people actually able to do and to be?" This approach revises common understandings of freedom to reflect the quality of possibilities an individual has: can someone who technically has the freedom of acquiring food reasonably act on that choice? If she does act on that choice, can she choose to do so in a way that leaves her more substantially nourished, perhaps even more morally nourished, or even simply nourished in a way that makes her happier? If she can't make a meaningful choice in this regard, what mechanisms does she have at her disposal to move herself into a position of choice in the matter–if she's interested in one?

Nussbaum defines ten capabilities that are required for human life to be "not so impoverished that it is not worthy of the dignity of a human being."[1] These are broad categories that include: life; bodily health; bodily integrity; senses, imagination and thought; emotions; practical reason; affiliation; the choice to meaningfully interact with other species when it's mutually agreeable; play; and control over one's environment.[2]

While this approach in and of itself can feel quite revelatory to how we might evaluate if human rights are flourishing or not, what's even more philosophically astounding is her application of this thought to non-human animals. Rejecting anthropocentric lines of animal defense that we should focus on protecting animals who are like us in terms of intelligence, or more utilitarian notions that we should at least be more sensitive to the lives of animals who we glean some sort of value from, she instead views each animal as an end, insisting that we should protect animals for what they are, in and of themselves. Her defense of animal rights is an extension of the capabilities approach she applies to humans. Just as humans have specific capabilities that enable their lives to flourish, so too the same can be determined for animals. With regards to animals that have historically had a great deal of human interaction, opportunities for intervention can be quite nuanced including everything from personal diet to legislation, while she suggests that with wildlife our best angle for support is environmental stewardship.[3]

Much of her philosophical work has revolved around questions of emotion and law, particularly the roles of human emotions, such as shame and disgust. While disgust may be a powerful emotion, she cautions that

---

1. Nussbaum, *Women and Human Development: The Capabilities Approach.*
2. Kleist, *Global Ethics: Capabilities Approach.*
3. She discussed these ideas during our interview on human rights and animal rights.

it is often rooted in irrational concerns. She says in her 2004 work *Hiding From Humanity*[4]:

> Disgust ... is very different from anger, in that its thought-content is typically unreasonable, embodying magical ideas of contamination, and impossible aspirations to purity, immortality, and non-animality, that are just not in line with human life as we know it. That does not mean that disgust did not play a valuable role in our evolution; very likely it did. Nor does it mean that it does not play a useful function in our current daily lives; very likely it does. Perhaps even the function of hiding from us problematic aspects of our humanity is useful; perhaps we cannot easily live with too much vivid awareness of the fact that we are made of sticky and oozy substances that will all too soon decay.

She goes on to argue that even with the potential usefulness of feelings of disgust, we should reject it as a basis for lawmaking, particularly because it "has been used throughout history to exclude and marginalize groups or people who come to embody the dominant group's fear and loathing of its own animality and mortality."[5] Throughout the corpus of her writings, she focuses on how notions of disgust have been used to oppress women, Jews, and homosexuals.

In her 2010 book *From Disgust to Humanity*, she specifically analyzes "the politics of disgust" with reference to legislation against homosexual marriage, relationships, and acts. Ultimately, she argues that in the realm of political thought, societies are better and more ethically served by functioning in line with the Harm Principle forwarded by John Stuart Mill, as opposed to seeking to codify feelings.

While rabbinic literature is filled with emotions that interact with texts and religious laws in a variety of ways, the Torah itself does not always clarify the role of human emotion in particular scenarios. While Nussbaum doesn't see the value of disgust within law, here we will see a case in the Torah where disgust can play a morally constructive role.

The case of the Eishat Yifat To'ar[6], the beautiful captive woman, is found in the 21st chapter of Deuteronomy, following the laws of the egla arufa–the process by which city elders atone for the death of a person whose body is found beyond their boundaries. The Torah introduces circumstances of war that were common historically and, unfortunately, are not unheard

---

4. Nussbaum, *Hiding From Humanity: Disgust, Shame, and the Law*.
5. Nussbaum, *Hiding From Humanity: Disgust, Shame, and the Law*.
6. Deuteronomy 21:10-14.

of in modern conflicts: a Jewish man, in the hormonal and emotional milieu of military victory, sees an enemy woman, finds her beautiful, and abducts her. The Torah does not condone his actions, but stipulates that, if he is to do this, he must bring her into his home, crop her hair, pare her nails, and discard her captive's garb. He must then allow her to observe a full month of mourning for her parents. Only after this is the soldier permitted to have her as a wife in every sense. If, following all of this, he rejects her, he must let her go free–entirely free–rather than selling her as a slave.

What is the Torah trying to achieve? Many traditional commentaries are firm in the assertion that the Torah is trying to prevent intermarriage–this woman is clearly an idol worshiper, and while the soldier might think that he is in control, she will use her charms to subvert his spiritual quest. Rashi goes so far as to say that the "captive's garb" is actually a seductive outfit she wore into battle for the purpose of luring an enemy soldier astray.[7]

Much of the interpretation of this text is meant to evoke feelings of disgust–whether this process is imagined as a way to "make" the woman physically repulsive to the man, or to help him see that she is spiritually disgusting.

Rabbi Ari Mermelstein analyzes how disgust is given form in the midrashic tradition surrounding Eishat Yifat To'ar, comparing her to "a gourd, a piece of dead meat, or rotten food."[8] (The gourd metaphor might fall a little flat in a world where people set pumpkins on their steps as a seasonal decoration, but it is nonetheless a deeply dehumanizing image.)

But this is all rabbinic conjecture. The Torah tells us that the man feels desire for her when he first captures the beautiful woman, but the only emotions we see after belong to her. For a full month, she is in full-fledged *aveilut*, in the house of her captor and she mourns and grieves the loss of her family. Even though she has been kidnapped, a violation of any number of her rights by modern standards, the Torah forces her captor to let her be in grief; Nussbaum refers to the capabilities of emotion, grief being one of the most profound among them. "When we love people," she says, "often there's loss and the grief that acknowledges that loss, I think, is a way of acknowledging the depth and importance of that love."[9]

Grief is something we typically share only in our most intimate relationships. It can be ugly–uncontrollable crying, running out of things to blow one's nose and dry one's eyes on, and occasionally some horrific

---

7. Rashi on Deuteronomy 10:13.

8. Mermelstein, *Beauty or Beast? The Pedagogical Function of Metaphor and Emotion in Midrashim on the Law of the Lovely Captive.*

9. A quote from our interview on human rights and animal rights.

wailing. And we might imagine that a woman who has been taken away from her people by force-who certainly must think that her loved ones are dead-has grief that goes to the marrow.

And the captor must endure this, must honor this, must provide space for this strange woman, as she mourns in his home the very enemies he sought to defeat.

Perhaps he will see her as disgusting in all of this- for it is often the case that we find others' grief to be unnerving. Even more so, perhaps he will find himself disgusting, in realizing the impact of his actions in warfare, in seeing that even idolators are human.

The Torah takes this woman who is painted as a moral enemy, and nonetheless defends some portion of her bodily integrity and her human dignity against a man's impulses. If the prescription is not morally generative for the imagined soldier, then it certainly has the potential to be for us, as we consider the reality that our whims and desires do not dictate rights or realities in the religious imagination-we are beholden to The Other. The Torah will not fully legitimate our desire to crush the enemy and see them as inhuman. Therefore, it forces us to confront the pain and grief of the other.

As we see in this case, and surely in many others from our own lives, trying to develop rules around anything related to the subjectivity of emotions is difficult. Jewish law moves around this with a general orientation towards translating mitzvot that appear to be about emotions into discrete actions. We have developed and codified ways of expressing love, joy, and grief, particular to weddings, holidays, and the loss of different family members.

In contrast to the disgust legislation that Nussbaum focuses on, we often see an individual's negative emotion-such as those associated with mourning-turned into an opportunity for the community to witness and support the aggrieved.

"It's a form of human love," says Nussbaum, "to accept our complicated, messy humanity and not run away from it."[10] Torah has mechanisms for helping us to do this, even when it's difficult.

How might our own emotions and impulses be a source for personal behaviors that limit the dignity, capabilities, or rights of others?

How is that politicized? How do we stop individual disgust from being transformed into fears of "social contagion?"

What do we do, whether guided by Torah or our own sense, to find the humanity in people we might at first find in some way disgusting? How do

---

10. From Rachel Aviv's extensive 2016 profile of Dr. Nussbaum in *The New Yorker*.

we challenge ourselves to focus on the dignity of the other rather than our own discomfort?

What strategies do we have for recognizing the disgust people feel about abortion, homosexuality, transphobia, public breastfeeding, menstruation, women's sexuality, the elderly, visibly disabled people, and various other demographics, ideas, and actions? How do we help people move past those feelings into recognition of shared humanity?

We can reflect, based on Nussbaum, upon how a capabilities approach might help us reorient our moral and political debates. We can also consider how much we have to take our emotions seriously in our legal and moral considerations.

45

Kwame Appiah (1954–Present)

WITH KANT OR ARISTOTLE or Plato or most of the philosophers we are discussing, you and I can read their writings and learn from what experts have written about their philosophies, but except maybe in a dream, we don't get to ask them questions or talk with them directly. Here, on the other hand, we are exploring the philosopher Kwame Anthony Appiah, and I have had the privilege and pleasure of emailing and talking with Prof. Appiah on several occasions. You can watch two of my recorded conversations with him online, and I encourage you to read his books.

Prof Kwame Appiah was born in the UK, of British and Ghanaian parents, descended of politicians and people of status from both lands. Prof. Appiah grew up primarily in Ghana, though also spending much time in England, and currently lives as a naturalized American citizen in New York City. He is a professor of philosophy and law in the Department of Philosophy at New York University, and he researches and writes about ethics, race, and political philosophy, among other topics. Prof. Appiah has written of his particular experiences growing up gay in post-colonial Ghana. He writes for popular as well as academic audiences, and he has written the Ethicist column in the New York Times for the past eight years. He has a real role as a contemporary public intellectual.

Prof. Appiah situates himself within the philosophical tradition of Cosmopolitanism. In his book called *Cosmopolitanism*, he traces the term back to the Cynics of the fourth century CE, with the paradoxical definition "citizen of the cosmos", and he marks the influence this notion of universalism has had in the development of the Christian Church and Enlightenment Liberalism, and how cosmopolitanism has been reviled by nationalist movements of the twentieth century.

Appiah describes his own conception of cosmopolitanism like this:

> So there are two strands that intertwine in the notion of cosmopolitanism. One is the idea that we have obligations to others, obligations that stretch beyond those to whom we are related by the ties of kith and kind, or even the more formal ties of a shared citizenship. The other is that we take seriously the value not just of human life but of particular human lives, which means taking an interest in the practices and beliefs that lend them significance. People are different, the cosmopolitan knows, and there is much to learn from our differences. Because there are so many human possibilities worth exploring, we neither expect nor desire that every person or every society should converge on a single mode of life. Whatever our obligations are to others (or theirs to us) they often have the right to go their own way. As we'll see, there will be times when these two ideals—universal concern and respect for legitimate difference—clash. There's a sense in which cosmopolitanism is the name not of the solution but of the challenge.[1]

He establishes a tension, between a universalist morality that considers all humans equally responsible for one another, and a belief that humans are diverse and different from one another—even in their values, their lifestyles, their moral systems. He does not deny that these two underlying assumptions—about the simultaneous sameness and difference of humans in terms of their morality—can come into conflict. But he attempts to show that they both derive from the same deeper belief in the value of diversity, which finds expression in the commitment that the individual must have freedom to diverge and choose one's own way. For this same reason, we must also dedicate ourselves to exploring and learning from many different attempts to gain wisdom.

Appiah understands cosmopolitanism as a moral obligation and also in terms of the character trait of curiosity. Though these two aspects are related, he teaches that curiosity and learning about other cultures certainly does not guarantee someone will treat people who are different from them ethically or with dignity.

Though Appiah emphasizes human freedom, he is not a relativist. For example, when I asked Prof. Appiah about the benefits and drawbacks of using European intellectual produce to address global issues, he responded "my view about theories . . . is that the question to ask about them isn't who invented them or where they come from, but whether they are any good."

---

1. Appiah, *Cosmopolitanism: Ethics in a World of Strangers*.

He believes that ideas can be evaluated for their morality and truth, using reason, and then applied in other cultural contexts. He is practical, though, in pointing out that reasoning one's way to truth in the abstract is not a direct route to actual progress in society. And he teaches that the transfer of ideas between cultures must be a relational process and not one-sided—every culture has something to teach and every culture has something to learn. When I asked him how American activists can serve as allies to gay Ghanaians suffering from government repression, he first contextualized the situation in Ghana for me, and then he said we should "be clear to [Ghanaian politicians] that we do think they have a responsibility to bring their country into compliance for human rights norms . . . I think we should just have this conversation, because I want *them* to be able to tell us what they think *we're* doing wrong . . . ." For Appiah, non-coercive dialogue, curiosity, openness, and relationship are important. Respect and dignity are important.

In his book *In My Father's House: Africa in the Philosophy of Culture*, Prof. Appiah explores questions of race, identity and social movements. He argues against racialism, the belief that humanity is divided into different races, and that members of a given race share traits and tendencies, deeper and more essential than physical appearance, which they do not share with members of other races. For Appiah, the idea of race and the notion of different biological races with different essential characteristics is provably false, an artificial construct that is not scientifically accurate, and is better understood as pseudo-science.

According to Appiah, racism takes on two forms, one extrinsic and the other intrinsic. Extrinsic racism, according to Appiah, is an ethical system that depends on racialist assumptions. It assumes that the essential differences between the races are reasons to consider people of different races differently in moral decision making. For example, assuming black people are more likely to be criminals and therefore treating them more harshly than white people in the criminal justice system.

Intrinsic racism, on the other hand, does not seek to divide up the world into a hierarchy of races, but is instead founded on the notion that one should treat members of one's own race differently than members of other races. Like a non-universalist ethical system that requires one to act differently to one's own family than to a stranger, the intrinsic racist believes in treating members of another race differently, whether or not people of the different races have different characteristics. Appiah says that these three ways of thinking—racialism, intrinsic and extrinsic racism—are certainly often related to one another, and hard to pull apart in particular cases, but that it is useful to keep their separate definitions in mind.

As mentioned, his view is that race is not real, it is an invented concept and not a useful one (indeed, a damaging one) for understanding humanity. But he still finds it worthwhile to understand the construct of race and the way it influences people's moral systems.

Prof. Appiah brings different examples to illustrate these ideas, but his primary case study in *In My Father's House* is Pan-Africanism. He discusses in depth the theory of Pan-Africanism that W.E.B. DuBois developed over the course of his long life, which is based on a notion that there are different human races each with their own gift and mission to bring to humanity. DuBois therefore called on the race of Africans—including African Americans—to become unified in order to discover and fully realize their role in human civilization. According to Appiah's analysis, DuBois' theory suffers from a lack of coherent definition of race. In rejecting pseudo-scientific notions of racial inferiority, DuBois also, justly, rejects the notion of a biological definition of race. But at the same time, he cannot escape it entirely, for the other groundings he attempts to give race—sociohistorical, linguistic, geographic, and even notions of shared historical oppression, each fail to provide an internally consistent concept of race that can serve DuBois' purposes. According to Appiah, DuBois lived the end of his life in Ghana, driven by a hope for a sense of home that he could not find in racist America, but was ultimately unsuccessful in being able to construct a theory of race that would support that dream.

Appiah further teaches that the notion of race is an invention of the West that has nevertheless made its way also into post-colonial African ideologies.

In dismissing theories of humanity based on race as not true to reality, Appiah offers us instead to see a post-essentialist world in which people have more in common than we might otherwise imagine. He also invites us to embrace a diversity of identity that encompasses more than just race. He cares deeply about culture, and sees overlapping identity variables like gender, socio-economic status, and nationality that should not be oversimplified. He further explores these ideas in his book *The Lies that Bind: Rethinking Identity*.

Prof. Appiah's work exploring questions of individual and group identity in relation to other groups and in relation to global humanity is particularly relevant to thinking about the Jewish experience in the world. He himself frequently refers to Jewish history, for example stating in the introduction to his book *Cosmopolitanism* that when Hitler and Stalin vilified "rootless cosmopolitans", it "was often just a euphemism for anti-Semitism." Because local Jewish communities are vitally connected to a wider, global community of Jews that transcended national borders, nationalists often saw them as embodying the ideals of cosmopolitanism. Also in Appiah's discussion of race and identity in *In My Father's House*, he explores historical examples of the Jewish people's racialized oppression, as well as showing how Pan-Africanism to Zionism developed in parallel in the nineteenth century.

One Jewish thinker I believe it is particularly worthwhile to think about in dialogue with Prof Appiah is Rabbi Lord Jonathan Sacks. Like Appiah, Sacks established himself as a public intellectual, writing and speaking about large and deep ideas for popular audiences.

Rabbi Lord Jonathan Sacks was simultaneously a universalist and particularist, in a way reminiscent of Appiah's cosmopolitanist framework. Sacks celebrated human solidarity, unity and equality, while also putting great emphasis on the particulars of different cultures. He demanded the world see him not just as a human, but as a religious Jew. And he said that all human beings should be seen for their uniqueness as well. We should honor the other, teaches Sacks, because of the ways in which they are different from us and in spite of them.

Appiah puts more emphasis on the nuance of identity—that diversity exists in a way that is too complex to separate people neatly into groups. But both argue for tolerance and dialogue and neither are moral relativists.

In today's globally interconnected world, Appiah and Sacks both speak to some of the greatest tensions of our time. The tension between tribalism—the idea that my group is superior and all others are inferior—and an absolute universalism that wants to abandon or eliminate historical particularities and differences. We see this tension in the wide world, and we see it in the Jewish world. Appiah and Sacks invite us to live within the nuance of holding both ideals of particular diversity and universal humanity.

Conclusion

I'VE OFTEN THOUGHT ABOUT the relationship between philosophy and religion. Rabbi Abraham Joshua Heschel offered an interesting reflection on this relationship:

> In our quest for forgotten questions, the method and spirit of philosophical inquiry are of greater importance than theology, which is essentially descriptive, normative, and historical. Philosophy may be defined as the art of asking the right questions. One of the marks of philosophical thinking is that, in contrast to poetry, for example, it is not a self-sufficing pouring forth of insight, but the explicit statement of a problem and the attempt to offer an answer to a problem. Theology starts with dogmas; philosophy begins with problems. Philosophy sees the problem first; theology has the answer in advance. We must not, however, disregard another important difference. Not only are the problems of philosophy not identical with the problems of religion; their stator is not the same. Philosophy is, in a sense, a kind of thinking that has a beginning but no end. In it the awareness of the problem outlives all solutions. Its answers are questions in disguise; every new answer giving rise to new questions. In religion, on the other hand, the mystery of the answer hovers over all questions. Philosophy deals with problems as universal issues; to religion the universal issues are personal problems. Philosophy, then, stresses the primacy of the problem, religion stresses the primacy of the person. The fundamentalists claim that all ultimate questions have been answered; the logical positivists maintain that all ultimate questions are meaningless. Those of us who share neither the conceit of the former nor the unconcern of the latter, and reject both specious answers and false evasions, know that an ultimate issue is at stake in our

existence, the relevance of which surpasses all final formulations. It is this embarrassment that is the starting point for our thinking.[1]

We need philosophy, theology, and religion. We need them to challenge each other and compliment each other. We need pre-modern thought, modern thought, post-modern thought, and metamodernism. Whether we embrace a monism (one truth and reality to be discovered) or pluralism (multiple truths being legitimate), we will need a rigorous process of intellectual inquiry.

Whichever intellectual approach we embrace, we will need to make ourselves spiritually open to receiving new ideas. *Pirkei Avot* describes different ways of processing knowledge by giving four practical metaphors:

> There are four types among those who sit before the sages: a sponge, a funnel, a strainer and a sieve. A sponge, soaks up everything; A funnel, takes in at one end and lets out at the other; A strainer, which lets out the wine and retains the lees; A sieve, which lets out the coarse meal and retains the choice flour.[2]

The point here is that we don't start from the premise that nothing is beyond doubt. Instead, we start with the premise that there is an abundance of information that needs to be sorted through and filtered out. In addition, we should reflect on who our teachers are and how we embrace an oral transmission of wisdom, in addition to a rich written tradition we've inherited. Every year on Passover, we do rely on handed-on knowledge, in retelling the Exodus story based upon how it's passed down from generation to generation. This is because we're told in the Torah:

> And you shall explain to your child on that day, "It is because of what the Lord did for me when I went free from Egypt."[3]

Here we see that the Torah commands a passing on of human knowledge, which we base not only on fidelity to the text, but also on collective storytelling and memory. This does not mean every word of the story must be interpreted literally, but there is value to be found in and drawn out from the knowledge we've inherited.

We have one life to live and an urgent calling to find our truth, discover our purpose, and make sense out of the chaos of the universe. This is not an academic pursuit but a deeply personal one. It is my hope that this

---

1. Heschel, *God in Search of Man*, 4.
2. Pirkei Avot 5:15.
3. Exodus 13:8

work here can be a small tool in that journey for seekers. May we all settle for some simple truths we need to live by as we continue to cultivate and refine our most complex truths. May we transform our learning into action to foster a more just, beautiful, holy, and kind society.

Bibliography

Adler, Rachel. "Jewish Women: A Comprehensive Historical Encyclopedia." *Jewish Women's Archive* (2021). https://jwa.org/encyclopedia/article/plaskow-judith.
Alter, Charlotte. "Exclusive: Effective Altruist Leaders Were Repeatedly Warned About Sam Bankman-Fried Years Before FTX Collapsed." *Time* (2023). https://time.com/6262810/sam-bankman-fried-effective-altruism-alameda-ftx/.
Appiah, Kwame Anthony. *Cosmopolitanism: Ethics in a World of Strangers.* New York: W.W. Norton, 2006.
Arendt, Hannah. *Eichmann in Jerusalem: A Report on the Banality of Evil.* New York: Viking Press, 1963.
Atherton, Margaret. *The Empiricists: Critical Essays on Locke, Berkeley, and Hume. Critical essays on the classics.* Lanham: Rowman & Littlefield, 1999.
Atkins, Zohar. "Are You Religious or Philosophical?" *What Is Called Thinking?* (2022). https://whatiscalledthinking.substack.com/p/are-you-religious-or-philosophical.
Avineri, Shlomo. *Karl Marx: Philosophy and Revolution.* New Haven: Yale University Press, 2019.
Bentham, Jeremy. *An Introduction to the Principles of Morals and Legislation.* Oxford: Clarendon, 1789.
Berkovits, Eliezer. "Hume und der Deismus" (PhD diss., Friedrich Wilhelms University, Berlin, 1933). Translated by Ruth Morris, provided by David Hazony.
Berlin, Isaiah. *Russian Thinkers.* London: Penguin Books, 1979.
———. *The Proper Study of Mankind: An Anthology of Essays.* New York: Farrar, Straus and Giroux, 1997.
Blau, Eleanor. "An unusual Rabbinic Court Judges Social Problems." *The New York Times* (1973). https://www.nytimes.com/1973/02/06/archives/an-unusual-rabbinic-court-judges-social-problems-attracts-young.html.
Boteach, Shmuley. "The Great (and Imperfect) Hope That Is Chabad." *The Forward.* https://forward.com/opinion/120594/the-great-and-imperfect-hope-that-is-chabad/.
Brill, Alan. "A Tiny but Articulate Minority," *The Book of Doctrines and Opinions* (2008). https://kavvanah.blog/wp-content/uploads/2009/11/wurzburger-article.pdf
———. "Prayer without Hoping- Rav Shagar." *The Book of Doctrines and Opinions* (2017). https://kavvanah.blog/2017/10/17/prayer-without-hoping-rav-shagar/.
Buber, Martin. *Hasidism and the Modern Man.* New York: Horizon Press, 1958.
———. *I And Thou.* Translated by Walter Kauffman. Edinburgh; T. & T. Clark, 1947.
———. *Tales of the Hasidism: Later Masters.* New York: Schocken, 1961.

———. *The Way of Man: According to the Teachings of Hasidism.* New York: Routledge, 1965.

———. *Thoreau in Our Season.* Amherst: University of Massachusetts Press, 1962.

Carr, Flora. "The Eerie Gravestone Where Frankenstein's Story Began," *Time* (2018). time.com/5133735/wollstonecraft-grave-mary-shelley-frankenstein/.

Chittick, William. "RUMI, JALĀL-AL-DIN vii. Philosophy." *Encyclopedia Iranica* (2017). \ http://www.iranicaonline.org/articles/rumi-philosophy.

Chow, George. "All Actual Life is Encounter: Martin Buber's Politics of Depoliticization." *University of Victoria* (2010). https://dspace.library.uvic.ca/items/c873c195-e90f-4435-98bd-54b497164a0b.

Cohen, Gerson. "The Blessing of Assimilation." *JTS commencement address* (1966).

Crenshaw, Kimberlé. "The Intersectionality Wars." *Time* (2020). https://time.com/5786710/kimberle-crenshaw-intersectionality/.

Davidson, Herbert A. *Moses Maimonides: The Man and His Work.* New York: Oxford University Press, 2005.

Dennett, Daniel C., & Caruso, Gregg D. "Just Deserts." *Aeon* (2018). https://aeon.co/essays/on-free-will-daniel-dennett-and-gregg-caruso-go-head-to-head.

———. "Quining Qualia." *Consciousness in Contemporary Science* (1988). https://philpapers.org/rec/DENQQ.

———. "The Problem of Counterfeit People." *The Atlantic* (2023). https://www.theatlantic.com/technology/archive/2023/05/problem-counterfeit-people/674075/.

———. "Dennett on Wieseltier V. Pinker in The New Republic Let's Start With A Respect For Truth." *The Edge* (2023). edge.org/conversation/daniel_c_dennett-dennett-on-wieseltier-v-pinker-in-the-new-republic.

Descartes, René. *Meditations on First Philosophy.* "Meditation I." The Classical Library, 1901.

de Spinoza, Benedictus. *The Chief Works of Benedict de Spinoza: Introduction. Tractatus theologico-politicus. Tractatus politicus.* Translated by Robert Harvey Monro Elwes. G. Bell and sons. New York; Nabu, 2012.

Dewey, John. *The Nature of Conduct: An Introduction to Social Psychology.* New York: Henry Holt and Company, 1922.

Dutton, Yasin. "The Introduction to Ibn Rushd's 'Bidāyat al-Mujtahid.'" *Islamic Law and Society* (1994). doi:10.2307/3399333.

Emerson, Ralph Waldo. *Ralph Waldo Emerson (The Oxford Authors)*, Oxford and New York: Oxford University Press, 1990.

Evans, Richard J. *The Coming of the Third Reich.* New York: Penguin, 2005.

Foucault, Michel. *The History of Sexuality.* New York: Random House, 1990.

Goodman, L.E. *Avicenna: Arabic Thought and Culture.* New York: Routledge, 2013.

Goodman, Mark Asher. *Life Lessons From Recently Dead Rabbis: Hassidut for the People.* Location Bayit, 2023.

Goodman, Micah. *The Last Words of Moses.* Jerusalem: Maggid, 2023.

Green, Arthur. *Your Word Is Fire: The Hasidic Masters on Contemplative Prayer.* Woodstock: Jewish Lights, 1993.

Green, Peter. *Alexander of Macedon.* Berkeley: University of California Press, 1991.

Greenberg, Yitz. "Personal Service: A Central Jewish Norm for Our Time." *Sefaria* (2001). https://www.sefaria.org/sheets/115016?lang=bi.

Gros, Frédéric. *A Philosophy of Walking.* London: Verso, 2014.

Guevara, Ernesto Che. *The Bolivian Diary*. Melbourne: Ocean, 2006.
Hallam, Henry. *Introduction to the Literature of Europe in the 15th, 16th, and 17th Centuries*. Boston: Little, Brown, 1854.
Haraszti, Zoltan. "John Adams and Rousseau." *The Atlantic* (1948). https://www.theatlantic.com/magazine/archive/1948/02/john-adams-and-rousseau/644045/.
Hertzberg Hanover, Arthur. "Voltaire and the Jews." *The New York Times* (1990). https://www.nytimes.com/1990/09/30/books/l-voltaire-and-the-jews-590990.html.
Heschel, Abraham Joshua. *God in Search of Man*. New York: Harper & Brothers, 1955.
———. *The Sabbath*. New York: Farrar, Straus and Giroux, 1951.
Hidary, Richard. "How Is the Passover Seder Different from All Other Symposia?" *The Gemara* (n.d.). https://thegemara.com/article/how-is-the-passover-seder-different-from-all-other-symposia/.
Hirschmann, Nancy J, *Gender, Class, and Freedom in Modern Political Theory*. Princeton: Princeton University Press, 2009.
Hobbes, Thomas. *Leviathan*. London: Penguin Classics, 1982.
Hodakov, Levi. "Wisdom from the Rebbe." *Jewish Press of Tampa Bay* (2020). https://www.jewishpresspinellas.com/articles/wisdom-from-the-rebbe/.
Hooper, Simon. "The Rise of the New Atheists." *CNN* (2006). cnn.com/2006/WORLD/europe/11/08/atheism.feature/index.html.
Horgan, John. "One of the World's Most Powerful Scientists Believes in Miracles." *Scientific American* (2020). blogs.scientificamerican.com/cross-check/one-of-the-worlds-most-powerful-scientists-believes-in-miracles/.
———. "Was Wittgenstein a Mystic?" *Scientific American* (2018). https://blogs.scientificamerican.com/cross-check/was-wittgenstein-a-mystic/#:~:text=Wittgenstein%20writes%2C%20%E2%80%9CNot%20how%20the,just%20this%20is%20the%20answer.
Hume, David. *A Treatise of Human Nature: Being an Attempt to introduce the experimental Method of Reasoning into Moral Subjects*. London: John Noon, 1739.
Ivry, Benjamin. "A Loving Levinas on War." *The Forward* (2010). https://forward.com/culture/125385/a-loving-levinas-on-war/.
Jasper, James M. *The Art of Moral Protest: Culture, Biography, and Creativity in Social Movements*. Chicago: University of Chicago Press, 1999.
Josephus, Flavius. *Antiquities of the Jews*. London: Virtue, Spalding, 1874.Kant, Immanuel. *Critique of Practical Reason*. Cambridge: Cambridge University Press, 2015.
Kant, Immanuel. *Groundwork for the Metaphysics of Morals*. Translated by Jonathan Bennett. Cambridge: Cambridge University Press, 2008.
Kateb, George. "The idea of individual infinitude." *The Hedgehog Review* (2005). https://hedgehogreview.com/issues/weak-ontologies/articles/the-idea-of-individual-infinitude.
Kellner, Menachem. *Maimonides on Judaism and the Jewish People*. New York: State University of New York Press, 1991.
King Jr., Martin Luther. *The Autobiography of Martin Luther King Jr*. Edited by Clayborne Carson. New York: Warner, 1998.
Kleist, Chad. "Global Ethics: Capabilities Approach." *Internet Encyclopedia of Philosophy* (n.d.). https://iep.utm.edu/ge-capab/.
Klotz, Myriam. "Finding God Through the Body." *My Jewish Learning* (n.d.). https://www.myjewishlearning.com/article/finding-god-through-the-body/.

Kook, A.Y. *Selected Letters*. Translated by Tzvi Feldman. Maale Adumim: Ma'aliot, 1986.

Korab-Karpowicz, W. Julian. *A History of Political Philosophy: From Thucydides to Locke*. New York: Global Scholarly, 2010.

Kushner, Harold. *How Good Do We Have to Be?: A New Understanding of Guilt and Forgiveness*. New York: Little, Brown, 1996.

Lebrecht, Norman. *Genius & Anxiety: How Jews Changed the World, 1847-1947*. New York: Scribner, 2019.

Levinas, Emmanuel. *Beyond the Verse: Talmudic Readings and Lectures*. London: Continuum, 2007.

———. *Difficult Freedom: Essays on Judaism*. Baltimore: Johns Hopkins University Press, 1997.

———. *In the Time of the Nations*. Bloomington: Indiana University Press, 1994.

———. *Time and the Other*. Pittsburgh: Duquesne University Press, 1987.

———. *Totality and Infinity: An Essay on Exteriority*. Pittsburgh: Duquesne University Press, 1969.

Lewis, Michael. *The Undoing Project*. New York: W. W. Norton, 2016.

Lewis-Kraus, Gideon. "The Reluctant Prophet of Effective Altruism." *The New Yorker* (2022). https://www.newyorker.com/magazine/2022/08/15/the-reluctant-prophet-of-effective-altruism.

Maimonides. *Guide for the Perplexed*. Translated by Shlomo Pines. Chicago: University of Chicago Press, 1974.

Marx, Karl, and Engels, Friedrich. *The Communist Manifesto*. Translated by Samuel Moore. London: Penguin Classics, 2002.

———. *Critique of Hegel's Philosophy of Right*. Stuttgart: Newcomb Livraria, 1844.

———. *Critique of the Gotha Program*. Rockville: Wildside Press, 2008.

Matt, Daniel C. *God and the Big Bang: Discovering Harmony Between Science & Spirituality*. Woodstock: Jewish Lights, 1998.

———. *The Essential Kabbalah: The Heart of Jewish Mysticism*. New York: HarperOne, 2009.

McGrath, Alister. Historical Theology, An Introduction to the History of Christian Thought. Oxford: Blackwell, 1998.

Mermelstein, Ari. "Beauty or Beast? The Pedagogical Function of Metaphor and Emotion in Midrashim on the Law of the Lovely Captive." *Journal of Ancient Judaism* (2018). https://www.academia.edu/37849552/Beauty_or_Beast_The_Pedagogical_Function_of_Metaphor_and_Emotion_in_Midrashim_on_the_Law_of_the_Lovely_Captive.

Moss, Stephen. "A to Z of Wagner: N is for Nietzsche, Nibelungs and Norns." *The Guardian* (2013). https://www.theguardian.com/music/2013/aug/13/stephen-moss-a-to-z-of-wagner-n-is-for-nietzsche-nibelungs-and-norns.

Muskat, Jonathan. "A Torah Perspective on Gun Control." *The Times of Israel* (2018). https://blogs.timesofisrael.com/a-torah-perspective-on-gun-control/.

Nadler, Steven M. *Spinoza: A Life*. Cambridge: Cambridge University Press, 1999.

National Geographic Society. "Adaptation." *National Geographic: Education* (2023). https://education.nationalgeographic.org/resource/adaptation/.

Navon, Chaim. "Intro to the Guide of the Perplexed: Negative Attributes." Torat Har Etzion (2015). etzion.org.il/en/philosophy/great-thinkers/rambam/negative-attributes.

Nietzsche, Friedrich. *The Gay Science*. Translated with commentary by Walter Kaufmann. New York; Random House, 1974.

———. *The Will to Power*. New York: Vintage, 1968.

Nussbaum, Martha. *Women and Human Development: The Capabilities Approach*. Cambridge: Cambridge University Press, 2000.

Olson, Walter. "The Origins of a Warning from Voltaire." *Cato Institute* (2020). https://www.cato.org/publications/commentary/origins-warning-from-voltaire.

O'Malley, Sheila. "'The Turin Horse': A tale of animal and human deprivation, and an invitation to feel Nietzsche's pain." *Politico* (2011). https://www.politico.com/states/new-york/city-hall/story/2011/09/the-turin-horse-a-tale-of-animal-and-human-deprivation-and-an-invitation-to-feel-nietzsches-pain-068822.

Pinker, Steven. *The Blank Slate: The Modern Denial of Human Nature*. New York: Viking, 2002.

Plaskow, Judith. *Standing Again at Sinai*. New York: HarperCollins, 1990.

———. "The View from Here: Gender Theory and Gendered Realities - An Exchange between Tamar Ross and Judith Plaskow." *Nashim* (2007). https://www.jstor.org/stable/10.2979/nas.2007.-.13.207.

Poole, Steven, "The Four Horseman review – whatever happened to the 'New Atheism.'" *The Guardian* (2019). theguardian.com/books/2019/jan/31/four-horsemen-review-what-happened-to-new-atheism-dawkins-hitchens.

Popova, Maria. "Either/Or: Kierkegaard on Transcending the Tyranny of Binary Choice and Double Regret." *The Marginalian* (2016). https://www.themarginalian.org/2016/05/05/either-or-kierkegaard/.

Prochnik, George. "What Gershom Scholem and Hannah Arendt Can Teach Us About Evil Today." *LARB* (2017). https://lareviewofbooks.org/article/gershom-scholem-hannah-arendt-can-teach-us-evil-today/.

Rawls, John. *A Theory of Justice*. Cambridge: Belknap, 1971.

Re, Justine. "Bronx rabbi ushers in the next generation of female rabbis," *Spectrum News* (2023). ny1.com/nyc/all-boroughs/religion/2023/07/14/bronx-rabbi-ushers-in-the-next-generation-of-female-rabbis.

Rebbe Nachman. Likutei Moharan, Tinyana. Sefaria.

Riemer, Jack, and Elie Spitz. *Duets on Psalms*. Woodstock: Jewish Lights, 2023.

Rofeberg, Lex. "Episode 369: Jewish Mysticism - Ariel Mayse Episode." *Judaism Unbound Podcast* (2023). https://open.spotify.com/episode/2UTbZDlotRSAccKVKLcdTW?si=2397dca3c6114838.

Rosenzweig, Franz. *Understanding the Sick and the Healthy: A View of World, Man, and God*. Cambridge: Harvard University Press, 1999.

Ross, Tamar. "Feminism Changes the Study of Jewish Thoughts." *Tablet Magazine* (2021). tabletmag.com/sections/history/articles/feminism-changes-study-jewish-thought.

Rotenberg, Mordechai. *The Psychology of Tzimtzum: Self, Other, and God*. Jerusalem: Maggid, 2016.

Rothman, Joshua. "Daniel Dennett's Science of the Soul." *The New Yorker* (2017). newyorker.com/magazine/2017/03/27/daniel-dennetts-science-of-the-soul.

Rousseau, Jean-Jacques. *The Social Contract*. Translated by Maurice Cranston. London: Penguin Classics, 1968.

Rowlatt, Bee, "The original suffragette: the extraordinary Mary Wollstonecraft." *The Guardian* (2015). theguardian.com/lifeandstyle/womens-blog/2015/oct/05/original-suffragette-mary-wollstonecraft.

Sacks, Jonathan. "Argument for the Sake of Heaven." *Jonathan Sacks: A Rabbi Sacks Legacy* (2018). https://rabbisacks.org/covenant-conversation/korach/argument-for-the-sake-of-heaven/.

———. *Ceremony & Celebration: An Introduction to the Holidays.* Jerusalem: Maggid, 2017.

———. *Future Tense: Jews, Judaism, and Israel in the Twenty-first Century.* New York: Schocken, 2012.

———. *Judaism's Life-Changing Ideas.* Jerusalem: Maggid, 2020.

———. *Morality: Restoring the Common Good In Divided Times.* New York: Basic, 2020.

———. *The Great Partnership: God, Science and the Search for Meaning.* New York: Schocken, 2012.

Schaeder, Grete. *The Hebrew Humanism of Martin Buber.* Detroit: Wayne State University Press, 1973.

Septimus, Daniel. "The Thirteen Principles of Faith." *My Jewish Learning* (n.d.). https://www.myjewishlearning.com/article/the-thirteen-principles-of-faith/.

Shannon, Jeff. "The Elvis of Cultural Theory." *The Seattle Times* (2006). https://www.seattletimes.com/entertainment/movies/the-elvis-of-cultural-theory/.

Sharma, Urmila, and Sharma, S.K. *Western Political Thought.* Washington: Atlantic, 2006.

Shenker, Israel. "Now, Jewish Roots." *The New York Times* (1977). https://www.nytimes.com/1977/03/20/archives/now-jewish-roots.html.

Singer, Peter. *Animal Liberation.* New York: Random House, 1975.

———. *The Life You Can Save.* New York: Random House, 2009.

Soloveichik, Aaron. "A Glimpse at Eternity from a Hospital Dungeon." *Tradition* (1984). https://traditiononline.org/a-glimpse-at-eternity-from-a-hospital-dungeon/.

———. "Redemption, Prayer, Talmud Torah." *Tradition* (1978). https://traditiononline.org/redemption-prayer-talmud-torah/.

Stack, Jr. Sam F. "John Dewey and the Question of Race: The Fight for Odell Waller." *The Journal of the John Dewey Society* (2009). https://docs.lib.purdue.edu/eandc/vol25/iss1/art4/.

Steinsaltz, Adin Even-Israel. *The Soul.* Jerusalem: Maggid, 2018.

Taylor, Mark. "What Derrida Really Meant." *The New York Times* (2004). https://www.nytimes.com/2004/10/14/opinion/what-derrida-really-meant.html.

Teutsch, David A., editor. *Imagining the Jewish Future: Essays and Responses.* Albany: State University of New York Press, 1992.

Thoreau, Henry David. *Walden.* Boston: Ticknor and Fields, 1854.

———. *Walking.* Cambridge: The Riverside, 1914.

Vereen, Linwood G., Wines, Lisa A., et al. "Black Existentialism: Extending the Discourse on Meaning and Existence." *Montclair State University Digital Commons* (2017). digitalcommons.montclair.edu/counseling-facpubs/14. Last accessed November 9, 2023.

Weijers, Dan. "Hedonism." Internet Encyclopedia of Philosophy (n.d.). https://iep.utm.edu/hedonism/#:~:text=f.-,Hedonistic%2520Utilitarianism,net%2520happiness%2520for%2520all%2520concerned.

White, Thomas.: "What did Hannah Arendt really mean by the banality of evil?" *Aeon* (2018). https://aeon.co/ideas/what-did-hannah-arendt-really-mean-by-the-banality-of-evil.

Wittgenstein, Ludwig. *Tractatus Logico-Philosophicus.* New York: Harcourt, Brace, 1922.

Wolf, Gary. "The Church of Nonbelievers." *Wired* (2006). wired.com/2006/11/atheism/.

Wollstonecraft, Mary. *A Vindication of the Rights of Woman.* London: Penguin Classics, 2004.

Wurzburger, Walter S. "Is Sociology Integral to the Halakhah?" ProQuest (1980). https://www.proquest.com/openview/d870417c3194b7a5cd5788e7878dc4fe/1?pq-origsite=gscholar&cbl=1817128

Young C, Brook A. "Schopenhauer and Freud." *National Library of Medicine* (1994). https://pubmed.ncbi.nlm.nih.gov/8005756/Int J Psychoanalysis.

Zion, Noah. "How Passover Customs Have Changed and Developed Over Time." *My Jewish Learning* (n.d.). https://www.myjewishlearning.com/article/changing-passover-customs/.

"Archives." *Stanford Encyclopedia of Philosophy* (n.d.).

"Babylonian Talmud: William Davidson Edition." *Sefaria.* https://www.sefaria.org/texts/Talmud/Bavli

"Biographies." *Encyclopedia Britannica* (n.d.). https://www.britannica.com/Biographies.

"Buddhist Jewish Dialogue." *SpiritPeaceLove* (2016). https://www.youtube.com/watch?v=wQys2HIW1ZM&t=821s.

"Daniel Dennett," *Institute of Art and Ideas* (n.d.). iai.tv/home/speakers/daniel-dennett/.

"Eastern Philosophy – Buddha." *The School of Life* (2014). https://www.youtube.com/watch?v=tilBs32zN7I

"Eastern Philosophy – Confucius." *The School of Life* (2015). https://www.youtube.com/watch?v=tUhGRh4vdb8&t=156s.

"Jastrow Dictionary." *Sefaria* (n.d.). https://www.sefaria.org/Jastrow?tab=contents.

"Jerusalem Talmud." *Sefaria.* https://www.sefaria.org/texts/Talmud/Yerushalmi

"JPS Tanach." *Jewish Publication Society.*

"Leading Women 1868-2018," *University of London* (2018). london.ac.uk/about-us/history-university-london/leading-women-1868-2018#. Last accessed October 17, 2023.

"Mishneh Torah." Maimonidies.

"Philosophy - Ludwig Wittgenstein." *The School of Life* (2015). https://youtu.be/pQ33gAyhg2c.

"Plato." *Lapham's Quarterly* (n.d.). https://www.laphamsquarterly.org/contributors/plato.

"Plato, Apology." *Perseus Digital Library.* https://www.perseus.tufts.edu/hopper/text%3Fdoc=plat.+apol.+38a.

"Rabba Sara Hurwitz." *Maharat* (n.d.). yeshivatmaharat.org/scholar/hurwitz/sara.

"Sacred Books of the East." *WikiSource.* Translated by James Legge. https://en.m.wikisource.org/wiki/Sacred_Books_of_the_East/Volume_3/The_Hsiao/Chapter_9.

"Wei Lei Gong." *Chinese Text Project* (n.d.). Translated by James Legge. https://ctext.org/analects/wei-ling-gong.

"Who Are the Brights." *The Brights* (n.d.). http://www.the-brights.net/.

www.ingramcontent.com/pod-product-compliance
Lightning Source LLC
Chambersburg PA
CBHW051632230426
43669CB00013B/2274